LAZY DAYS IN SUMMER

BY
BERNIE HOWGATE

The Travelling Man Enterprises

WEBSITE
www.berniehowgate.com
Email
info@berniehowgate.com

LAZY DAYS IN SUMMER
First Edition

WRITTEN
Bernie Howgate

EDITED
Joanna Ebbutt

COVER MAPS AND ILLUSTRATIONS
Bernie Howgate and Wendy Reger

PHOTOGRAPHS
Bernie Howgate
Duplessis Tourism and Newfoundland Tourism

PUBLISHED
The Travelling Man Enterprises
General Delivery
Mud Lake
Labrador
A0P 1K0
CANADA

FIRST EDITION
2002

Printed in Canada

ISBN-0-9694419-4-0

for me
meeting people is the name of the game
a special thank you
to

Mick and Tish Emmens

CJ and Christopher

Books in Print

Tales of a Travelling man:
based on an eight year round the world cycle trip
ISBN-0-9694419-0-8
$30:00 postage included

Journey through Labrador:
based on an eight month snowshoe and sea kayaking trip up the Labrador coast
ISBN-0-9694419-1-6
$25:00 postage included

Newfie or Bust :
based on an eight month 9000km cycle trip across Canada from Victoria, British Columbia to St John's, Newfoundland
ISBN-0-9694419-2-4
$25:00 postage included

Lazy Days in Summer:
based on a 4500km sea kayaking trip from the Great Lakes down the Saint Lawrence river to Goose Bay, Labrador
ISBN-0-9694419-4-0
$25:00 postage included

Contact: for book purchase

Bernie Howgate's Home Page:
http//.www.berniehowgate.com

Email:
berniehowgate@info.com

Snail mail:
Bernie Howgate, c/o Travelling Man Enterprises, Mud Lake, Labrador, A0P 1K0, CANADA

CONTENTS

MAP ILLUSTRATIONS

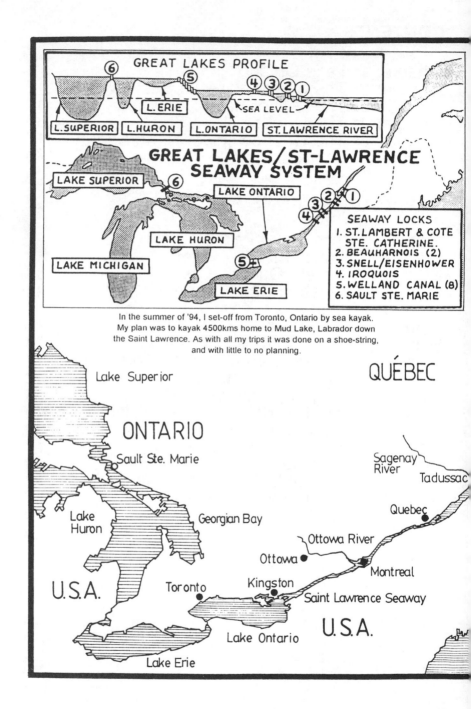

GREAT LAKES PROFILE

L. ERIE

SEA LEVEL

L. SUPERIOR | L. HURON | L. ONTARIO | ST. LAWRENCE RIVER

GREAT LAKES/ST-LAWRENCE
SEAWAY SYSTEM

LAKE SUPERIOR

LAKE ONTARIO

LAKE HURON

LAKE MICHIGAN

LAKE ERIE

SEAWAY LOCKS
1. ST. LAMBERT & COTE STE. CATHERINE.
2. BEAUHARNOIS (2)
3. SNELL/EISENHOWER
4. IROQUOIS
5. WELLAND CANAL (8)
6. SAULT STE. MARIE

In the summer of '94, I set-off from Toronto, Ontario by sea kayak.
My plan was to kayak 4500kms home to Mud Lake, Labrador down
the Saint Lawrence. As with all my trips it was done on a shoe-string,
and with little to no planning.

Lake Superior

QUÉBEC

ONTARIO

Sault Ste. Marie

Sagenay
River

Tadussac

Quebec

Lake
Huron

Georgian Bay

Ottowa River

U.S.A.

Ottowa

Toronto

Kingston

Montreal

Saint Lawrence Seaway

U.S.A.

Lake Ontario

Lake Erie

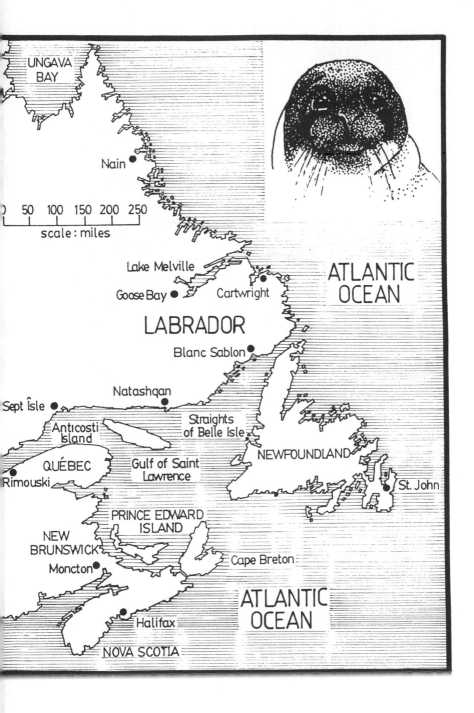

UNGAVA
BAY

Nain ●

0 50 100 150 200 250
scale: miles

Lake Melville

Goose Bay ●   Cartwright ●

LABRADOR

Blanc Sablon ●

Natashqan

Sept Îsle ●

Anticosti
Island

QUÉBEC

Rimouski ●

Straights
of Belle Isle

Gulf of Saint
Lawrence

NEWFOUNDLAND

St. John ●

PRINCE EDWARD
ISLAND

NEW
BRUNSWICK

Moncton ●

Cape Breton

Halifax ●

NOVA SCOTIA

ATLANTIC
OCEAN

ATLANTIC
OCEAN

FOR MY FATHER
A MAN OF TRUTH

March 21st 1914
November 6th 2001

Chapter 1
The Great Lakes

I left Ward Island before the break of dawn. It was like a walk in the park. Even the geese encamped by the side of my tent didn't stir. The city of Toronto was just starting to flex its muscles and its skyscrapers, outlined in jet black against a pale pre-dawn sky, were still checked with lights. The drone of early morning traffic from the Queen Elizabeth Highway was only just audible and Toronto Island's commuter ferry was still thirty minutes away.

I was more than two hours into my paddle and had detoured round the harbour's landfill project just east of downtown, before the city finally woke. The conditions were ideal for kayaking. Lake Ontario was as smooth as a baby's bottom and empty of traffic. The sun had just popped its brilliant gold head above the horizon, and its rays were rushing over the lake to greet me. Downtown now brushed off its cobwebs and burst into colour. Its towers, tinted in brilliant flashes of bronze and steel, looked like a huge pyramid of reflective glass, and its roads filled with the sights and sounds of commuters, its arteries that gave it life. It was a sight to remember. I decided on one last taste of city life before turning the page. I pulled up my kayak besides the Balmy Beach Club; left it under the watchful eye of its attendant on the boardwalk, then walked up to Queen Street and treated myself to a full breakfast.

All morning, Scarborough's Bluffs drifted by slowly. Bleached white and eroded by the elements, these soft white sandy cliffs looked like the colourless folds of aged skin. For four hours they rose and fell; sometimes opening up in deep cuts of green and sometimes topped by huge houses with views that only money can buy.

At Rouge Hill, some fifteen miles east from downtown Toronto, I stopped to watch a Via Rail train thunder over a bridge, and just before Frenchman's Cove, I was stopped by yet another sight. I had spotted a group of

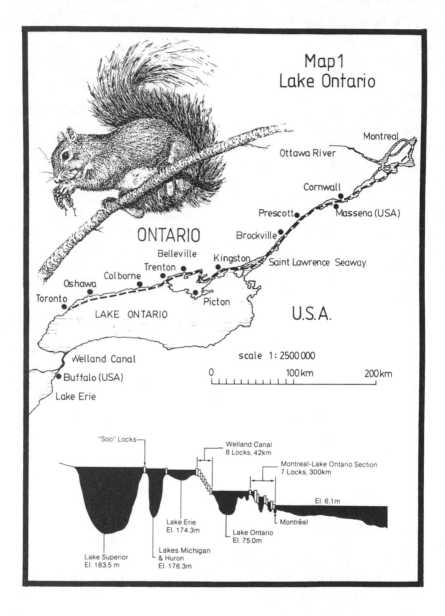

Map 1
Lake Ontario

Montreal

Ottawa River

Cornwall

Prescott

Massena (USA)

Brockville

ONTARIO

Belleville

Kingston

Trenton

Saint Lawrence Seaway

Colborne

Oshawa

Toronto

Picton

LAKE ONTARIO

U.S.A.

Welland Canal

scale 1: 2500 000

Buffalo (USA)

0   100 km   200 km

Lake Erie

"Soo" Locks

Welland Canal
8 Locks, 42km

Montreal-Lake Ontario Section
7 Locks, 300km

El. 6.1m

Lake Erie
El. 174.3m

Montréal

Lake Ontario
El. 75.0m

Lake Superior
El. 183.5 m

Lakes Michigan
& Huron
El. 176.3m

youths playing volley ball on the beach and yet another group, no less animated, half in queue and paired in twos and threes, talking with each other around an enclosed barbecue pit. It was a typical summer scene and I turned into its gaiety, then beached close to the action.

I had just dug out my wallet. I was just making my way to the barbecue pit when the sight of a huge pale white blubbery mass stopped me in my tracks. He looked like a beached walrus with folds of insulating fat to spare. He was as naked as a newborn baby, oblivious to his fellow sun worshippers and only slightly interested in my gaze. It almost seemed that I was being reeled in. I got the distinct impression that like the venus fly trap, his bulk was his bait, and that if I entered the arms of his invisible boundary, that he would snap back and devour me. He had this strange decayed look, but it was his eyes, half closed, half smiling, and utterly self-satisfied, that gave me the willies. He had the beginnings of a Charles Mason look, not quite mad, but certainly getting there. How he got away with laying naked on the beach while everyone else was costumed, was anyone's guess.

By now a small crowd had gathered around my kayak. I was just giving my blubbery friend a wide berth en route to the barbecue when he moved. Maybe he felt upstaged by my kayak or maybe he just wanted to impress, but for whatever reason, he rolled sufficiently over onto his side to display his rather impressive sex organ. Then, having caught my attention, he rolled back into his slumber.
"Don't pay any attention to him no one else does."
In my awkward attempt to round him, I'd walked straight into the arms of a woman.
"Sit down and join us". She wasn't so much inviting me to sit down as giving me a command. It turned out that I'd paddled into a wedding reception. Not any kind of wedding reception, but a unity of two different cultures, Italian and German, under the umbrella of alternative lifestyles. The walrus turned out to be the bride's eccentric father, and the ample lady I'd walked into the bridegroom's mother. I was

into my second glass of wine and had my mouth wrapped around a delicious vegetarian burger when all hell broke loose. The bride had been simmering like a pot under boil ever since her father had rejoined the group. Ten minutes before, she had shouted out something to him in Italian. He'd got up and disappeared, and now he was back, dressed in a pair of Bermuda shorts with only a tie around his neck and a blush on his cheeks. They kept up a steady banter, each trying to out do the other, when suddenly he stood, turned to face the food, then dropped his shorts and did a moonie for the guests.

She exploded like a hand grenade. Spit like shrapnel spread itself out like a fan and hit everyone within earshot. It happened so quickly and without warning, that I was speechless. It wouldn't have mattered anyway. There was only one voice that mattered at that moment, and it wouldn't stop until it had run its course.

"She's just letting off steam boy."

It was the walrus. As large as life, and then some. *"That's my girl."*

He reared back, gulped in some air and burst out laughing. His whole body started to wobble and clap in unison to his laughter, then his daughter joined in, and soon everyone else had fallen into step, till the whole beach was roaring with laughter.

"God help the guy she's marrying. She's a temper like her mother."

By the time I left, I had a full stomach and a head cushioned in an alcoholic glow, but I soon sobered. I was just approaching Richardson Point. Black clouds had been appearing out of the north west ever since I left the beach. Every now and than sheet lightning would light up the dark clouds in mushrooms of light and the distant sounds of thunder echoed like subterranean depth charges. Just past the point, the wind picked up and within minutes the rain started, followed by the hail, and then rain again. At its height, the thunder was deafening.It split the silent pauses between flashes like the report of cannon fire, and the rain beat down so hard that it turned the lake,s surface into a boiling cauldron of bubbles. I was less than three hundred meters from shore, but couldn't see a thing.

For some unknown reason, I have always felt a little naked in lightning. Once, I had dashed from a golf course for shelter in a sudden thunderstorm and today was no exception, but this time I had knowhere to go. I was starting to get frightened. The rain had now stopped, but the dark clouds were whirling around like angry whiskers in a breeze. It felt like being in the eye of a hurricane, waiting for the inevitable back lash, when I spotted a loon. I only saw him for a few seconds, but it was enough. Suddenly I felt relaxed. Like a young child who finds his mother in a crowded station, my fears melted away. The clouds didn't look as threatening and when the rain returned it had lost its bite.

The storm stopped as quickly as it had started, and almost immediately the sun popped out overhead. The lake began to shimmer in a heat haze, then the inevitable happened. The fresh rain, still invisibly puddled and trapped on the lake's surface started to evaporate and gather. It started as a white surface cloud, climbed, moved towards the shore, then swallowed everything up in its wake.

I would have passed right by the harbour had not a yacht crossed my path. Its sails were down and its small engine purred out, then back into the fog. I quickly turned into its sound, followed the cut it had made through the water, then attached myself to the shapes forming in front. It took me straight into the yacht club, and once inside everything fell into place. I pulled up my kayak onto its slipway, erected my tent on its lawns, then visited the yacht club to ask for permission to stay. I was welcomed with open arms as not only did I win their favour with my story of kayaking home to Labrador, I was also given the keys to the club. I showered, used their laundry service to dry my clothes, and as if to top off my good fortune, one of the ladies made me some sandwiches from the kitchen.

That evening, I joined some members for a drink. They came in all shapes and sizes, from the professional ranks to a local labourer who liked to sail his pint-sized dingy in fog. They were both men and women, from loners like myself to a family who had dropped out for a year to live out their dream and sail round the Pacific Islands. I enjoyed their company thoroughly. Our love of the water transcended all our differences on land, and our recounted experiences as shared that evening - although dressed differently - came from the same source. I must have travelled thousands of miles that night from Fiji in the Pacific to the Bahamas in the Atlantic, from Panama to Cape Horn, and from the Liverpool Docks in England to Halifax harbour. Each story was worth listening to, and I laughed and cried, as we each in turn held the torch of story teller. That night was akin to a religious experience. We had all talked in tongues; each in turn used the language and sentiment that only lovers of the waters can understand, and as the evening stretched so did the stories. I lost count of the drinks I'd had and forgotten their names and faces, but it didn't matter. A good story once shared takes on a life of its own, and when I woke to find a hand written message of good luck taped to my kayak, I knew that my story, like theirs, had found a new home.

I left that morning in good spirits and almost immediately hit a rhythm. The weather was beautiful. The light breeze off the lake kept the humidity down, but the scenery I was paddling through was boring. At Raby Head I caught my last glimpse of Toronto. The CN Tower disappeared behind some trees and was gone. I had been ten hours in the saddle and covered 40 kilometers and just before Bowmanville, I called it a day.

It was a bitter sweet night. I had got too close to the city, trapped in a one-way street of manicured gardens down by the lakeshore. The light had been fading fast, and I had been forced to camp on a plot of municipal land. It was small and narrow, and far enough away from the lakeshore road to be spotted, but I wasn't its only guest. This small piece of open greenery used for boat launching, was also a haven for geese and goslings. At first they kept their distance, but once I had finished cooking and retired to my reading material inside my tent, they got more brazen. Initially, I was amused. My kayak and equipment must have looked like a Disney World of gadgetry to them. At first I enjoyed watching them at play, but that was before the squadrons of day shift workers returned. They swoop down in large V formation, taxied along watery runways, then greeted their neighbours in a gaggle of noise. It was as if a call had gone out, and every neighbourhood flock had turned up at my door step. I was turning into the main event, and their constant chatter kept me up for most of the night.

Possession is nine-tenths of the law, and when I rose and stuck my head out to greet the predawn chill, they were still there. Maybe they had surmised the only harm I could inflict was on myself, but when one - probably a sentry on guard - rushed forward, neck stretched to the limit, coiling around like an excited snake and snapping and hissing at my ankles, I'd had enough. The place was littered with their fresh soft pellets of shit. They had even got up onto the barbecue table, stained my stove and knocked over my white gas container. The sun was just starting to rise, and I could hear the main flock - no doubt readying themselves for take-off, just the other side of the slip-way down on the beach. I picked up my paddle, raced down to the water and surprised them.

I had never experienced anything like it. In Labrador you're either a lucky man, or a damn good hunter if you can get within spitting distance of a flock of Canada geese. I swore I could have chased them down and battered at least half a dozen of them out of their slumber, and had I have been on the Labrador Coast, I wouldn't have hesitated. To see so much food beat a hasty retreat was like watching a carton of chicken fillets disappear off a supermarket shelf. I watched them beat a path for the water, then like jumbo jets that require extended runways, slowly raise their bulky bodies into the air.

The day's paddle was a repeat of yesterday's. The

scenery in front was a border line of green. Green upon green with only the distant haze of some lakeshore industrial plant which I could rest my eyes upon. Sometimes I would spot a bulk carrier of grain, probably from Thunder Bay en route to Montreal, or Lakers full of iron ore pellets en route to Hamilton or Chicago from Sept-Îles. I would watch them pass, then disappear, and sometimes wished I could go with them. I was paddling point to point; in a groove and making good mileage, but I just wasn't enjoying myself. I had experienced these feeling before, at the beginning of a new adventure, and had always reached the other side, but this time I knew it was different.

The trip's foundation rested on a six-pack of beer. A stupid bet I had made six months ago. Since then, for my sanity and pride, I had loosely wrapped the paddle around the need to make a practice run. I had planned to kayak around the coastline of Newfoundland the following summer, and I had told everyone that I was taking this trip to test my endurance. I had kept this story up during interviews on radio and television, putting on a brave face, even agreeing with interviewers who praised my courage, told me what a personal achievement it would be. The story would fool people some of the time, but you can't kid yourself. The questions why was I on the water ? Why was I kayaking home and not flying? buzzed around my head like a pesky fly.

That night, I was in the mood for a pick-me-up. I made it to Cobourg; called in at its yacht club, put up my tent, gained permission to stay the night, then got drunk. For a guy who had been practically a teetotaller for twelve years, getting drunk two nights on the trot was too much for my body to take, and the next morning I felt like death warmed-up.

Today, I had something to shoot for. The thought of staying one more day in the lake was just too much to bear. I had an alternate route in mind. I have always liked lakes from the shoreline, especially those small enough to see details on the opposite shore. Lake Ontario is over 48 kilometers wide and 240 kilometers long. It's the smallest lake in the Great Lakes system, the flattest, and has the most habitation along its shoreline. Its waters are neither clear or drinkable anywhere near human habitation, and its shore-line is festooned with the flotsam and jetsam of city life. I wanted out. The thought of cutting from Proctor Point to Nicholson Island and then onto Long Point along Lake Ontario's shore was too much to bear. It had been my orig-inal plan, but now I was about to change it. I was fast approaching the point of no return at Proctor Point. I was still in two minds on whether to portage my kayak over the neck of land in front to Presqu'île Bay, then proceed down the Murray Canal and into the open waters of the Bay of Quinte, or stay in Lake Ontario when the wind picked up.

Without warning, the lake suddenly filled with steep chopping waves. I had never seen anything like them. It was as if someone had dashed down a flight of stairs, slipped on a loose-fitting carpet and pushed up a mass off folds. The waves didn't so much build as materialize from nowhere, and no sooner had the wind died, the waves flattened and their steep folds stretched back into the four corners of the lake. Twice more the wind picked up and the lake's surface chopped and slapped me about. The last time it changed direction, came out of the south west and blew me ashore down at the bottom of Popham Bay. The wind had made up my mind for me. I now had a one-kilometre portage along the beach, up and over a Provincial Park access road, then through the marshy channels into the shallow waters of Presqu'île Bay.

After five days of open scenery it was a pleasing sight to be enclosed on all four sides, but no sooner had I relaxed into the change of scenery when the mosquitoes struck. They were so big they could arm wrestle with you, and the noise they made buzzing around my ears sounded like 'the chain saw massacre.' They were relentless. They struck from every side at once, and no sooner had one filled up with my blood, when another took its place. I let them bite, it was useless to do otherwise. I closed down my ears, bit down hard on my paddle and telescoped my will down to the end of the Murray Canal. Ninety minutes later, I found myself bathing in a fresh breeze at the throat of the Bay of Quinte.

That night, I celebrated my good fortune on hearing about the Murray Canal with a huge fire. I'd spotted the canal's entrance at the top of my map, but because I didn't have its adjoining mate, I didn't know where it went to. I had only bought my seaway charts a few days before leaving, and as I didn't expect to take any short cuts down the lake, I hadn't checked them closely enough. It had been during last night's drinking session; an overheard conversation at the bar; an exchange of information, and I had left with the old sail boat and barge route from Trenton (at the beginning of the Trent-Seven Waterway from Georgian Bay,) to Lake Ontario under my belt. It was a stroke of luck, and so was my fire. I had fuelled it with arm-fulls of wind-dried dead marsh reeds. It kept the dancing mosquitoes away and its smoldering embers crackled and spat deep into the night.

The next day was like a Chinese Water Torture. The monotonous drip came from the distant flashes of reflected sunlight, and its bearer came in the form of the Belleville to Picton Bridge, some 24 kilometres away, whose traffic mirrored the sun's rays.

The wind that day was sometimes so strong that it picked up spray and jetted it into my eyes. Together with the strobe lighting effect caused by the vehicles crossing the bridge, it wore me down like a soap stone. I had little to no enthusiasm to give the armada of sail boats who raced up and down the bay that morning, and even less for the lone speedboat who dropped by for a chat in the early afternoon, for no sooner had I stopped to chat, when I went into reverse. It was a prime example of two steps forward, one step back, and when I eventually turned the corner at Grassy Point, I found little in reserve to take advantage of my newfound tail wind. I was bankrupt, and as if to underline the fact, quite suddenly an argument erupted. My left hand wouldn't agree with my right. I wanted to push not pull. For five minutes my head refereed this imaginary fight like a ping-pong match, and had a passing boat witnessed the incident they would have presumed I was suffering from sun stroke.

It was only late afternoon, but my shoulders and lower back were screaming out in pain. My eyes were sore from the constant spray and the palms of my hand were blistered and raw. I made camp on a small open point, erected my tent, laid down my roll-o-mat, then fatigue overtook me. I fell asleep on top of my sleeping bag, and didn't wake until the sun was setting on the day.

I was just starting to make my evening meal. I had boiled some water and had just opened one of my freeze-dried packets of food, when some one hailed me.

"Would you like to join the party ?"

There are times in one's life, when no means no, and others, when it means maybe. I did say no, and I thought I meant it, but I was so tired, so physically and mentally spent, that the thought of cooking an evening meal looked like a mountain I couldn't climb. I was wavering somewhere between fatigue and hunger when my new friend thrust a beer into my hand. Immediately the mountain face tilted vertical and I surrendered. I accepted his invitation, drank his beer on the spot, and thirty minutes later found myself propped up against his fridge with another beer in one hand and a burger in the other. I was paddling through cottage country, and in Canada, one's cottage, plus a long weekend, equals 'party time'.

Questions came thick and fast:

" Eh mate, where you from ?"

"What, in a kayak !"

"You're crazy".

"Give him another beer."

Then,

"Are you married..........! ! ! "

Now that line of questioning I like. It always leads to a sister, a distant cousin or even an ex wife, but they always lead to destinations that under the normal circumstances of my everyday life, seen to be beyond my reach. It's not that I have a woman in every port, far from it, but just like a beautiful lady who likes to get laid, but doesn't want the baggage of a commitment. I don't mind being that interesting person, the one that a lady can look back on in later years and say 'Yes, I knew him.' I know my limitations, but when I am into a trip, I seem to sprout wings and fly.

The girl I was about to meet didn't so much walk towards me as glide. She was the kind of girl who lives for a crowd, who knows how to play an audience, and the short distance she covered across the kitchen was like watching a skillful model walk down a cat walk. We are all a product of our faults. You are handsome, but vain. I am rich, but poor in spirit. She is intelligent, but plain. But I kid you not, when I am flying I can see the person under the skin, and this girl was beautiful, outside and in. Within minutes, she had read me like an open book. I am no social butterfly in parties. I like to watch and listen, speak when spoken to, and try my best to stay in the wings, but if I am left unattended for too long, I either pass out from nerves, drink or leave.

Julie was like my little tornado and that night I became her landing pad. She gave me her jacket, her purse, her ego and took off. I had no idea some one could talk so much, be so flirtatious, yet have so much energy to burn. It was as if her audience was willing her on, and wherever she was in the room that is where the action was. I felt as though I was in the eye of her tornado, both exciting yet still. The time flew by, and I was still sitting where she had left me, on the stairs overlooking the dining room, when the party eventually broke up. Then it was my turn.

I opened the door and she stepped out of her world and into mine. The night sky was amazing. The stars were so bright and the air so crisp, you could reach up and touch them. My camp set against the silvery flow of water looked as romantic a place to spend the night as a French chateau. My tea, she jokingly tasted like champagne, and the perfume from the bank was as seductive as musk oil. We must have talked for hours, exchanged secrets and dreams, but always there is a dawn, and just as she had held my hand at the party and given me a story to carry with me, so I did for her.

I cannot remember if it was something I said, but she started to cry, then she suddenly stood up and left. Every ounce of my being wanted to stand up and follow her, but I couldn't. I knew if I followed her back into the cottage, I wouldn't want to leave. I sat watching the water praying she'd come back, but I knew she wouldn't. I continued to stare into the water until the night sky began to melt into the dawn.

I broke camp just as the colours started to appear, and I left as the sun's rays broke free of the tree tops. They say the scent of a beautiful woman can linger for a long time and to replay her memory only makes it worse. I never did look back over my shoulder, but it was a hard page to turn, but I knew that I would.

The day was blistering hot. The banks were bleached of colour and the waters were without ripples. My heart wasn't in the paddle, and even after I had turned the corner at the bottom of Long Reach, and gained some colour and depth to the scenery, I couldn't rise to the occasion. I stayed in the cockpit all day. After no sleep the previous night, I was running on pure adrenaline. I drank milk and water, finished off the remains of the pizza Julie had given me, and had a Mars bar. I was unable to give my Bay of Quinte detour the justice it deserved. I had covered it in two days, paddling almost 100 kilometres, and its sheltered channel - sometimes stretching for up to two kilometres across - had given me all the colour and balance I could have hoped for. Its shores were open to both industry and agriculture; it had the manicured lawns of private homes and was dotted with the rustic retreats of weekend cottages; it had points of land, islands, and in places was deeply wooded, but that day the only picture I carried was of Julie.

Kingston had been the only town on Lake Ontario's

shore I wanted to see, and that evening its shoreline echoed to the sights and sounds of tradition. I saw a manpowered lawn mower being used; watched a skilled carpenter at work renovating a large open veranda, and even a stonemason touching up a delicately patterned rising sun above a door-way. Gardens were in the old British style; bordered with hedges, cut and manicured like signatures, and filled with colour. Its lazy riverside beaches, its rectangular parks and its heavily treelined roads had sprung from a heritage that crossed the Atlantic, and its towering high tech university is the flowering bud of its future. Kingston, with a population close to 90,000, is your typical backwater town. Laid back not only in its architecture, but in its people. That night I was forced to take shelter on a small patch of land, sandwiched between the lakeshore and some garden properties. All I had to do was walk up a garden path, knock on a door and announce my presence.

It's always been my experience that it is better that people know you are there, than not to know.As on that night, one small act of kindness is always replaid ten-fold. The old lady who answered the door insisted I stay for a cup of tea, which stretched into a sandwich, and on leaving into a tupperware container filled with oven-fresh cookies.

I woke up blistered and burnt. My nose was a bul-bous mass of burning sensitivity. My right elbow was a rash of minute water-filled bubbles, and the skin on my temple felt as though it had been stretched on a rack. I had not only forgotten to wear my hat under yesterday's sun, but had for-gotten to immunize my skin, with ointment and now I was paying the penalty.

Today, I had two options. I could take the south side of the lake and follow the Seaway's shorter route between Wesley Island and the States, or stick to the Canadian north shore and skirt past Gananoque. Both routes looked pic-turesque. The lake had tapered in and the view in front had cracked like a pane of glass. Lake Ontario was starting to empty through its splintered shoreline into the headwaters of the Saint Lawrence River. I was now paddling in a notice-able current. At this point my Seaway Chart had me 75 meters above sea level. From here to Montreal, I would have to paddle 300 kilometres, portage three locks and drop over 65 metres. Finally, I could put Lake Ontario behind me. I felt relieved. It was as if my trip had just started. At last it had a spirit if not a purpose, and as I wound around the numerous islands in front of the Canadian north shore, I found myself for the first time also since leaving Toronto with a landmark to shoot at, The Thousand Islands Bridge.

As soon as the day was more advanced, I stripped. The sun's rays were now beating down without hindrance and the islands were starting to wobble. They don't call this region a Thousand Islands for no good reason. The land mass that span the river looked like the fragmented pieces of a dropped slab of slate. The colours were amazing; bronze, brown, grey and all topped with a coating of lush green ferns. Thank God, I had a landmark to shoot for and a river current to push me along, for without them that day, I would have definitely been in trouble.

I've never been one to court history, visit museums or search out man-made landmarks, but some landmarks you can't escape from. Thousand Islands Bridge towers above the surrounding country side like a giant flexible ruler. Its primary function was, and still is, to carry freight from Canada to the U.S.A., but as the numerous postcards of this picturesque region will attest to, it's fast becoming the region's most popular tourist attraction. It had dominated my progress all day and now I was approaching it rapidly.

In my excitement at seeing the bridge up close, I'd drifted into some mini rapids on the north side of Ash Island. I was now in the grip of a strong current, full of whirlpools, and I was dancing to a different drummer. My paddle took little purchase and as I shot under the bridge, I could hear the dull drone of wheels on tarmac overhead. I now could care less if I was tipped by a half submerged log, or washed ashore in the rip current. I was transfixed by the sights and sounds above. The whole scene was one of mass chaos. A vast colony of birds, like the residents of a dozen beehives, were coming and going, banking this way and that, and peeling away from the bridge's support like soggy paper from a wall. There must have been thousands of them and one could only guess at the din they made, if only the vehicles would stop.

The river had given me an amazing two minute-adrenaline rush, and it was worth the price of admission. At this point, the current was so strong it was bubbling and muttering to itself in a way that was almost human. It bore me away from the bridge in overdrive, deposited me in a back eddy, and spun me around behind a point of land into a quite cove of rock and sand.

I didn't paddle much further that day. The current I'd just paddled through had announced the beginning of the Saint Lawrence Seaway. Lake Ontario was officially behind me, and I wanted to camp early and celebrate.

Chapter 2
The Saint Lawrence Seaway

I woke early to the mysterious beauty of pre-dawn mist. The view from my campsite on the back side of Hill Island was amazing. It was like looking through Alice's Looking Glass, to where shear cliffs, topped by mysterious objects, rose above their blankets of gloom. I sat mesmerized watching the river's currents bubble and ferment under my gaze, tracing its patterns of liquid silver into still pools of jet black oil. Two birds materialized from nowhere, then a jumping fish shattered my mirror. Only to return minutes later, in a frame of bronze as the sun started to rise. Two melancholy loons sang out to each other and a low flying flock of geese disturbed by my movements and woken by the sun - banked away from my camp and were soon lost in the mist. I didn't want to leave. Only a fool rushes a meal, and this morning I had been presented with an a-la-carte menu of moments to savour. In only a few more minutes the sun would start its inevitable course through the mist, and within the hour the whole scene would be bleached white, but this morning I was in luck.

The curtain of haze didn't bleach as it went, and by the time I was in the water and paddling, the early morning sky had turned into a crisp royal blue. I was full of enthusiasm. There was no wind and the river's surfaced was mirror perfect. Thousand Islands had lifted its skirt, and its pleasures were in full view. Every outcrop, tree, branch and twig had a reflected twin and the colours were vivid and bright. High in the sky, a flock of white tipped birds fluttered like pieces of paper, circled, then descended in small formations onto the river. Downstream and to the left of the bridge, a long peninsula, formed by a bend in the river and striped in gold and green by narrow fields of corn, extended like fingers down to the water's edge.

The islands were now starting to fan out, and for the first time I could catch more than just a glimpse of how the

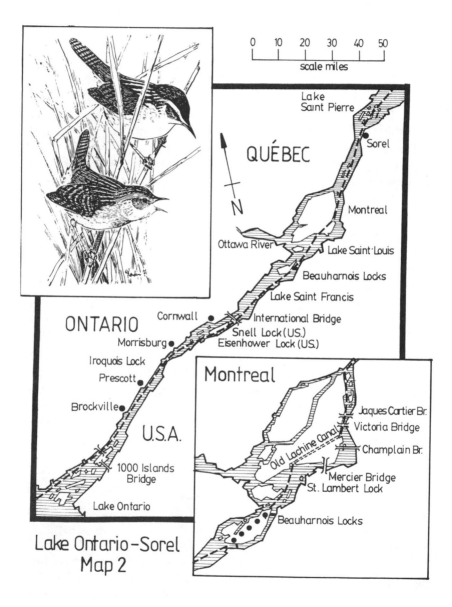

0   10   20   30   40   50
scale miles

Lake
Saint Pierre

QUÉBEC
• Sorel

N

• Montreal

Ottawa River
Lake Saint·Louis

Beauharnois Locks

Lake Saint Francis

ONTARIO   Cornwall •   International Bridge
Snell Lock (U.S.)
Morrisburg •   Eisenhower Lock (U.S.)

Iroquois Lock

Prescott •

Brockville •

U.S.A.

1000 Islands
Bridge

Lake Ontario

Montreal

Old Lachine Canal

Jaques Cartier Br.
Victoria Bridge

Champlain Br.

Mercier Bridge
St. Lambert Lock

Beauharnois Locks

Lake Ontario–Sorel
Map 2

other side lives. I was now paddling in the playgrounds of the rich and famous, and as the islands shrunk in size, their cottages grew.

When I emigrated to Canada, my dream was to own a cottage by the water. It would be my weekend retreat. Rustic but homely; heated by a wood-fired stove; lit by lantern light and water would come from a 'little house on the prairie', hand-pumped well. So much for my idea of getting away from it all. God knows where these people live normally. My dream cottage would fit in their out-houses and no doubt their generators could produce enough hydro to light up a small Ontarian township. Yachts seemed to be the vehicle of choice, although I did spot three float planes and a flotilla of multi-coloured seadoos. Manicured gardens were the norm, and the weeping willow with its branches hanging down into the river like rope bells, the tree of choice. White granite seemed to be most favoured by these home owners, and three stories their preferred height. I did pass one highly futuristic wooden chalet, with angles so sharp and panes of glass so big it seemed to defy all the known architectural laws of logic, and I even spotted a medieval fortress. None of these mega-cottages were my idea of a home-away-home, but then the old saying that 'you can tell the size of a man's penis from the size of his car' may have a lot to do with their construction.

Once past Grenadier Island the river started to pull in again. The shipping lane, lost for two days now, made a lazy diagonal turn and came back to the Canadian northern shore.

Just before Brockville the river's current picked up again, and I began to motor. The river tapered, then narrowed into a fast-flowing channel between some islands. It was just past noon. The sun was high and trees were detaching themselves from the bank. I had fallen victim to a mirage. A boat manifested itself in front of me, then turned into a floating log. Objects were starting to wobble, split and reunite into different shapes, then abruptly a huge object plugged up the channel ahead and everything fell into place.

It was a 'laker'. It looked like a huge rectangular red and white box, underlined by a thick band of white. It didn't so much cut a passage through the water as push up a tidal wave in front of it. The dull rhythmic drones of its engines echoed off the islands and tickled my ears. It was travelling much faster than I thought. I'd never seen one up so close before and as it passed, I turned to face it. It was awesome. Twice as long as a football pitch and maybe five stories high, it glided by as gracefull as a swan, then the swells hit. I watched them build, drop and build again. The swells picked me up and passed me gently from one to the other.

Suddenly a seadoo appeared from nowhere. It shot directly across and behind the laker, crashing into the first swell and rearing out of the water like an excited stallion jumping a fence. I followed it, playing in the swells and enjoying the view of a giant, close-up. Its propeller cut up the surface into a sea of bubbles, and my rudder and paddle found no purchase in its wake. I had the feeling that if I flipped, I would fall through the water and wouldn't stop until I hit the river's bottom. Until today, I had only seen lakers from a distance, and when another two appeared just past Brockville, I paddled out to a seaway buoy, anchored myself to it, and replayed the whole scene again.

That night, I made camp just before Maitland. I had noticed a small group of boys fishing; some perched in nooks on the bank and a couple clung precariously to bare roots of trees. At this point, the river's current was sluggish. Maybe I was passing over a deep pond full of fish. I'd brought along a folding rod, an accessory meant for spending a pleasurable interlude more than any need to eat fish. I headed for the shore, anchored myself to a fallen tree, attached one of my flies, turned on my radio and then stretched out in my kayak with the chord between my toes.

I stayed until the boys had gone. I had notice a small postage stamp of grass and I wanted to camp on it. I had passed many choice camp sites that morning, but since Brockville the few I had seen were; either too exposed, too overgrown, private property or municipally manicured with signs declaring 'no overnight camping'. I pulled my kayak over a broken bank, and hid it as well as I could in some willows. The spot I'd chosen for my tent just fit the bill, and the pebbled beach it faced was an ideal spot for an elicit camp fire. I was not afraid of being spotted by the police. I had a tailor-made story. 'Eh, I wasn't your average paddler', I told myself. After all it's not everyday that some one kayaks down the Saint Lawrence en route to their home in Labrador.

At first light, a time I was beginning to accept as a normal time for waking, I broke camp. Once again, I paddled out to the shipping lane, picked up the river's current and headed east. By mid morning the sun was hot on my face. I was beginning to applaud my decision to bring a baseball cap along. Even with my expensive sun screen, the sun's glare was already frying my second layer of skin, but at least the cap had saved my temple from the same kind of treatment.

At Cardinal, I skirted too close to an industrial wharf and swept past it as if in overdrive. The river was dropping a little, which coupled with the natural blockage at Gallop Island, only increased its current.

I was now fast approaching my first natural barrier at Iroquois Dam. Erected as flood gates to stabilize the river's depth, it stretches from one side of the river to the other. I was in two minds whether to shoot their 18 inch drop, or to take the old discussed Gallop Canal route and portage over its fill-in. I had summarized that if lakers could steam up and through the opening in the flood gates, then I could surely pass down through them, but that was before I got close.

The current suddenly picked up, 1500 meters up from the flood gates. I could see the river ahead slip into a natural trough, then pick up speed on route to the gate opening ahead. At 1000 meters, I notice a piece of driftwood shoot past. I was still out of the trough of fast flowing water, but at 500 meters, I bailed out, doubled back to the canal, paddled down to where it dead ended at a land-fill, and then portaged up and over it to the other side.

That morning, the radio had announced the begin-nings of a heat wave, and even with a river breeze, I was now boiling. It was so hot, the sun's light shimmered and danced in a heat haze. I was now stripped to the waist and trying to acquire a more uniformed tan, but the exercise did-n't last long. The river reflected the sun's rays like a mirror on dried grass and within the hour my shoulders had turned a shiny red.

At Morrisburg, the landscape flattened out as if it had been pressed by a rolling pin and at Cooks Point, where the river opens into Lake Saint Lawrence, I called it a day.That night, the sun set in technicolour. It changed slowly from gold to a deep saffron, and then loosing itself in an early evening mist, it shattered into millions of orange fragments. I should have felt on top of the world, but I wasn't. For some strange reason, the sunset had reminded me of the ones I'd seen so many times in Asia and Africa. Had I seen this all before?

I know why I take these trips; I know what they give me, and I know what I have sacrificed when I return. I've never glorified travel. For me it's a drug, a glorious escape with highs and lows. I've watched friends come and go like a sea tide, and over the years, as the perennial world trav-eller, I've become uncle Bernie to my friends' children. The rush of not knowing what lies around the next bend has sus-tained my travelling habits for over twenty years, but some-thing was missing. That night, I must have replayed in my head every love affair, every farewell and every missed opportunity to settle down. Five days before starting this trip, during an interview in Toronto, the interviewer had tweaked and prodded me at every turn. She wanted to get under my skin, asking why I always travelled solo, and did I ever get lonely? I am no stranger to this line of questioning, and in the past I have always been able to deflect it. But this time, the interviewer hit a nerve.

"Are you scared of commitments ?"
Her question came straight out of left field, and before I

could gather myself, I was into melt down.

"I'm a selfish bastard", I replied. I could hear my words, but I just couldn't believe what I was saying.

"When I leave on a new trip, I cut all ties. I can't afford the baggage."

My trip aren't exactly walks in the park. Whether I'm cycling through a civil war in Uganda, mountain climbing in the Himalayas, or snowshoeing through a blizzard, I can't afford sentiment to cloud my judgement.

"I never look back over my shoulder."

When the interview was finished, I felt like a repentant sinner. Like I'd just visited the confessional and been given absolution, but the feeling didn't last long. I'd just got to the stage door, and was just about to leave, when her last words stopped me in my tracks.

"You must have a heart of ice." I turned into her words. There was no malice in her tone, and nor the trace of a smirk on her face.

"*Yes you're right,*" I replied. *"That's why I'm still alive."*

At the time I felt cocky. I took her comment as a compliment, but now I wasn't sure. Her comment had turned into an itch I couldn't quite scratch. Neither positive or negative, but one I couldn't quite wrap my mind around. Until now, I had managed to file it away, but it had returned. That night I picked away at it, like an old scab. This would continue for the next 960 kilometres.. then, when least expected, it would burst.

The next day my second hurdle and major headache was put to rest, but before I reached the Eisenhower Locks on the American side of the Saint Lawrence, I fell victim to a most unusual incident.

Again, I had broken camp early, paddled to the shipping lane and caught the current, and was just within sight of the navigation sign warning of the locks ahead. I had paddled over to the American side, spotted a beautiful sandy beach besides a golf club, and had decided to take a break. I was into my second cup of coffee when a huge container ship steamed by. I watched its swell form, but thought nothing more of it. Five minutes later the beach drained. I may not have notice it, had it not been for my kayak. I had left it half in and half out of the water. There was no current in the small horseshoe cove. I had been too lazy to pull it out of the water and now it was high and dry. It was as if someone had pulled the plug out of a bath tub. All this time, a flock of geese had been congregating on a lip of grass, half way between the golf green above and the beach below. They had turned into the central focus of my break. Maybe six adults, and God knows how many young. They were mostly at rest, preening and cleaning themselves as if they'd just returned from a morning swim, when quite suddenly they burst into life.

A wall of water swept over the point of land at the end of the beach and erased the geese like a silent avalanche. The water didn't so much crest as pancake out. It picked up my kayak, smashed it against the bank, then snapped it back like a rubber band. I was in the water within seconds. At first the surge of water propelled me towards my kayak, but as the water rushed back, my feet sank into the sand and the kayak literally broadsided me. Luckily, I took most of the impact on my thighs and was able to stay upright and hang onto it. I could hardly believe my eyes. I would never have imagined that a passing container ship could raise such a surge of water. They were no warning signs posted on the beach, nor any visible signs of erosion on the bank that surely would have been caused by such continuous surges of water. Even the geese couldn't be that stupid!

I would retell this incident to people again, and again from here to Montreal, but no one came up with an answer. Maybe it had been a fluke, a boat overloaded, passing too close to shore, but I doubt it. I think the answer lies in the beach itself, in its unusual shape and its drop-off into the river. If anyone from Massena is reading this section, READER BEWARE. The beach is dangerous.

It was past noon before I got to the staging quay at Eisenhower Locks. This system of locks had been on my mind since Kingston. I wasn't only worried about the portage from one end of the lock system to the other, (small boats cannot pass through the locks) but I had forgotten to pack away my passport. Now, I was standing on American soil; the owner of a British accent and with no documentation to prove my Canadian citizenship. As far as the American Customs would be concerned, I wouldn't exist.

"So you're the guy with the kayak."

My saviour had a Texas drawl, loved kayaks and as luck would have it, had been the person to answer the phone when Julie had called from her home in Kingston to see if I had passed through yet. The old saying 'What comes around goes around' , had saved my bacon. The gods were smiling on me. Not only did my new found saviour pass on Julie's best wishes for my trip; he also insisted on taking me the 11 kilometres by road, from one end of the lock system to the other, in his pick-up. It all happened so quickly, I hardly had time to thank him. He was on his lunch break, so speed was of the essence. We quickly threw everything into the back of his pick-up, tied my kayak onto the roof and thirty minutes later I was back in the water.

Have you ever seen water tilt? I have. I'd just pushed off from the shore. The foot of Cornwall's hydro dam was to my left, and I was approaching Massena Point on my right at mark speed. The full force of the Saint Lawrence was now about to make a man made ninety degree turn between two islands, and its current now gripped me like a vice.I was right in the middle of the fast flowing current and there was little I could do, but go with the flow. I rounded the bend in overdrive, shot out of it like a bullet and minutes later squirted between two man-made barriers of rock like wet soap under pressure (the rocks were there to break up the river's current as it returns to its natural course in the Seaway). All this time I had been aware of two fishermen on the rocks ahead, but as I passed them, one almost fell into the water with surprise. I grabbed onto their boat, spun around in the back eddie, and with only the time it takes to exchange introductions, was feasting on their sandwiches.

There are some things best left to others to write

about, but seeing is believing, and I can only relate what I saw, and how I felt about it. Ontario's outlandishly high cigarette tax was in its second year, and I had already bought some under-the-counter packets at a much reduced rate. I heard about the cross-border smuggling around Cornwall, but in this technological age of super cops, I didn't think it possible. Cigarette smuggling had been in and out of the news on a regular basis. I had never heard of anyone being arrested, and now could understand why.

It all started just past Hopkins Point when two young bucks from the reserve (on the U.S. side of the river) shot out of nowhere and began doing donuts around my kayak. I was more frightened than angry. You have to have been in a kayak to know how naked and weak you can feel when being attacked by two powerful seadoos. I know they weren't trying to capsize me. They were just having fun, but to capsize in the middle of a fast-flowing river at the mercy of two kids, young enough to be my sons, is no laughing matter. The incident only lasted minutes, but by the time they left, I was full of fear.

I had noticed two houses on the bank of an island, and I judged by their size and lack of normal upkeep to be part of the reserve. I was worried the two young bucks would return, so I'd paddled towards the houses, thinking that I could shout out for help in case they returned. I was within five hundred meters from the bank. I could just make out some native markings on a gold flag hanging besides the house, when two men appeared with binoculars, looking in my direction. They weren't exactly dressed in civvies and when they didn't return my waves, I felt uneasy. Suddenly, a deafening noise, like that of a jet engine preparing for take-off, startled me, and no sooner had their boat come into view, than it had shot across the river like a guided missile. It must have been travelling in excess of 160 k.p.h. and in less than a minute, had turned into a silver streak. I watched it go down the river, then rear up, turn and stop about four kilometres down stream.

What happened next had all the hallmarks of an

army maneuver. The boat had not even come to a full stop when a medium sized truck appeared on the road above. Four men jumped out; chained linked, then passed one carton after another from boat to truck. The whole maneuver lasted less than ten minutes and before the truck's back shutters had been closed, the jet boat had fired up its engines and was streaking back across the waters towards me.Looking back on the incident it was like being a bit player on the set of a Sylvester Stallone action movie. And when, thirty minutes later, I was back paddling on the Canadian shore, within sight and sound of the Saint Lawrence's monotonous border of manicured suburbia, I was more than a little relieved.

I ended the day some two hours later. I had had enough excitement for one day and when it started to rain lightly, just the excuse to turn in for an early night night.

I woke to another world. Last night's rain must have incubated billions of flies. The air was thick with them, the ground underfoot carpeted with their dead and dying bodies, but nothing compared to the sight of them rising off the river's surface. They fluttered in yellow pools of movement and got everywhere, and I mean everywhere. They followed my progress all day, forcing me offshore into the shipping lane and it wasn't until early evening when they mysteriously disappeared, that I retuned to the shore.

Once again, I overshot good campsites for the sake of added mileage. The sun was now sinking, and so were my spirits. Willows knotted the banks I was paddling past, and what clearings they offered looked uninviting. Marsh reeds don't exactly inspire me with confidence. There was a complete absence of current close to shore. The slight bend in the river had turned into a catchment pit for silt and dead flies. There wasn't a hill, blip or grassy knoll to camp on that I could possibly paddle to before dark. It was depressing Only an hour before, the shoreline had been a haven of campsites. I had passed acres of cultivated pasture, and even some manicured lawns with their chance invitation of an evening meal. All had dangled before me like bait on a hook, but I'd been cruising. Looking for that ideal spot to pitch my tent, I had, so to speak, missed the boat.

It was getting distinctly cooler. There was a hint of mist in the air, and a pungent smell of stagnant ponds wafted in from the shore. The dull pain at the base of my spine was slowly working its way up to my shoulders, and my knees were starting to hurt. They were all signs of tiredness, but there was nothing I could do but grin and bear it.

I kept on paddling until the sun had set. Only the gloom of early evening and a slight drizzle drove me ashore.I had probably had the most incident-filled day to date, but that evening it was of little consolation.

I ended up on a postage stamp of elevated dry ground, surrounded by swamp and clouds of mosquitoes. The smell was suffocating and the blood thirsty flies attacked without mercy. That evening, I couldn't even muster the energy to cook. I ate my remaining chocolate bars inside my tent, drank the cans of orange juice I had been saving for just such an occasion, then slipped into my sleeping bag for an early night.

Usually, I can fall asleep the moment my head hits the sack, but not tonight. I was still unwinding from the adrenaline rush those two young crazy seadooers had given me earlier in the day. As if I hadn't enough on my plate, I was now beginning to add these machines to my already expanded list of potential obstacles. It's at moments like these when my brain cries out for a diversion; for some mindless background hum to latch onto and swallow me up. It's one of the reasons I carry a radio and that night my valium came in the soothing tones of CBC's Fireside Al', aka Alan Maitland. He's a natural charmer. He's like your favourite uncle; the one you curled up with when you were a child; who kept you spell bound with his stories, and who was so familiar you would be lost without him. It's not the stories he reads out on the radio that I find soothing, but his voice. Alan has the pipes of a good base tenor and the gravel tones of a two pack-a-day smoker. I have lost count of the times he's lulled me to sleep or given me cheer on a dull day, and this evening was no different.

I was now fast approaching the lip of the Laurentian Escarpment, and with it, my first distant horizon since leaving Lake Ontario. After two weeks of restricted river level views from my kayak, crossing Lake Saint Francois the following day was almost like flying in a helicopter. The view was tremendous. To the southeast, the forest-covered mountains of the American Adirondacs were tapering off in shades of green, while in the distant north, rising above the rich farmlands of the Ottawa River like a cresting wave, were the Laurentian Mountains of Quebec. This whole area is rich in history, and its strategic importance, let alone its majestic panorama, hadn't escaped me. The Coteau and Cascade Rapids around Salaberry Island had been the fur traders' last major hurdle before they could exploit Canada's rich interior. They are the main reason the city of Montreal was built where it is, and also the reason it's Canada's second largest port, behind Vancouver. I am not a nostalgic person, but the combination of tremendous views and rich history dominated my crossing of the lake. It wasn't until I had entered the man-made and characterless high-walled Beauharnois Canal system, that I came back down to earth.

Thank God for telephones and the nature of gossip. It's not that the canal's management had rolled out the red carpet for my arrival, but I was expected, and I now took full advantage of their hospitality. I showered and changed, used their kitchen to cook-up my evening meal, and most importantly, secured the promise of a morning lift around the locks.

For whatever reason, I always seem to have problems with men in uniform. Until the moment I was stopped by the river police, my morning's paddle had been relatively uneventful. My lift had materialized on queue, transporting me and my kayak around the locks. I had paddled past the junction of the Ottawa River. I had traversed Lake Saint Louis before the midday heat and was now half way across the Saint Lawrence River en route to the

Lachine Yacht Club on Montreal's western island. I judged myself to be well above the dangerous Lachine Rapids and was drifting in its lazy current, taking in Montreal's glittering skyline. I hadn't a care in the world. I had friends to meet, a place to stay, and I was at that very moment visualizing the night's a-la-carte menu of scallops, salmon and cheese cake. I was, so to speak, in a different world, when suddenly the police boat came out of the blue and burst my bubble. *"ATTENTION! ATTENTION!"*

Now, my French isn't good at the best of times, and, when faced by a uniform, almost non-existent. To say we got our wires crossed was to put it mildly, and what happened next was more fitting a 'Drew Carey' comedy sketch than a close call with nature.

It all started innocently enough. The police stopped me to give me a polite scolding for not wearing my life jacket. One of the officers had held out his own, pointed to mine strapped on my kayak, then put it back on. Even a complete moron could have understood his meaning, but it was when he began pointing in two different directions at once, upstream, that I lost him.

I give the officer his due, from the very outset he tried to use mime instead of talking. Maybe it was my initial bewildered look, or perhaps I have a tattoo on my forehead that reads 'ENGLISH ONLY'. Whatever the reason, we became locked in a game of 'Give us a Clue'. For about five minutes we danced together, him leading the way with animated movements, while I, my brain working in overdrive, tried to follow. He was pointing this way and that. Sometimes scolding with his looks and sometimes throwing his arms up in dismay. It's not that I was treating it all as a joke, but when he called out *"RAPID"*, then pointed downstream, the dime dropped.

I was in deep shit. I was on the wrong side of the marker buoys he'd pointed out. I was approaching dangerous waters in overdrive. The river was dropping away all over the place. It was as if I was standing at the top of a hill, looking down. I had drifted into a lagoon; a noman's land of dry water; cut off in three directions by rapids. I had obviously misjudged my traverse of the river; undershot the safety buoys and was now perilously close to the rapids. Even my route to the marina was fraught with danger. I had been told that, even for a seasoned river kayaker, the Lachine Rapids can be dangerous. For a novice like myself, paddling a top heavy sea kayak, it was near suicidal.

It's not that I was frightened. In fact the only thought that went through my head when the police boat finally left, was that being sucked down the river and shooting the rapids would make a great story, but that thought didn't last long. The current suddenly gripped my kayak and swung it around 180 degrees. I was now looking down the throat of the rapids. My brilliant story had been replaced by a sombre eulogy. What I saw, I didn't like. The river had tilted and was starting to boil. I could now hear the dull background drone of water rising and pitching over rocks. I'd never shot rapids before, and I sure as hell didn't want the experience to be my last. They stretched for as far as the eye could see, and the waters flowing under the Mercier Bridge looked a nightmare.

I back paddled, turned against the current, then paddled back up-stream as if my life depended on it. When I eventually made it back over the lip of the rapids into the lagoon, I immediately set a course for the nearest buoy.

An hour later, I was paddling into the marina. I passed the police boat at its entrance like a wet puppy dog, with my tail between my legs. The officer whose animated warning had saved my bacon had a coat hanger in his mouth. He was smiling from ear to ear. One can only imagine the story he would tell later, and who could blame him? For once I had attached myself to one buoy, when the rest fell into place like a jig-saw puzzle. Notices warning of the rapids were both in French and English, and you'd have to be blind not to see them when leaving the marina. In my defense however, I had crossed from the opposite shore.

I've been told, 'A good lie is better than the boring truth', and that night surrounded by a friendly atmosphere, eating a lobster supper in the old quarter of Montreal, I stretched the story of my 'near death experience' to the limit. By midnight, all the day's memories had been washed away by red wine, and when I woke with a hangover, they were only a foggy memory.

I took two days off with my friends, and I needed them. I was tired, but most off all, I wanted to check out the old Lachine Canal through downtown Montreal. It was built to take traffic above the Lachine Rapids, and has long been put out of business by its high-tech brother, the Saint Lambert Lock system on the southern shore. Over the years, it has fallen into a bad state of disrepair, it still looked worth while investigating. Six years before I had used the cycle path besides the lock, which runs from behind the Lachine Yacht Club to Montreal Harbour on the east side of the city. I hadn't made it to the end, but from memory it looked feasible. Its lock gates had been stripped, and all that remained were three mini waterfalls, but portaging around them from memory shouldn't pose too much of a problem. It sounded fine and dandy except for one vital detail. It was illegal. The canal is closed to any kind of traffic, but to be the first person to paddle down it since its closure over twenty years ago seemed worth the risk. After all it was why I crossed over the river in the first place. There was no way I was going to negotiate another characterless lock system. Turning back didn't enter the equation. It would be the Lachine Canal, or a ride through town.

I spent one whole day cycling up and down St. Patrick Street by the side of the canal. I memorized the portages, their slip-ways, the dead-ends that split away from the main route, and the best way of crossing the busy inter-section at the back of the Lachine Yacht Club. There was only one section I couldn't check, and as luck would have it, it was probably the worst.

Just after the Moulins Road Bridge the canal sud-denly disappeared under a huge railway siding for freight trains. It was all a dark mystery, and when I eventually picked it up again on the other side, it was even darker. There was no current. I had no idea if this invisable section of the canal, had been drained and filled-in, or if its current had been redirected by some kind of overflow dam. I couldn't see a thing, and to compound my situation, there was no one to ask.

It really was a mystery, but one that didn't deter me. I was more determined than ever to tackle this canal. I had seen numerous cyclists, and I guessed they would all be quite willing and able to stop and help me with my portages, if needed. If worse came to worse, there was always my friend's car. Securing my kayak to its roof wouldn't be a problem.

To be up and about before a great city awakes is awesome. To watch a city wake up is akin to kicking an ant hill. One minute all you see is empty space, and the next mass confusion. The following morning, I was across the road at the back of the Lachine Yacht Club and into the canal before the first commuters took to the streets, but it didn't last long.

Soon, I was right where I like to be. Front and centre of attraction. Cyclists, joggers, roller bladders, and morning walkers with their dogs were stopping by the dozen. They were all gob-smacked. Even the car commuters now clogging up St. Partrick Street honked their horns and waved. I must have looked like some rare bird returning after many years to nest. I had been told that the canal hadn't been used in eons. I had also been warned about its pollution, but was finding it nowhere near the sweaty armpit of Montreal's waste. Sure it wasn't pristine - I would hate to capsize in it - but it wasn't raw sewage, either.

I was now paddling through the district of Lasalle and closing in on the city's downtown pyramid of concrete and glass. Montreal's three great bridges, the Champlain Bridge, Victoria Bridge, and Jacques Cartier Bridge, now rose above Verdum's industrial skyline in viaducts of steel. The dull drone of the traffic they carried filtered down from above, like the sounds of a storm at sea. The circle was complete. I was now surrounded by the prying eyes of rush-hour at the peak of its aggression. Even if I could have escaped the stop-go sounds from the traffic on St. Patrick Street, the constant beat from above was suffocating. This rare bird was losing his feathers. I felt naked, and it wasn't until after I had portaged around my first lock, and entered the concrete jungle of downtown that the doors closed and the noise of rush-hour finally filtered itself out.

I was now within sight of Moulins Road. I could see its bridge and the black hole I would have to paddle through. I stopped paddling, and screwed open my flask of coffee. I was weighing up my options - the width of the tapered canal in front, its current, the space under the railway bridge behind, and its shaft of seductive light. Deciding to go for it. I put paddle to water when a sudden down draft of wind churned up the canal. It was a helicopter with a zoom lens pointing in my direction. Holy smoke! Caught in the act. I was either being recorded for the evening news, or was it for tomorrow's court appearance? Then, no sooner had the helicopter turned away than I spotted a police cruiser parked on the bridge in front.

Nothing, and I do mean nothing, was going to deter me. I am a stubborn son-of-a-gun, and when I have made up my mind to do something not even wild horses can hold me back. I had already portaged three locks; two with the help of cyclists. I had been framed in film, recorded on video and no doubt this morning would be the topic of conversation around many an office cooler. I had in turn felt used and abused, and also been pampered like a prince. Somehow, I had got it into my head that I wasn't just paddling down the canal for me, but for all those nine-to-fivers who'd seen me. Whether I liked it or not, I was now public property, and if the little people wanted to live out their Peter Pan dreams that morning through me, then who was I to disappoint them? I paddled straight up to the bridge, waved at the two police officers, then continued underneath.

The noise from the vehicle traffic came in waves, but

didn't last long. As soon as I disappeared under the neigh-
bouring railway bridge, my whole world tapered into an eery
silence. I could now almost touch its roof with my hands and
its walls with my paddle. I was passing under some kind of
concrete platform, built to span the canal, and to carry the
freight trains above. It had for all intents and purposes
turned the canal into a watery tunnel.

The canal now made a slow, ninety-degree turn into
the shaft of light I had spotted earlier. It was as I had
guessed, an overflow dam - a short off-shoot from the main
canal, and as I paddled past it, I saw the Saint Lawrence
River below.

After five minutes of paddling, I finally hit the light of
day. The canal opened, then deadened in front of a wall of
cultivated grass. I was home and dry; for, rising behind the
knoll of grass, was the harbour.

I still had three more obstacles to negotiate. The first
got rid of the second. The helicopter had indeed carried a
film crew, and a reporter was waiting to interview me. The
police, never patient at the best of times only stayed long
enough to see the camera roll, then left. And finally the short
portage across the park into the harbour was made with the
help of a small group of happy-go-lucky extras, who - on
finding out that they would be on the evening news - were
only too willing to help me carry my kayak from canal to harbour.

The day was not even half over before I started to put
some mileage between myself and its harbour. In all hon-
esty, I was glad of it. Unlike Toronto's Harbour front which
has reinvented itself into a lively lakeshore community of
marinas, luxury condominiums and a compact freight terminal, Montreal's Harbour looked depressingly colourless and
dead. Where once the sounds of metal upon metal was a
twenty four hour industry, only silence and decay remain.
The port looked only a shadow of its former self. Cranes lay
idle, and its grain elevators near Verdun were only echoes
of dead space. Huge warehouses, windows boarded or broken, were now an economic testament to a new order that

doesn't take prisoners, and its miles of deserted wharf - where once a proud army of men worked - was living proof that all man-made things eventually surrender back to nature. Bushes were now pushing their way through cracks in concrete and the river's current was beginning to reclaim the rest. There was a smell of death in the air; not human but one of the spirit. The harbour was obviously too big for the tonnage it handled, and in drastic need of some major surgery. Thankfully, the harbour flew by at a jogger's pace. The river's strong current pushed me along, and by nightfall I was camped on a small sandy beach on the south shore of Vercheres Island. It had been my best day yet in terms of mileage. I had paddled across Montreal Island and then put over 40 kilometres between me and the city without break-ing sweat.

There is something almost therapeutic about lighting a fire after a long hard day, and that night I needed one. I had been glad to put Montreal behind me. There would be no more locks to portage. Soon the Saint Lawrence's river banks would rise into the shoreline cliffs of open sea. I now couldn't wait for the rolling surface of ocean swells; the noise of surf rubbing up against pebbled beaches and the cries of sea gulls. My eyes were sore from the constant change of daily objects, they rubbed up against, and I now craved the soft sea horizons that dilute themselves into the sky. I was tired of kayaking through an industrial corridor of pollution. I missed the salt-laden sea air, its perfumed gar-dens laced with the scent of seaweed drying in the sun. I wanted to be woken by a refreshing sea breeze, and air that was fresh and crisp, not humid. But most of all, I missed the daily bookmarks of a good sunrise and sunset and a canopy of stars to sleep under. True my kayak trip from Toronto to Montreal had been filled with incident, but it was time to turn the page and start a new chapter.

That night the Saint Lawrence must have read my mind. The sun set into the foothills around Montreal in a blaze of colour. Wind-blown clouds were like the wings of a giant grey bird dipped in blood, and as the clouds changed so did the technicolour. A purple necked giraffe, a pale blue beard, then a snake-filled pit of royal blue serpents. Finally a brilliant white streak coming from a jet, miles high, was my only memory of a great sunset. And as I turned in for the night to the crackling sounds of dying embers, the stars popped out on queue into an ink black sky.

I broke camp in a heat wave. It was hot, unusually hot so early in the morning. The humidity was as sticky as molasses, and you couldn't buy a breath of fresh air for love nor money. It held its breath like that for two hours, then the rain came. At first it drifted down as fine as mist, then in pulsating waves like a fluctuating shower. It stung my face with the pin point force of needles and in turn churned up the river's surface into a cauldron of bubbles. It lasted less than thirty minutes and as soon as it stopped, a thick fog descended. The morning now turned into one of those stop-and-go affairs, where shoreline sounds come and go with the land, and it would only get worse.

The only consolation about being lost on a river, I've been told, is that if you go downstream you are bound to arrive somewhere different from where you started. A river's current, like gravity, falls in one direction only, but this law doesn't always apply to the Saint Lawrence.

Just past the town of Sorel, the river splinters into a maze of narrow channels, picks up steam, then suddenly opens like a yawning mouth. Lake Saint-Pierre is a natural water shed. It's caused by a sharp bend in the river at one end and a narrow cut through the hills at the other. It's a place where the current dies and, today, an ideal place for the fog to settle.

With no visible current, the thick fog pushed my panic buttons. I hadn't expected to use a compass so early into the trip, and now that I needed it, my compass was nowhere to be found. I had started to hop from one shipping lane buoy to the next, but the thick fog made it an impossible task on my nerves. I saw my first buoy at the lake's entry, but when an unseen laker passed and its powerful wake rocked

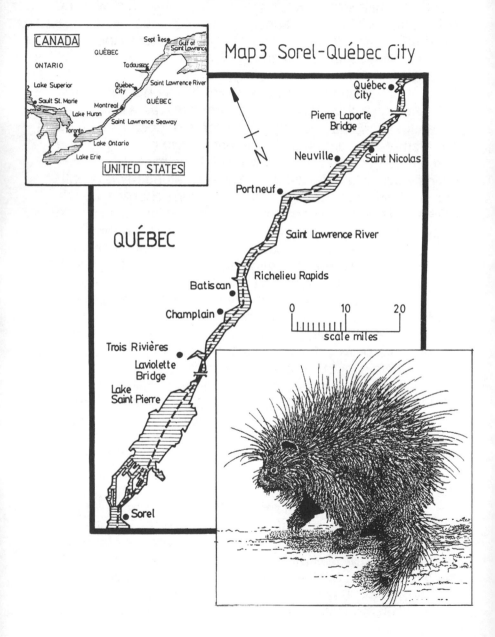

CANADA

ONTARIO

QUÉBEC

Sept Îles

Gulf of
Saint Lawrence

Tadoussac

Lake Superior

Québec
City

Saint Lawrence River

Sault St. Marie

QUÉBEC

Montreal

Lake Huron

Saint Lawrence Seaway

Toronto

Lake Ontario

Lake Erie

UNITED STATES

Map 3 Sorel–Québec City

N

Québec
City

Pierre Laporte
Bridge

Neuville

Saint Nicolas

Portneuf

QUÉBEC

Saint Lawrence River

Richelieu Rapids

Batiscan

0   10   20

Champlain

scale miles

Trois Rivières

Laviolette
Bridge

Lake
Saint Pierre

Sorel

me only minutes later, I scuttled the idea and paddled back to shore.

I was now passing through a surrealistic world of eerie shadows. An upturned tree with roots frozen as if in the throws of death loomed up out of the gloom. Ducks materialized in bursts of sound, but before my eyes could wrap around their shapes they would melt back into the mist. Meanwhile the sun was starting to force its way through the fog. Diffused shafts of light offered up enticing pools of colour, but like the wavering 'northern lights' they were constantly in motion. I was still paddling through acres of colourless vapour, still clinging to the lake's hemline, but gradually the fog began to lift, and with it my spirits.

Somewhere ahead, I heard the distinctive high-pitched purr of a power boat's engine, but before I could pin-point its location it died away. Then, I spotted a red buoy. At last my eyes had something to fix onto, and within minutes, three more buoys fell into place.

I now gingerly paddled through the mist from one buoy to the next until one hour later - stretching across my shortened horizon - the long dark line I had been paddling towards took shape. Life now returned to the lake. A thickly wooded point came into view, and as I drew near, the sound of cars told me I had finally got to the other side.

I chose to camp just above a beautiful sandy beach within a stone's throw from the old abandoned lighthouse at Pointe Du Lac. Everywhere the sweet smell of nectar hung in the air. I had pitched my tent on a quilted garden of colour. They were pockets of yellow, flashes of red and bordering the beach in a carpet of white, some late-blooming wild strawberries. It was a glorious end to the day. The sun was just starting its slow descent, but its rays washed over the beach without hindrance. The sky was cloudless; the lake glass calm, and what fog remained had long since retreated into the folds of its shorelined foothills.   I   now   found myself alone on a deserted beach with time on my hands and a playground to play in. I was in my element. I'm never lonely on my own and never lost for words when talking to myself, especially when I am walking. I love taking walks. I like best the unrestricted ones. The walks where I can choose my own rhythm and unwind at my own pace. That evening, I walked and walked and walked. After being a prisoner to my wet suit all day, the feel of a light breeze on my skin and the tickling sensation of fine sand underfoot was invigorating. Time just ticked by, but who was counting?

That night, I took a moonlight dip. There were flocks of ducks everywhere, but they all kept their distance. Some turned on spotting me and paddled away in silent ripples, while others, much more vocal, beat their wings like pistons in the water, while all the time crying out their displeasure. At one point, I startled a family of geese, who's neat little band of goslings dropped under the water's surface like a scattering of stones as soon as they saw me. It was a night to remember.Later, the appearance of a lone white tailed deer on the beach was just icing on the cake.

The next morning everything was wrapped in a haze. The lake was still and the hills that loomed above its dense-ly forested banks were, at first light, so indistinct that they seemed only to be a figment of my imagination. It was going to be another hot day and, by the looks of the sky, a rainless one.

Once again the Saint Lawrence cut a course through high banks. That morning, I shot under the Laviolette Bridge in overdrive; past the industrial city of Trois-Rivieres at a jog-ger's pace, and all before its rush-hour of commuters had revved up their engines.

Rocks were now starting to sprout up on the shore and the bordering farmlands were in full retreat. Gradually the river banks were starting to climb, taper in and become vertical. The river had once again turned northeast and was beginning to pick up momentum. I was within striking dis-tance of tidal waters. The river was still pristine in places, and drinkable, but I knew that once I had shot the Richeliue Rapids, those days would be over. From here to Quebec City, I could expect very strong currents whenever the tide was falling. Before I could exploit them however, I had to call it quits.

I cut my day short just past Saint-Charles des Grondines. It's not that I was tired from paddling - a moderate current had pushed me along all day - and it's not because it was late - rush hour was just starting to make its way back to the suburbs. No, it was because I was suffering. My head was in a tail spin. It had been a blistering hot day. The glare from the river had pounded my head with the relentless rhythm of a bass drum. I just couldn't escape it. My fuel tanks were empty and I had been running on pure adrenaline since mid afternoon. I had all the symptoms of sunstroke. A pounding headache, fever and the shakes, and when I experienced a sudden surge of blood to my brain and fell getting out of my kayak, any thoughts I had of continuing vanished as my head hit the sand.

The hours that followed were utter torment. I had this unquenchable thirst but I couldn't keep a drop down. No sooner did I douse its flames when my throat would be consumed by this irresistible urge to bring it back up again. My stomach was gripped with cramps and my hypothalamic skin by pins and needles whenever I moved. My only relief came when laying completely still. I finally gave in to sleep more out of relief than fatigue.

The next morning, my body felt like it had been through a fifteen round title fight with George Foreman. I ached all over, but at least my head was clear. My sleeping bag was soaked in sweat and a musky smell of fever pervaded my tent. I now had this humongous appetite, but not the energy to cook for it. I packed in slow motion, then walked to the nearest roadside diner and straight into another sickness.

When I am struck by hormonal imbalance, I tend to walk like a disjointed giraffe and talk in tongues. Some people call it love at first sight. I call it a sickness.

Perhaps on any other day the girl that served my table might have just have looked attractive at best, but after last night's fever, she looked like an angel. She had neither the classic lines of a model, nor the well-rounded figure of a sex goddess, but this girl had character, oodles of it, and that's what attracted me. It was in the details. The easy flow of her loose fitting skirt. The confident bounce in her step, and the defiant way she pushed her shoulders back. I can still remember the scorpion tattooed on her left shoulder, the shock of purple in her hair, and the squeaky nervous laugh she forced through a gap in her teeth. But it was her eyes that reeled me in. They were as large as moons and as deep as any ocean. She flirted constantly and hovered around my table like some kind of humming bird. She was powerful medicine and just the right tonic to wash down my food. Before I left the diner, I had made a miraculous recovery.

I broke camp that morning and pushed off into a falling tide. The sun shone from a cloudless sky and there was a gentle cooling breeze from the northwest. The river's current was now more powerful. I was about to enter the section known as the 'Rapids' I had initially planned to paddle down its northern shore, but I discovered it was shallow and festooned with boulders. A laker, maybe two miles away and what looked like hundreds of feet below me, was slowly edging its way upstream in the shipping channel. I could already hear its powerful engines, but just as the boat approached Richelieu Island, it slipped down a gear and started to turn. A huge wash seemed to hide its bow, it looked as though it would flip at any moment. It was all an illusion caused by the strong current, but it was still an amazing sight.

The current was so strong that, in places, I didn't have to paddle, just adjust my rudder and go with the flow. Banks had become high cliffs and the river just dropped at their feet. I crossed paths with the laker at speed. Its crew members were clearly visible and as we exchanged waves, the ship's horn let go a deep blast. I shot the Richelieu Rapids in no time. I covered the 10 kilometres in less than a hour, turned its corner at Pointe-au-Platon and was now gliding in still waters, but the best was yet to come.

There are times when I wish I could see the Saint Lawrence from a speed boat. Sure, I would miss all those subtle details close to shore - the natural breezes off the river, the unique scents and sounds of its life - but sometimes speed is better, and the faster the picture it flashes, the more memorable. The sudden sight of Pierre Laporte Bridge and the deep vertical chasm it spans was like a towel being dropped. It's the sudden nudity. The unannounced view imprints itself in your mind in a way that prolonged association rarely achieves. I had been travelling so slowly that these sudden views were a rarity, for not only was the view ahead clear and sharp under the sun, but set against a contrasting backdrop of menacing dark clouds, a spectacular one.

I have experienced many thunderstorms over the years, and the more exposed I have been the better the experience. I had already been caught out twice on this trip, but each time they had approached from the side, gave little warning and passed quickly. This storm was different. It gave me time to prepare, as it formed before my eyes and headed straight towards me.

I was paddling in a purple patch. It was the calm before the storm. The air was still, the atmosphere charged and the sky and river empty of birds and ducks. The clouds were mushrooming like germs under heat and the bridge was already lost to a curtain of rain. I was paddling like crazy towards a Seaway buoy. I wanted a front row seat. I wanted to experience the storm from the water and not from the shore, and when I reached the buoy, I tied on and waited.

The light show from a distance was riveting. Zig-zag streaks of pulsating light lit up the clouds like Christmas trees and its thunder rippled and echoed from point to point. Dark curtains of rain danced on both sides of the river, then gathered in force and united as one. The storm now raced towards me like a runaway truck. It tore up the surface of the river, atomized its spray, then sucked it along in an ever thickening cloud. I now braced myself for the inevitable, but when it hit, it hit with a vengeance.

I was bushwhacked and blinded at the same moment. The first gust of wind threatened to lift up the kayak. Anything that wasn't tied down became airborne. I lost my baseball cap, my gloves, and my paddle was ripped from my hands. My kayak took on a life of its own. It swung like a pendulum on a short leash behind the buoy and I was powerless to control it. By now, all signs of the sun had been eclipsed. Lightning flashed, then burst in my ears like depth charges. The storm came in waves. The rain beat down, vertical one minute then, driven almost horizontal the next. Then the hail struck.

It sounds almost biblical by today's standards. The nineties generation are the children of technology. We live in an age that has been blunted by science and cushioned by insurance companies. Natural wonders are for the 'Weather Channel', or the storm junkies who chase them down, but to be centred in one, to be alone, to be past the point of fear, is to be exhilarated and deflated all in the same breath. I swear, I saw lightning strike the river only yards away. I saw its steam pattern rise and smelt its vapour. I caught ice pellets as big as marbles and experienced gusts of wind that threatened lift-off. It was one of those experiences that money can't buy. Had it struck on land, I might be writing a different story.

Thirty minutes later, peace returned. The sun burst out again, scattering the clouds. Steam rose, vapourized and stained the air with the sweet smell of grass. Slowly life came back to the river. Once again, I could hear the sound of cars from the shore and speed boats were returning to the water. I now had the time to count the cost of the storm. My cap and gloves had gone the way of the river, and I was now paddling with my spare, but the experience: PRICE-LESS.

The next morning, I woke with a jolt. One moment it was all peace and tranquility and the next chaos. I had been trying to ease my way back out of a restless sleep, to savour the last dredges of night, but it wasn't to be. The predawn groan of traffic over the distant Pierre Laporte Bridge had at first been like background music. I was still tired. I had not fallen asleep until the wee hours. The metallic sounds of city life had kept me awake. At first, I had been afraid of being seen that the police - or even worse, a crowd of drunks - would add me to their list of nightly experiences. My camp-site was within a stone's throw of Sainte-Foy and, to say the least, exposed. The only thing in my favour had been its location at the bottom of some cliffs. I had chosen a small piece of industrial wasteland on Cap-Rouge. It had a natur-al slip-way of seaweed coated rocks I had been more afraid of losing my kayak to a rising tide than of being spotted. I had judged the cliffs difficult, at best, to descend and defi-nitely not for the fainthearted. Still, if someone was persis-tent enough to pay me a visit, it could be done. I had final-ly drifted off under the secure blanket of chatter from a near-by flock of geese. Now I wanted badly to sleep in, but Quebec City's early morning commuters were on the move.

A sharp blast of road rage had woken me. I could hear voices from the pedestrian walkway above, and judg-ing by their excited tone, spotted. I shot out of my tent in overdrive and started to frantically pack. I was illegally parked and I knew it. 'PROPRIETE PRIVEE' signs were posted everywhere. I was almost packed. I was just secur-ing my last bunji chord with only my sleeping bag to be put away in my cockpit, when the voices I heard from above materialised in front of me.
"Please, I take picture?"
I was suddenly surrounded by a group of well groomed Japanese tourists.
"Please? Thank you mate."
They clustered around me like a battery of paparazzi. They were recording my every movement, and didn't stop until I had tailed away out of view - having turned to wave to them for the umpteenth time. Boy, I was famous!

It was now full-tilt to Quebec City. I passed under the bridge at racing speed. The tide was falling. The deep chasm the river flowed through was fermenting, full of mini whirlpools and back eddies, but I didn't care. I was on the crest of a wave. I could smell salt in the air. I knew that the Gulf and its endless horizons were just around the corner.

At Point a Puiseaux, I was passed by a flotilla of yachts and then crossed paths with two huge jet black Canada Steamship Lines lakers bound for the Seaway. Just past the point, I caught my first glimpse of Quebec City's historical Citadel - Saint Lawrence's fortified gateway - and only moments later, Quebec City rose above the cliffs like a Manhattan skyline. I was home and dry, and when I spotted the Hotel de Ville's pale green leaded roof glistening in the sun, it was a magical sight.

I know I should have stopped. At the very least, lingered and taken time to explore the outdoor festival whose colourful sights and sounds now filled the harbour front, but I was on a mission: on that day, nothing was going to seduce me ashore.

Chapter 3
The Gulf of Saint Lawrence

The Gulf of Saint Lawrence with its bearing teeth of high banks was a sight for sore eyes, but it didn't last long. I was now facing the Île d'Orleans Bridge. I had just passed the Saint Charles River estuary and its magnificent yacht club. To the west, down an open channel between Point Levis and the Île d'Orleans was the shipping lane and the Gulf, but the wind was against me. It blew with such force its gateway was scarred with surf, and the choppy seas beyond looked far too intimidating for me to try so early in the trip. But the decision to pass under the bridge and take the sheltered inside passage behind the island was to turn out no better.

Till now, I had consulted my charts no differently than your average motorist would a road map between cities - infrequently. I had only checked them on a few occasions; once when plotting a course through the Thousand Islands, second on approaches to locks, and once again just before Montreal's 'Lachine Rapids'. Many of the charts' icons and almost all its informational bells and whistles were still a mystery to me, and I was about to pay the price.

I should have guessed there was something amiss, when I realized I was the only person heading north up the inside passage, and it should have become crystal clear when I noticed a deep long band of clapping water - but who would have guessed that a river's current would suddenly rise to the surface? If only I had taken the time to check my chart I, would have seen that, in places, the river bed rises from 40 to 2 meters in less than half a block. Obviously a zillion years ago the island had been connected to the mainland. Its exposed causeway may have long gone the way of erosion, but, as I was about to find out, its underwater foundations were intact. I was now passing under its subteranean cliff and what river current hadn't been deflected west

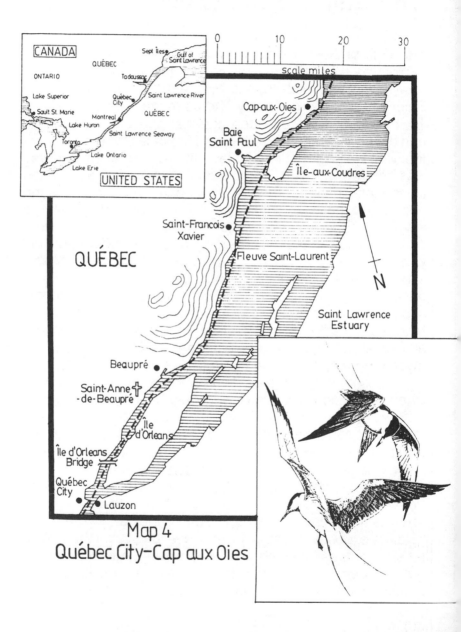

CANADA

ONTARIO
QUÉBEC
Sept Îles
Gulf of Saint Lawrence
Lake Superior
Tadoussac
Sault St. Marie
Québec City
Saint Lawrence River
Montreal
QUÉBEC
Saint Lawrence Seaway
Toronto
Lake Ontario
Lake Huron
Lake Erie
UNITED STATES

scale miles

Cap-aux-Oies

Baie Saint Paul

Île-aux-Coudres

QUÉBEC

Saint-Francois Xavier

Fleuve Saint-Laurent

N

Saint Lawrence Estuary

Beaupré

Saint-Anne -de-Beaupré

Île d'Orleans

Île d'Orleans Bridge

Québec City

Lauzon

Map 4
Québec City–Cap aux Oies

into the Gulf by the wall of rock now rose to the surface with such force it was literally jumping out of the water.

Despite the tide and current in my favour, I was going nowhere fast. It's not that I was in danger of capsizing from the steep waves, but I was being slapped around like a ping-pong ball. It was the constant braising this way and that, not knowing from which side the next wave would strike, that was wearing me down. It seemed to take hours to get to the bridge. Then, to make matters worse, I realized the whole shoreline was turning into one huge tidal mud flat. Just under the bridge, the two shorelines almost kissed each other. I was now cutoff from either shore by a kilometre deep mud bath, and all I could do was grin and bear it.

I kept going until late afternoon, but my heart wasn't in it. Even the tantalizing sight of the Gulf ahead with its distant mainland wall of mountainous cliffs and numerous islands, couldn't raise my spirits. My eyes were glued to the shoreline. I had been hoping the tide would change quickly and swallow up the mud flats so that I could get ashore, but it hadn't. I was now scouring the shoreline for any hint of a channel that could help me beach. Twice I misjudged the shoreline and bottomed out, and twice I lost my feet and calves to its oily grey suction of mud while attempting to drag my kayak into deeper waters.

I threw in the towel within sight of the famous landmark church steeple at Sainte Anne-de-Beapre. I had been spotted from shore and now was following their directions. My guiding light stood on a small point of dry land in the mud flats. By now a small expectant group of happy-go-lucky spectators had appeared to watch me beach, and I didn't disappoint them.

I cannot find the words to describe the feel of mud pushing its way up between your toes and forcing its way into your wet suit without being pornographic. I had just taken a few steps to find my balance, and a few more to judge the suction, when I stepped into a submerged pocket of water, stumbled and fell. I must have looked like Lasarus prostrating himself at the feet of Christ. Immediately all pretense of me playing the know-it-all adventurer flew away with my pride, but I wasn't about to show it.

At first, I tried skimming my kayak over the mud. In the beginning all went well. The mud surface was smooth and slick from the incoming tide. When the gradient changed and entered a cut, however, the kayak almost immediately imbedded itself. It was like trying to extract a coffin from its grave. It just wouldn't budge. One of the spectators, encouraged on by the shouts of his mates and encased in waist-high waders, came to my rescue, but still it wouldn't move. I was stuck alright, and by the looks of it, until the evening high tide. I ended up securing the kayak to my paddle stuck in the mud, then portaging my tent and sleeping bag ashore.

By now, I had attracted quite a crowd and as the confusing barrage of untranslatable questions came my way, a figure stepped out of the noise and grabbed me.

"Je m'appelle Denis. Viens avec moi."

Well, let's say this guy didn't so much save me from the group as kidnap me. He was built like a brick shithouse and then some. Apparently, I was being invited to a party and as any Quebecois will testify, polite refusals don't go down well in Quebec. Here you are expected to enjoy your vices. It's part of the culture and anything less than full participation is unacceptable, but there are, always, exceptions.

It's common knowledge throughout Quebec that English-speaking Canadians are a constipated lot, and some more than others. I am definitely what you would call a partygoer. Poser, yes. A person who would rather be seen and not heard, so I certainly wasn't prepared for what happened next.

Denis is what some people would call a 'party animal'. A person who's alcoholic glow over the years had turned into his second skin. He was full of beans and had this contagious laugh that was hard to resist. As the house he was leading me to was only a stone's throw from the beach, and the tide had still a long way to go before it reached my kayak, I surrendered to him. It didn't seem to matter to Denis that I couldn't understand a word he said, and for the moment, I was just glad to hang on to someone's coat tail.

The house we entered was packed to the rafters and the music - after the peaceful sounds of the river - was deafening. It was obvious from the rebelrousing that I had some catching up to do. I had just started into my third beer, just started to mellow into my surroundings, when I made a big mistake and opened my mouth.

Denis had just introduced me to one of his bilingual friends. In the background, the Beatles were playing. One thing led to another; my age; place of birth; music, then out popped the inevitable question.
"Have you ever seen the Beatles?"
"Yes," I answered, then I put my foot in it. *"I use to be the lead singer in a sixties pop group."*
God knows why I told him. It's true, I had been a lead singer in a group, but we were no more than a local band. None of us had pretensions other than playing at local dances, but it was too late to back track. I was trapped.

Looking back on the incident, it was the word 'group' and the word 'sixties' used in the same sentence that lit the fuse. I was now front page news. I mean, who in their right mind cares about someone who is kayaking home from Toronto to Goose Bay anyway? That kind of news gets lost somewhere between page six and seven, but to have been a lead singer of a sixties band in your midst and even better at your party, now that's worth shouting about.

The music stopped and an announcement was made. I was being asked to sing a karioki version of 'SHE LOVES YOU'. To be honest, I was petrified. All eyes had fallen on me. This wasn't the kind of stage I like to stand on. Even shooting the Lachine Rapids paled to singing in front of more than forty people, but I did it.

I downed my beer, closed my eyes to the music and gunned it. To my relief, everyone joined in. They sang along with the chorus and la, la the verses. I think I was somewhere between the third and fourth verse when it happened.

Pressure had built up from the word go. I was belting out the words *'with a love like that'* when suddenly, I popped out of the house like a champagne cork.

The next morning, Denis - beer in hand - accompanied by his friends, woke me as promised at the crack of dawn to catch the falling tide. They looked no worse for last night's drinking binge and were still in good spirits. Someone gave me a cheese and ham sandwich, and Denis insisted I take a beer for the road, then out came the cameras. I posed with each in turn. Denis wanted his picture in the kayak on dry land. He still didn't believe this 'chose' thing as he called it could take me to Labrador, but it was said in jest. I was genuinely upset to leave them. They had all helped in their own ways with my kayak, my tent, making me feel at home, and all had forgiven me for leaving the party early. They had swept me into their weekend revelry and were now taking time out to see me off. I appreciated their warm farewells more than I cared to show.

The Gulf was still sleeping and shrouded in mist as I left, and soon my friends were swallowed up by it. I was now passing the small town of Beaupre, at the mouth of the Sainte-Anne River. Behind the town a steep range of hills rose out of the gloom. In front arching around the flatlands, its eastern arm jutted out into the sea like a defiant chin. There was almost an entire absence of colour. The heavy, low lying clouds soaked up the sun rays like a sponge and its sounds like a muffler. The river was almost invisible and only its bridge, and the town's white steepled church could be seen. Just as I began to notice houses on its shoreline the mist rolled back and buried it.

I was now paddling in a strong current. I had past Pointe Argentenay on Île d'Orleans, and had caught the outgoing tide. I should have been on a high that morning, but I wasn't. My mind was not on the present but on the future. Although I was more than three weeks into my trip, I knew that it was only just starting. The Saint Lawrence River hadn't tested me. Its Seaway locks had tamed the rapids and the river's width whatever the wind could throw at me. I had been spoiled by its forgiving corridor of sandy banks and by its numerous campsites, slip-ways and manicured gardens. I knew that from here on, the shoreline would only get rockier and more exposed, and that some day soon I would be tested by a strong easterly wind.

Already, I had noticed the subtle changes. The salt water was colder and darker than the river, and this morning I had been woken for the first time by its tidal alarm clock. The background hum of waves rubbing up against the shore had drowned out the metallic noise of its shoreline traffic, and the river's sometimes distasteful flotsam and jetsam of city life had given way to the seaweed of open sea.

By midday the mist had burnt itself out, and I experienced my first blue horizon. I was now hugging the shore and skipping point to point, under the tree top cliffs I'd seen yesterday. I was going at a joggers pace, squeezing out of every drop of ebb tide and, wherever possible, cutting corners to decrease my day. Each point rounded offered a different view and with each picture a different story. The shoreline road had disappeared inland long ago and with it, its constant sounds, but I wasn't alone for long.
Hoo..Whoooooooooo..ratatatat.........ratatatat.
It was a freight train. It's appearance on the shore at the foot of the cliffs came with its sound, but disappeared in slow motion. For the next ninety minutes, I caught glimpses of its snaking tail of empty iron ore freight cars again and again, rounding points, until finally loosing it. By now, I was tired. The mid afternoon sun was searing down, and I was as thirsty as hell. I had forgotten to top up my water bottle and Denis' beer had only made matters worse.

Saint-Francois Xavier is a limpet of colour stuck to the side of rock. A pocket of life connected by a thin thread of gravel, and why it's there, out of sight except from the sea, is anyone's guess. Soon, I was basking in the sun. I had beached close to a brook outside the village. I'd topped up my tanks, stripped and was now catching the rays. There was a pleasing sound of rushing water, and in the distance

I could hear a container ship steaming by. It was hypnotic, too hypnotic.

I woke to find myself high and dry, and a long way from the tide. The sun was starting to disappear behind the cliffs and there was a chill in the air. It was now a race. I had no intentions of camping under the cliffs. For once I wanted to see a sunset without craning my neck, and I wanted to see it from Île aux Coudres, out in the Gulf.

I made it to the island in no time at all. Athough the tide had changed and was coming in, the Saint Lawrence's current just pushed me along. By now the sun had dropped below the hills and the sky was deepening in colour. I beached at the village of Saint Bernard's public wharf, pulled my kayak up its slip-way, secured it to a metal railing above the high tide mark, and began to climb. I was searching for a small plateau of land above the town. I had all I needed in my hockey bag for the night: my tent; my sleeping bag; my roll-o-mat, stove, food, water and smokes. All I wanted now was a room with a view.

'Nothing worth having in this life comes easy', my father used to say and he was right. By the time I found my little spot of heaven, I was bathed in sweat. The mosquitoes were having a field day, and my tent poles just didn't seem to want to unite, but I was content. I was alone, but it was the kind of solitude I like. The hills around Quebec City were bathed in bronze, and as the sun set further, its afterglow dyed the whole scene red. Light drained rapidly from the night sky, and it wasn't until the first stars appeared that I thought of my stomach.

The next morning, I woke into a violent thunderstorm. It rained with such force that the ground around my tent immediately started to puddle. I must have camped in a small hollow and soon the bottom of my tent turned into a waterbed. It was like being caught in a tropical downpour. Sheets of lightning exploded into thunderclaps and the wind propelled rain that beat on my tent was deafening. I was beginning to curse my choice of campsite. Inside the tent, I was fighting a loosing battle with my towel. Puddles of water were forming in the corners and their streams were slowly uniting under my roll-o-mat. At any second, I expected the dams to burst, but fortunately it stopped before that happened.

The scene outside was no better than within. Last night's crusty surface was now a bog. The ridge I had camped above had turned into rappids and the brook it emptied into a fast flowing river. The low land below my tent was lost to a slow-moving lake and the rocky cliff above had turned into a mini-waterfall. It was both a morning to remember and forget. By the time I'd broken camp, walked back to my kayak and pushed off, I was lost in fog.

Paddling with only the sounds of my paddle as company, I felt strangely content. I knew the fog would soon break up. Already the sun had burnt away its roof top and it was only a matter of time before it burnt the rest. I was paddling on a due north bearing, going nowhere in particular except towards the mainland. I was kind of drifting, waiting for something to break up the silence. Just before Cap Saint Joseph came into view, something did. I spotted my first seals. Three in fact - standing head and shoulders out of the liquid grey calm with their jet black snouts raised to the sky. They didn't give me a second glance. As I passed them, two white objects broke the surface ahead.

There is something about encountering a new experience when least expected especially when it's in someone else's back yard. Simply put, it's an incredible adrenaline rush. The two white objects closed in rapidly, then guided effortlessly under my kayak. They were belugas. I had read about them, seen them on television, but nothing prepares you adequately for these albino white whales in the flesh.

I was riveted to the moment. I stopped paddling the instant I saw them. Normally, I am frightened of whales; can't wait actually to get the hell out of their way, but these after all were, the aquatic equivalent to the cuddly Koala Bear, and just as rare. In fact it was a toss-up who was the more curious. For five minutes they circled my kayak.

Sometimes shooting underneath like bullets and sometimes banking and rolling away to the sides in elegant curves of slow motion. Once they both breached cheek to jowl, almost vertically beneath my kayak. For a moment, I was worried they would capsize me, but at the last moment they arched away whilst all the time peering at me with their jet black eyes. Maybe they were checking on my kayak's white underbelly? Maybe they thought I was a distant cousin? Who knows? Who cares? I was glad of their company, and when they finally disappeared, so had the fog.

There was now a strong ebb current, and I was glad that I had checked my sea charts before leaving. Wavy lines rainbowed every point and the same icon of information appeared at the mouth of almost every river. I wasn't one hundred percent sure what they meant, but as I approached Cap aux Oies, and heard the distant drone of an express-way where none existed, I knew for certain I was going to be in for a rough ride.

Seeing, in my book, is believing. I wanted to experi-ence the icons first hand and it was the only reason I pad-dled straight into the noise. It was like paddling in a bath tub. Waves were high fiving everywhere. Some rose almost ver-tically, then - for no discernable reason - flattened out. They were reflective waves from the cape, waves built by the wind, and some seemed to join in just for the hell of it. Next came the whirlpools and back eddies, then the strangest sight of all. I hit it at speed. A foot high picket fence of water. It was a shoreline tidal bore. A localized build up of water caused by the conflicting forces of a strong outgoing river current sling-shooting around the cape and a powerful incoming tide. I could have easily passed the lot of it, but it was an education and worth the ride.

By noon, a strong southeasterly had set in. Waves were building in uniform layers and starting to crest close to shore, but I was in good spirits. My kayak was handling the waves with ease and bracing against the occasional broad-siding one was a piece of cake. If anything, my spirits rose to the occasion. This, after all is what I had come all this way

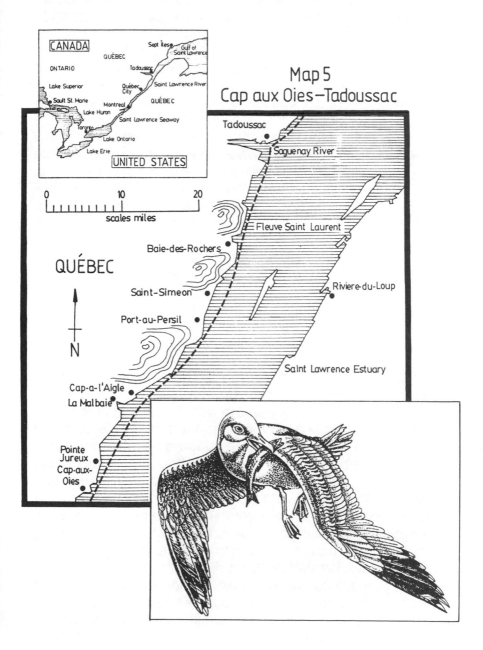

Map 5
Cap aux Oies–Tadoussac

to experience, and I wanted to savour my first wind-blown seas for all they were worth. The seas surged higher and I was swamped by a wave, but nothing dampened my spirits. Everything now looked larger than life. The cliffs, with their beautiful rusty coloured surfaces topped and washed lush green in the afternoon sun, looked magnificent, and so did the deep opal sea. I was just beginning to think I owned the picture I was paddling through when I spotted Kontiki.

Summertime has a habit of awakening the little boy inside all of us. It's a time when everything seems possible and usually is. I have travelled long enough over the years, and seen the A to Z of travellers neither to judge someone's motives or their method of transportation. We all take off for different reasons, have our different goals and choose our own poison. But the sight of David's Kontiki-like canoe, weighed down with gear, rudderless and with a makeshift canvas sail being blown towards the edge of disaster was an eye opener.

To be honest, David had the balls, it's just that his canoe wasn't up to the occasion. He was awash and sinking before my eyes. I didn't realize, at first, the extent of his predicament, or that he had lost his paddle until I was almost on top of him. The wind had carried away my shouts and his furious attempts to bail himself out my view. The lip of his canoe was almost level with the water. One good broadside and he would have been a goner; not him, but his boat and equipment. We were only three hundred metres from shore, but that was his problem. He had drifted into some coastal shoal water. The waves had steepened in the shallows, crested with the wind, and he was now taking in water faster than he could bail it out. I was sure it was just a matter of time before he sank, but David was cast from an unusual mould. Under the circumstances I did the only thing I could do. I retrieved his paddle, then guided him ashore.

Sometimes you need an outside jolt to put life into perspective. All too often my thoughts and actions during my trips revolve around my own needs. I become selfish. It's only natural. People come and go like a revolving door.

Some make lasting impressions, but most never reach the filing tray. I am normally attracted to the radical outsider, the individual who swims against the tide, and David certainly fitted the bill.

On dry land, David resembled a survivor of a shipwreck more than someone who was thoroughly enjoying himself. He was wearing a gentle, almost childishly naive smile, had a kind open face and a gaze that seemed fixed on something in the far distance, so to get his attention, I rose into it.

"What the hell do you call this?"
I was trying my best not to laugh aloud. I had helped him drag his canoe ashore and curiosity had got the better of me.

"It's a tepee," he replied
I couldn't believe my eyes. His equipment alone must have weighed a ton. David was certainly not your average wilderness canoer. Just being in his presence was like being transported back in time. He must have been carrying everything but the kitchen sink, but that wouldn't have been 'traditional' as he put it. It turned out that his tent was a full blown canvas Indian tepee big enough to house a sweat lodge of elders. God knows where, en route, he had chopped down the six tent poles.

It took a full hour to sponge dry his canoe and transport his equipment up the beach. Once laid on the sand, his bric-a-brac of survival must have looked from the shore like some kind of native yard sale. Besides his tepee he had with him a large wood-fired tin stove and enough pots and pans to cook for an army. This guy was certainly in for the long haul, and - going by his axe and bucksaw, his heavy duty army surplus sleeping bag and assorted cotton and wooly work clothes - for the whole winter as well.

I left David fiddling with his equipment to comb the shore for driftwood and soon had a roaring fire going. I had just brewed up some tea and we were relaxing into its heat when David started to unravel before my eyes. Like a spinning top left to unwind, all his pent-up emotions from today and previous days unravelled. All those replays. His ex wife, his child, why he was making the journey, the highs and lows he'd played out in his head and craved to share popped out of his mouth and whirled around the fire. He was close to tears. A Martian from an alien world, unable to explain his problem with only his body language to rely on.

I hadn't planned to spend the night on the beach. It was a little too exposed for my liking, but I didn't want to leave David either. I knew more than he did that at that moment, some solid advice was needed more than a good ear. I knew if he didn't make some major changes and edit out some equipment, his dream of crossing the Saint Lawrence at Saint Simeon and continuing east to the Gaspe Bay Peninsula would probably self destruct in the first storm. For the remainder of the day I acted as his sounding board. I had no experience of canoeing, but I did know from past experience what he could expect from the sea. He'd never canoed in open water before, and I told him that today's seas, whipped up by only a moderate wind, was the tip of the iceberg compared to what he could expect from a full-blown storm.

It's not that my warnings fell on deaf ears, or that my suggestion that he purchase or make a sea skirt for his canoe didn't take hold, but the mere mention that he should consider exchanging his tepee for a more conventional all-season tent or his wood-fired stove for a gas one, saw his heels dig in. I was walking a fine line and I knew it. I wanted to stress caution, but the more I carried him away from his traditional path, the more he dug in. I had become an unwelcome wedge between him and his goal, and when I refused his request to let him accompany me as far as Saint Simeon, the crack grew even wider.

That night, I didn't get a wink of sleep. I was racked with guilt. I had lost too many friends over the years through just the same kind of pig-headedness that David was showing, but that is why I liked them. This was David's trip, not mine. I didn't know the demons that fuelled his passion and didn't want to know them, either. I had told him to take time out; to think of what we had talked about and to make some adjustments. I had wanted him to climb back into the driver's seat. I knew I'd dented his confidence, and now I didn't know how or whether I should repair it.

I slunk away at the break of dawn. Thankfully, David was still asleep, but no sooner had my paddles hit the water when his thin wiry frame appeared on the beach.
"Thanks for your advice, Bernie."
His cheery words picked me up like a feather in a breeze. He was all smiles and a bounce had returned to his step. It felt like a huge weight had been lifted off my shoulders. I never did see David again, and I would have to wait two long years to hear that he had lived out his dreams. He made the crossing of the Saint Lawrence, tepee, stove, sail and all. *'God looks after his chosen Fools'.*

Today, I found a silver lining sandwiches between two mountains, and they call it La Malbaie. Set in the folds of hills at the mouth of its name sake river. I had initially wanted to stop and investigate its colourful promenade, but an offshore wind was picking up steam, and I wanted to get across the bay before it chopped it up. I knew from past experience in Labrador that when wind starts fluting down between a corridor of mountains, they soon reach gale force.

I was less that half way across its high walled bay, and concentrating on Pointe le Heu's lighthouse. I was crossing my fingers that the white line of clapping waves between myself and the other side weren't to steep, when I got blasted. It was like sticking your head in a wind tunnel. For thirty minutes it was all I could do to stay up right. The wind was so strong, I could lean into it without fear of capsizing and the waves - chopped up where the river's current collided with the sea - were now steep enough to punctured a hole in. It was crazy. I was ahead of the day's game plan, so why was I pushing it? It's time like this when arguments erupt in my head and accidents happen. I become vulnerable. My concentration shatters and my guard drops. It's a proven fact that most accidents happen when you are distracted. A wasp lands on your lap, a raised skirt in the wind, a loud noise, or a flash of light. I was never in any danger until I started to turn back. I was inching my way around, braising this way and that, when the river's narrow bridge came into view. Maybe it was the dust created by the bridge's construction crew or the cracked echo of an engine backfire, but suddenly I jumped through a hoop and was gone.

My paddle hit fresh air....! One moment I was running away from a tribal war in the streets of Kampala in Uganda, and the next tasting salt water. It was a flashback so vivid I could smell the riot fires of burning rubber, the report of rifles and the distinctive taste of African sand on my lips. Thank Christ, the waves were steep and my flashback only momentary. I didn't have time to think. Another wave slapped me, and I popped back up like a rubber dildo. My head was bursting; my heart pounding ten to the dozen, and before I could gather my senses, I was paddling like a mad man for the beach.

I was almost ashore, just about to surf in, when I was spotted. Half a dozen families, children in tow, and a group of men from one of the cafes, spilled out onto the beach. I held back, let the wave I was surfing pass under me, then watched as the crowd developed. Everyone seemed genuinely delighted to see me and - to be honest - after my fright, I to see them. Eyes flashed, teeth gleamed and youthful hands waved like windmills under the sun. I was back paddling, sucking in the last drops of welcome and enjoying every minute of it, if not quite understanding where it stemmed from.

At times like these when you are swimming in total confusion, not knowing what the fuss is about, but knowing full well that the attention attributed to you is built on a shaky foundation, it is better to surrender quickly to the person who talks the loudest and hope he takes pity on you when the false hopes have been dashed.

I half guessed why all the attention had fallen at my

feet. Last night, David had told me about another kayaker. An Acadian student from Moncton who was attempting to paddle up the Gulf of Saint Lawrence to Montreal in aid of a charity, and somehow, I think, I had got caught up in his coat tails. I don't exactly court the media. I usually set off on a whim, and if I trip up and fall into the media's lap, as in Montreal, all is fair and well, but covert their attention? No, thank you! I had forgotten it was the height of the 'silly season'. Nothing of any note happens in summer. Serial killers go on hiatus; bank robbers are busier spending than planning bank robberies; politicians are out to lunch, and as for sports, everything is on cruise control until the World Series in October. In short the media are short for words. The airways are full of empty spaces just waiting to be filled with you and me, your average Joe. This guy, from what David told me, had been the answer to their prayers. He had filled the airways with his youthful exuberance, and his colourful anecdotes, so David said, had been the talk of many a phone-in both on the French and English stations.

"ICI Monsieur."

A rather large oval-shaped individual with a reddy brown face the size and shape of a soccer ball, fronted by an impressive handlebar moustache and underlined by a checkered set of teeth befitting a fine piano pushed his way to the front.

"Suivez - moi".

He held out his hand like a life line, and the second I touched it, I knew it would take infinitely longer to retract. He sped me through the crowd like a minder does through stage door groupies, and parried questions that followed our progress with the art of a well-heeled lawyer. I was now his prize and he wasn't going to let go of his catch until I was safely in his house.

We sped down the promenade as onlookers turned their attention to my kayak. No sooner had I crossed the threshold of his house, and sat down at the kitchen table, when his phone started ringing off the hook.

"You are the Anglais paddling from Toronto. Mr. Bernard,

yes?"
"What!" I was speechless Not only did he know from where I started, but my name. Apparently, I had partied the night away with his brother and a couple of his friends near Kingston. He had seen my yellow kayak the day before, en route back from a shopping trip to Quebec City. He had put two and two together, and then spotted me turning round in the bay. Now he was giving me the red carpet treatment.

No one could accuse this man of being stilted. Every sentence was punctuated with a "Qui" and underlined with the royal finger. I couldn't totally understand his pigeon English, but I certainly understood his sentiments. I was being swept along by his contagious enthusiasm, and when a handful of his relations appeared at the doorstep,I readily gave in to their hugs and kisses.

There is something special about Quebec's hospitality that the untrained pallet might find hard to digest. It comes attached to litres of red wine and mountains of traditional, high-cholesterol food. How his wife managed to fit everything on the small kitchen table with so many different cream cheeses, cubes of artery clogging 'cretons', breads, diced vegetables, sliced tomatoes, dips, mustards and wine was beyond me, but she did. And how I managed to talk, consume everything in sight within an hour, then walk back to my kayak without suffering cardiac arrest, or at the very least a severe bout of constipation, speaks volumes to my stomach's flexibility or to its thick internal skinned construction.

It was now as if my engines had been injected with rocket fuel. I sped off from the beach, punctured through the corridor of clapping waves as if they were non existent, and didn't slow down until I spotted a group of pilot whales feeding under the shadows of Cap-a-l'Aigle's face of rock. I was just purring along. The wind had now died away completely. The seas had flattened out and just before Cap-au-Saumon, I found myself paddling towards a living oil slick of jet black sea ducks. At first they parted to greet me, but as I passed, they took off in mass confusion, collected themselves down wind, then banked against the high cliffs like a huge 'Stealth Bomber'. Twice, I was circled, then as if by some silent command, in groups of six to ten, they returned to the sea and were soon pooled, as before, in a flock of chatter.

I was on cloud nine. The scenery was magnificent. Cliffs tailed away on the northern shore for as far as the eye could see and its flat southern shoreline tapered into infinity. I felt as though I could paddle for ever and probably would have, had I not have noticed a beautiful secluded cove just before Port-au-Persil.

I woke into a purple haze. The early morning car ferry had just left Saint Simeon en route to Riviere-du-Loup on the southern shore. If only I could relaxed into this beautiful scene I told myself, but I couldn't. To say the least, my nerves that morning were on edge The 5:00 a.m. Marine Weather Forecast was calling for moderate to strong northwesterly winds in the morning, turning to strong to gale force westerly winds by evening. A low pressure system was sweeping down from the Arctic and Quebec's North Shore would be catching the tail end of its storm.

All morning, I had one eye trained on the clouds forming above, and the other on the sea. The Saint Lawrence's current had noticeably increased since yesterday. Îles aux Lievres had, for all intents and purposes, cut the Gulf in two, and now the outgoing tide - aided by the river's current and squeezed in by the island - was racing out.

The cliffs now rose vertically out of the sea, but their protective walls were a mixed blessing. Although they baffled out the north west winds, I was bushwhacked twice by strong down drafts. Once while crossing Baie-des-Rochers and once again - although less severely - as I paddled across Anse du Chafaud aux Basques. Even the powerful current had a sharp edge to its push. I nearly lost it at Cap de la Tete au Chien. I misjudged its angular tidal bore rounding the point, and broadsided its stepped up wall of water at speed.

By midday, I was fast approaching the mighty Saguenay River. I had been going hell for leather to beat the outgoing tide. I wanted to cut across the barrier of sand-banks at its mouth and nip into its sheltered waters before they exposed themselves. There was absolutely no way I was going to cross its estuary four kilometres out in the Gulf. It wasn't the added distance that bothered me, or the strong river current, it was those bloody wavy icons denoting chop-py seas, that festooned the estuary's mouth on the sea chart.

I ran out of tide within spitting distance of Pointe-aux-Alouettes. The sandbanks were now fully exposed far out into the Gulf. I had been paddling down a narrow channel close to shore and it now deadened. I beached, put up my tent to wait for the incoming tide, then catnapped.

By mid afternoon, I was back in the water. I had picked my way through a shallow maze of channels and was now paddling down the river against a strong wind. For nine-ty minutes, I watched the river's shoreline, as banks of sand and silt passed in slow motion. My wrists were on fire and my eyes, soaked from the constant assault of salt-spray, were killing me. I was dog tired, but past the point of no return. Even if my body wanted to rest, my mind wouldn't give in. I had been told that the mouth of the Saguenay on a stormy day could look like Dante's Inferno and on a calm day, like heaven. I had seen enough heavens on this trip. I wanted to test my metal, and I wanted it tested surrounded by escape routes. I am no fool. I don't have a death wish. It had always been my intention to paddle down the river, then scoot across at a point where the current and winds were the strongest, and today's conditions were ideal for the exer-cise. The river was just over a mile across from the Pointe Noire ferry terminal to Tadoussac, and here I took a break.

Looking down the river from the ferry terminal was like looking into the jaws of hell. Its dark corridor of menac-ing rock made my stomach churn, but the feeling didn't last long. I immediately shut out the scene, focused onto a point of land at the other side of the river, concentrated on it until everything else was blocked out, and then started the long paddle across. By now the sun was setting, and immediately a cold damp wind cut right to the bone.

Only ten minutes into the crossing I changed my game plan. Rolling waves pushed up by the wind and compressed by the opposing forces of an incoming tide and an outgoing river current were starting to crest. It was increasingly difficult to angle into them. I turned, not much but enough. I don't like surfing with the wind, but I had no choice. When you paddle with the wind, the waves lift the kayak out of firm water. Your rudder gets exposed and it's like driving on ice. Your momentum from paddling and your nerves are all you have. Your steering is shot and your tail takes on a life of its own. I was digging in for all I was worth. Tadoussac's ferry terminal was already slipping away, as were the houses in its sheltered cove. I couldn't believe the current. My sea charts had said 6 to 7 knots, but I was already more than one mile downstream from my start point and not yet half way across. If anything, the waves were higher. These were not like the slow moving ocean waves you see building close to shore, but more like the back combed eddies of rapids, and, boy, were they moving! I had visions of being carried into the Gulf Stream, but I didn't care. The conditions may have been appalling, but I was exhilarated. I had hit a rhythm. I was now inside my protective shell of concentration and enjoying the challenge.

It took me ninety minutes to traverse the Saguenay. I finally beached close to the rocky Pointe aux Vaches, and, in no time at all, I'd crashed for the night.

Tadoussac didn't gain its reputation as being 'The Whale watching Capital of the World' overnight. True, whales have been swimming up and down the Saint Lawrences since time began, but paying to see them is what makes the world go around in these parts. Sure, the early explorers wrote about them in their journals, but in those days you paid to use their oils. Even the Group of Seven, who captured them in paint and imortalised them on canvas, added little to Tadoussac's economy. For a thousand years Tadoussac had all the right ingredients for a booming eco tourism industry except for one small detail, and then came the 'ZODIAC'.

Until today, I could have counted on one hand the number of whales I'd seen, and all but two of them had been from a distance, but by day's end, if one had popped out of the water right besides me, with a ten dollar bill in his mouth, I would not have batted an eye lid. To say I saw fifty would not have been an exaggeration, but they were all wasted on me. I am not a wilderness snob, but it's hard to get excited about seeing a whale break surface when surrounded by a battery of lenses or for that matter to be frightened by two swimming directly towards me while I was sandwiched between two other kayaks whose occupants are wetting their pants with excitement.

Chapter 4
The Quebec North Shore

Between Tadoussac and Escoumins had everything, whales, seals, porpoises, ducks, hidden coves and slabs of rock that dropped directly into deep water, but most of all, it had tourists. The day should have been a golden opportunity for me to overcome my stage fright of whales, but I was never alone for an instant. Kayakers, speed boats and especially zodiacs turned the shoreline route into a six-lane freeway, and when I was crossed by two youthful seadooers out doing donuts, I turned to shore and called it a day.

As luck would have it, I beached in a sandy cove fenced off from the outside world by dunes. I was now seasoned in the nightly routine of campsite organization. First, I parked my kayak in sight but out of harm's way above the high tide mark. Then I pitched my tent, facing west to catch the sun, and tucked in at the foot of a large sand dune topped in golden stalks. I was within a two-minute walk of a lazy brook, and I judged my closest neighbour - a rather futuristic style wooden chalet with a huge open balcony - far enough away that once evening fell, its occupants would be hard pressed to sense my presence. Driftwood was in abundance, and I had ample time to light a fire, eat, wash up and bed down before nightfall. By the look of the clear sky the evening promised a beautiful sunset, and at that very moment, the only thing I missed was some friends to share my good fortune with...............

"Bonjour..."

I turned into the words so fast, I fell flat on my back.

"Desole. Je vous ai supris."

'desole' ..that means sorry doesn't it??? I had fallen in more ways than one. I had managed to latch onto one word, but the *Je vous*..whatever had me stumped. From my new vantage point in the sand the man looked huge and the length of his arms, swaying like disjointed pendulums down to his

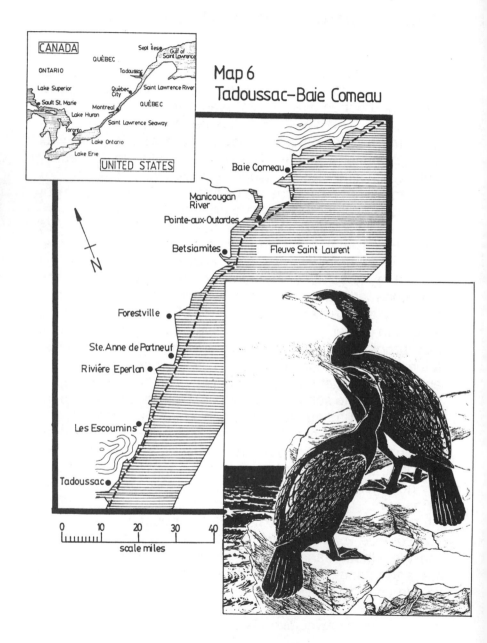

CANADA

ONTARIO

QUÉBEC

Sept îles
Gulf of Saint Lawrence
Tadoussac
Québec City
Saint Lawrence River
QUÉBEC

Lake Superior

Sault St. Marie

Montreal
Saint Lawrence Seaway
Lake Huron

Toronto

Lake Ontario

Lake Erie

UNITED STATES

Map 6
Tadoussac–Baie Comeau

Baie Comeau

Manicougan River

Pointe-aux-Outardes

Betsiamites

Fleuve Saint Laurent

Forestville

Ste. Anne de Portneuf

Riviére Eperlan

Les Escoumins

Tadoussac

N

0 10 20 30 40
scale miles

thighs, only enhanced my view. I immediately transformed into the skin of a wild cat. Sometimes my Jekyll and Hyde character has a will all of its own. It's a knee jerk reaction. Call it a survival instinct if you want, but over the years I have learned to accept the good in people, but to be prepared for the worst. Was I camped on his property? I'd done that before now. It had never been a big deal, but there was always a first time. I got up, brushed the sand out of my hair, then introduced myself.

"Je m'appelle Bernie Howgate."

"Bonjour. Je m'appelle Jean. Ma femme, elle vous vendu fait ton l'encampment."

'Encampment' another piece of the jig saw puzzle fell into place. Here it comes, I thought. I am definitely camped on this guy's property.

" Ma femme m'a demande de te demander si tu voudrais souper avec nous.

'souper' .. I was still half a street behind him, still trying to paste his words together. He certainly didn't look angry and if he was an out-of-uniform policeman checking me out, he sure had passed his undercover examination with flying colours. I was weighing up his body language, still not knowing whether to embrace it or turn tail and run, but I was melting, so I tried again.

"C'est moi. Je habite a Labrador. J'ai commence mon voyage a Toronto."

"Ah oui. We thought you were the kayaker from New Brunswick. My wife heard him being interviewed on the radio. Wait until she hears this. Where in Labrador do you live.....?"

I immediately gave into his English, and if Jean was disappointed to find out I was not the Acadian kayaker, he didn't show it. We talked for a few more minutes, then he pointed to his house.

"What about my camp?", I said. Past experience has taught me that invitations at this time of day never seem to finish with the meal. After dinner conversation invariably stretch into a night between clean sheets, and I didn't want the night

spoiled by worrying about my kayak, my tent, or my equipment.

"Don't worry, no one comes here. It's all private property."
It was a deal. I searched out my wallet just to be on the safe
side, showed him my equipment inside the tent, then before
my feet had time to touch the ground, I was inside his
house.

After a short interval his wife appeared. She was tall
and elegant and dressed in one of those loose fitting skirts
that I was beginning to believe that only the women of
Quebec could transform into something eye-catching. She
radiated all the best that her gender can offer a man, confidence, cheerfulness and sex. Jean, her husband and a
lawyer who commuted daily to Quebec City, I guessed was
fortyish, but looked ten years older in her presence. That
wasn't a put-down just a fact. He made the ideal foil. Whilst
she obviously enjoyed the game of flirting, he was as solid
as a rock. She had waited in the wings, like a good actress
waiting for the applause to settle, before introducing herself
and now she owned the space she occupied.

It was Natalie who had invited me for supper, and it
was Natalie who insisted I spend the night in the guest
room. She would accept no excuses. I was to make myself
at home, to have a shower, and to put on one of Jean's old
track suits so that she could wash my clothes. She was a
darling. I could have hugged her on the spot and probably
would have, but before I had time to fall in love and make a
fool of myself, she left for the kitchen to prepare the food.

Audience over, Jean showed me the bathroom and
after a refreshing shower gave me the guided tour. *"This is
the living room... If you want to watch television..this is the
remote...If you want to watch some videos......"* He went on
and on. I am sure he would have given me the keys to their
safe had they had one, so earnest he was in making me feel
at home.

After the tour we returned to the dining room, then he
took me onto the veranda. The sliding doors were enormous
and the view over the Gulf of Saint Lawrence was magnifi-

cent. Then I was introduced to their children, two young boys and a girl. They had been waiting to be introduced to me and it showed. For the meeting they assumed a suitably solemn expression, but really they were as lively and full of beans as their mother, and within minutes they had warmed to my presence.

I have always liked children, especially the ones who still have the wide-eyed innocent look. Karyne, Paul and Claude; the Three Musketeers as I like to call them, were a joy... if not a handful. I am not a disciplinarian and they instinctively knew it. When they asked if they could see my kayak, I couldn't refuse.

We ate outside. The sun was going down and it bathed the hanging glass ornaments hanging above the veranda. A school of whales past and two lakers steamed by. The night was turning into one of those end-of-the-day experiences to be treasured; to be put away in one's pocket and relived when trapped in the wind and rain, and it only got better once the meal was finished.

By now I had turned into the centrepiece of the children's attention, a new toy to be played with. As soon as we went inside, they started to fight over my attention. I was pinched and teased at every turn, while Jean cleaned up the dinner table, Natalie smiled on regally from the sidelines. I was bathed in warmth. Tonight, I would be adopted like a long lost brother. I was being spoiled and they knew it. For at least one night, their children were allowed extra liberty, and by ten o'clock, two of the three had fallen asleep - lost to a world of Uncle Bernie's creation, with tales of volcanoes, lions and sundrenched tropical beaches.

I woke the next day to the reality of wind and rain. The children were still asleep. Jean was making coffee. Natalie had prepared a smorgasbord of sandwiches and cookies for my journey ahead. I drank my coffee in silence, so much emotion from last night's playtime had left me exhausted.

After breakfast, Jean accompanied me down to the

beach. We exchanged small talk, then it was a time to leave. Reluctantly, because it seemed certain I would never see them again, I turned into the wind and rain, to wave. Jean was where I had left him on the bank, and Natalie was now with her children on the veranda. I called out each name in order of age, then Natalie. I would have been disappointed to leave without seeing them again. I turned for one more look at Jean, but he had turned back towards the chalet. My head dropped and I gave way to tears.

Hello and goodbye. It has been the story of my life for the last twenty years. I had not spent more that twelve months anywhere since leaving home as a teenager. I have bought and sold three houses during that time, lost count of the apartments I've lived in, and must have spent hundreds of nights as a house guest, and hundreds more under the stars. I used to look at home ownership as a millstone round my neck, and until last night believed that my presence in someone's house as guest-cum-storyteller was payment enough, but today the price of my chosen lifestyle seemed too high. They had given me more of themselves than I could ever repay. My tears had been genuine, but they had only started once I was out of site. The pain stemmed from that timeless question that dogs all travellers. Where was I travelling to? When a nomad starts questioning his nomadic lifestyle, he starts to question the core of his being, and his foundation starts to crumble. Was I a nomad? It wasn't the first time I'd ask myself this question, but today's emotions had cut deep. I truly didn't want to leave. Sure, I managed to push back the question to the back of my head. In fact it hid itself as soon as the chalet was lost to the bend, but I knew its germ had taken root.

Today was also another goodbye of sorts. The high cliffs and rugged deep water shoreline that typified my progress since Beaupre had levelled out. From here to Baie Comeau, some 200 kilometres to the northeast, all I could expect was sandbanks, mud banks and shoals of rock. I had hoped to put in some good mileage during this section. They were no river crossing of any note to worry about, no points of land to churn up the Gulf's current and no slabs of rock to deflect its waves. Everything was going to plan, but the weather wouldn't cooperate. The promised Arctic low pressure system had petered out over Montreal, and now the weather forecast was calling for moderate to strong southeasterlies. The Atlantic was starting to flex its muscles.

My mood on long trips usually follows the weather's atmospheric pressure curve. I can put up with the extremes of hot and cold, and fog and rain, but wind is another matter. On this particular section, westerly winds are the best, and - depending on the shoreline - a northerly wind poses no problem. An easterly wind, so deep in the Gulf, would have to be gale force to anchor me ashore, but a south easterly wind blowing over shoal water is a back breaker.

The only bright spot in the day came in the morning. I paddled past a flock of nesting gulls on Ilets Boises, but no sooner had I passed its bleached white rocks when the Gulf's bed rose up to greet me, and the gloom set in. I have used the word before, and no doubt I will use it again, but the only word to describe the rock-filled sandbank exposing itself in the Hautes-fonds de Mille-Vaches is 'MINEFIELD'. Thousands of sea-smoothed rocks were popping up before my eyes. Despite my efforts to cut a bypass course on their seaward side it was too dangerous. Just when I least wanted it, as if on cue, a southeasterly started to blow. Soon waves were streaking the deep waters of the Gulf and rafting in the shallows. The only protection I could find was between the rocks in the sheltered waters close to the beach, but it was frustrating. Every now and then my paddle or my rudder would bury themselves in sand. The falling tide was forcing me slowly back into the Gulf, yet it seemed pointless to head all the way out to the open sea. It would have meant paddling 4 kilometres offshore, but it wasn't the distance that concerned me. The sandbank's front guard of rocks were few and far between, and just visible to the eye, but they looked a dam sight more menacing in the waves than the numerous rearguard of sheltered rocks I was zigzagging through. Even when the wind died a little, their potential danger was easy to resist.

At one point, needing to stretch my legs, I wedged my kayak between a cluster of rocks and waded ashore. But even that didn't raise my spirits. It took me eight hours to cover 16 kilometres and once I reached the small peninsula of land that I had been crawling towards all day, I called it quits. I put up my tent, ate, then fell soundly asleep.

I woke into the breezeless atmosphere of a thick fog. That morning, the Marine Weather Forecast called for 'strong southeasterlies', but it hadn't mentioned fog. This fog bank was obviously localized, and probably caused by the peninsula. It may, indeed, have been the only patch of fog on the North Shore. Fog has a dampening effect on the wind. It literally blocks it out, but not the waves. There hadn't been a hint of wind to rattle the tree tops surrounding my tent, and as I was camped some way down the west side of the peninsular, I had no way of knowing that a sea swell was pounding its eastern arm.

As instruments of navigation your eyes are useless in fog unless you're close to shore, but where did the shoreline end and the sand begin? That was the question. I had no trouble finding the peninsula's lighthouse beacon stuck on a sand dune at its point. The fun started when I turned the corner and got lost on the wrong side of the sandbar, at the headwaters of the Portneuf River. It was a brutal section of shoreline. Rocks stuck up out of the water like dull fangs, threatening to split the underside of my kayak in two.

I was paddling along at a snail's pace, totally disorientated, when I heard a bell. It was the sound of Sainte-Anne-de-Portneuf's harbour buoy. It was a welcome relief, but only momentarily. I was on the wrong side of the sandbar. Somehow I had missed the sheltered lagoon I had been aiming for in the fog. I suppose I could have followed the sandbar in my sight all the way to the harbour, but large sea swells were starting to crest at the boundaries of my vision. I didn't want to let go of the sandbar's beach; nor did I want to paddle in a corridor of powerful surf. I felt that at any moment a wave would crest in the fog, rush out of the gloom and flip my kayak. The thought of capsizing didn't worry me, but the thought of being pulled under by a shoreline rip tide - that I was sure existed under the surface close to shore - did.

Knife edged sandbars like the one I was following that had formed like pencil thin islands out to sea, are visible markers to the invisible forces that have made them. Just as I know that bees are attracted to honey, so sand is to a current. A rip tide's current can suck you under in no time. Even with a life jacket, you can fall like a stone through its aerated waters, and - just like quicksand - the more you fight, the quicker you sink. I didn't have to wait long to weigh up my options. A wave swamped me. Immediately, I turned tail, searched and found a narrow channel that led to the sheltered tidal lagoon on the other side of the sandbar, then started the slow paddle towards the harbour.

For what seemed an eternity, I half dragged and half paddled down the shallow lagoon with only the sounds of pounding surf on the sandbar's seaward side as guidance. The fog just refused to lift, and it was only when the lagoon tapered in and houses started to materialize, that I relaxed.

I was now heading for a narrow shallow channel cut through the sandbar that my map showed as uniting the tidal lagoon to the river estuary and the harbour. Preparing to beach, I was suddenly descended on by a hornet's nest of noise. It was a group of village kids. They'd been out fishing, seen my bright yellow kayak emerge from the mist, and now I had become the centre of their universe.

There arrival was a blessing in disguise. They guided me to a better landing spot, aided me with my gear, fought over the rights to carry my kayak over the sandbar to the river, and before nightfall would turn into welcoming messengers of good fortune.

That evening, I was visited by one of the young boys and his elder brother. I was greeted in French, but the elder brother soon broke into fluent English. I was being summoned into the village to visit their uncle, and like all young boys entrusted with an adult message they were are proud as peacocks. As I had hardly started to unpack, all I had to do was change my clothes, zip up my tent, and then I was theirs.

The house I was led to, had the look of a cabin that had expanded over the years to accommodate their uncle's once growing family. His wife had died some years before and his children - pictured in B/W and colour on his living room wall - were now either married and living in their own homes close by, or working in Montreal. He'd adopted the two boys from his sister's overflowing family of sons, and was now content with their company.

The evening unfolded like a dream. I couldn't have wished for a better end to the day. Their uncle had already warmed up yesterday's fish stew and fresh bread appeared in the hands of another visitor. The elder boy translated all questions at speed, and although I was sure the boy was reconstructing all questions to his own liking, everyone seemed to be happy with my replies. I was slowly gaining an ear for French. At first it had grated on me, but now, two weeks into 'La Belle Province', I was beginning to understand why people say it's the language of passion. It has a rhythm like no other in Canada. It's like a song; sweet and clear, and as expressive as its Latin linguists.

It was well after dark before I left, and I was glad the boys accompanied me. The fog, if anything, had got thicker, and because the tide was in we had to use a different route. There was a chill in the air. I was cold, damp and tired from the day's excitement. But when I saw my camp hallowed in light, illuminated by a driftwood fire and surrounded by the same group of boys who'd helped me earlier, I hadn't got the will to turn my back on them.

I must have stayed up until the early hours of the morning. Where else, I ask myself, except in a small village can so many pre-teens go missing so late without being missed? I didn't stay up because I was worried that they would tamper with my equipment, far from it. I stayed up because they wanted me to. I felt, I owed them, and their continual stream of questions was small payment. When I finally gave in to fatigue and fell into a deep sleep to the sounds of their friendly chatter, I knew I'd paid my dues.

I woke with the sun, but broke camp in fog. There was a pleasant sound of rushing water coming from the beach and a sweet smell of grass in the air. I hadn't got up in time to hear the Marine Weather Forecast, but I was sure yesterday's strong winds had passed. When the wind eventually picked up, some hours later, and pushed the fog bank ahead of it, I was cheerfully surprised.... It was a moderate tail wind.

I struck a rhythm early and stayed with it all day. For once, my surroundings went unnoticed. I had slipped into my bubble and felt nothing other than a warm breeze on my ears. I was in cruise control. I was paddling 2 kilometres off shore, taking full advantage of the wind and surfing. In fact, the conditions were so favourable that the day was two-thirds over before I took a break. I spotted a family group of clam diggers, spading small castles of sand down at the bottom of Baie Blanche. The tide was fully out. I could smell the exposed kelp wafting in from the shore and see the encrusted growths of dark mussels on its rocks. It was a scene worthy of investigation. I nipped in behind a rocky point, beached, left my kayak against a knob of rock, then finished my flask of coffee within shouting distance of the diggers.

Tiredness set in almost immediately. I should have made camp there and then, played catch-up with my sleep, but I was too lazy to pull ashore my kayak. It was an error of judgement. If only I had taken time out to look at the sky.

When the storm struck, it struck quickly. I hadn't noticed the build up of clouds to the east until I was back in the water. By then, it was too late. The wind had already turned 180 degrees and the temperature had plummeted. I had initially planned to spend the night in the Indian reserve at Betsiamites. I had wanted to experience some traditional native culture and hospitality, but now it was out of the question.

By the time I had found a decent campsite with a sheltered approach, the heavens had opened. It was pouring down, but I was a lucky man. I had found a small oasis of dried ground surrounded by some high spruce trees, and by the time the rain had passed, I was already changed, warm and dry, and cooking supper inside my tent.

The next day was no different. The strong wind once again passed the seas through its shredding machine and white lines - as if drawn by a ruler - streaked the Gulf. Wind blown rain peppered my tent incessantly and thunder rolled. I wasn't going anywhere.

I have never been a handy man; a person who likes details; who enjoys fiddling with his equipment or replacing it. I am a go-with-the-flow type of guy. A person who will adjust into the vacuum caused by a breakage, or bend into its weakness. I had a pin hole fracture somewhere in my kayak, but I had chosen to sponge out its leak rather than find and repair it with fiberglass. My rudder also required attention. I had clipped a submerged rock some days back, but instead of replacing with my spare, I had just made allowances for its new shape. Even my cockpit seat needed adjusting, but instead of tightening up the adjustment chords, I had, over time, adjusted my back into its angle. No, I didn't relish the thought of these tasks. When Bernie has some down time on his hands he likes to write letters - long involved letters.

The spells I like to weave and the pictures I like to paint. It's a craft I have learned not from reading, but through life itself. It's the main reason I became a writer and letters home were my apprenticeship. I wanted my family to touch, taste and smell what I did, and sometimes just to add a splash of colour and to give their imagination something to latch onto, by adding a free hand sketch as well. All this takes time, and on that day - instead of adjusting and repairing my equipment - I filled it with my pen. I wrote all day and deep into the night, and throughout the next day as well.

It was late into the second day before the wind finally abated. The storm had held me captive in my tent for
almost thirty-six hours. My body felt rested; too rested. I now
felt like a spring under tension. I needed to stretch and
breath in some fresh air, and as soon as the rain stopped, I
took a walk.

From a distance, the scene looked like some World
War One aerial assault. Black objects circled, then dropped
in steep arcs onto an unseen object. My interest was
peaked. I had time on my hands and nowhere to go, so I
backtracked. I headed for the trees and approached silent-
ly. Three crows were harassing the living daylights out of a
lone dog. I was down wind, so there wasn't a chance the
dog could sense me, and the crows were too busy enjoying
themselves to care.

They don't call crows the winged brains of the sky for
nothing. It was obvious they only had eyes for the meal the
dog was guarding and with each assault they made, his
barks grew more feeble. It was a war of attrition and soon
the only visible deterrent the dog could muster was his teeth
which were now barely visible through the froth of his spent
energy. When the end came, it came quickly. One crow
brushed his back. He struck at fresh air, cartwheeled back
after his tail and just as he was rising, another clipped his
head. He now surrendered what he'd been guarding. A
dead seal. The crows didn't wait long. Once the dog had
retreated to a safe distance, the victors dropped onto their
supper. Floor show finished, I too returned to my food. I may
not have covered any distance that day, but it had had its
moments.

I broke camp early, more from a need to break out of
a restless state than to gain any mileage. The wind was
howling and the skies looked dark and threatening. Just
before Point a Michel it started to get worse, and the rain
began as I rounded its point. I had only been paddling for
one hour, but it seemed pointless to continue. The story
close to shore was of pounding surf and the one still being

written out at sea was getting choppier by the minute.

As I aimed for the beach, my rudder bit into a building wave. Suddenly it peaked, crested, then rolled me over. I exited the kayak somewhere between the first and second onrush of surf. I was actually more angry with myself than the wave. I'd only capsized in eighteen inches of water, but that's all it takes to get a soaking. Now I had to dry out.

First, I had to get out of the wind and get warm. I lit a driftwood fire in some dunes. It was a little exposed, but I didn't have to wait long for the rain to stop and once the sun had bust out, I was stripped and soaking up its rays.

I waited until the tide was full in and the breakers had lost their punch before pushing off again. Gradually, the wind that had tormented me today and kept me pinned to the shore yesterday died down, and by midday it had almost completely gone. The fog banks that had began to form once the rain stopped now rolled into shore. They weren't thick and with the sun shinning through them, it was as if the shoreline was suspended in a bowl of melted butter, then it cleared.

I was now approaching the mouth of the Betsiamites River. Ahead, jutting out from the shore, there was a long narrow sand dune and at its end, cut off by a narrow band of tidal water was its tip. A huge pile of rocks topped it, but as I got closer, the rocks swayed and moved, and before I could make sense of it, the whole scene shattered and rushed into the water. I had never seen such huge seals in my life. Seals may look like a heard of legless cows flopping around on land, but take it from me, they have a sprinter's power and a ballerina's grace in the water. They found me so quickly that, I neither had the time to be frightened or to take pictures. The only thing that worried me was being capsized by their sheer enthusiasm. For, once they had given me an initial pass and deemed me of no threat, they decided to give my kayak a closer inspection. I didn't want to irritate them by hitting out with my paddle, but I also didn't want to encourage their growing enthusiasm at finding a new toy to play with. All I could do was head for shore and hope my paddle didn't take an eye out.

They followed me right into the shallows and once ashore they kept a safe distance, but before I could finish my coffee they were encroaching on my territory. Or was it theirs? I left without asking.

On any other day, I may have found shelter and cut my day short, but today I had energy to burn and miles to tick-off. The afternoon winds were strong and the waves steep in the shoal waters. Initially, I had set a course across almost 20 kilometres of open sea to Pointe-aux-Outardes, but my nerves weren't up to the task. I gave up after only thirty minutes of paddling, and was now surfing like an express train into the throat of the bay. In the late afternoon sun, the shoreline looked lush and enticing. It was full of golden beaches, indented with sheltered coves and dotted with numerous fern-topped rocky islands. Then I caught a pungent whiff in the air. At first, I thought it was coming from the decaying carcass of a whale, but as it got stronger and sharper, my nose told me it was coming from two islands to my right.

Cormorants are no strangers to these parts. In fact, I had first spotted these birds at the head waters of the Saint Lawrence, but I had never seen a nesting colony of them before, or, for that matter, witnessed the destruction they can cause to the environment.

The only way I can describe the destructive forces they can unleash and the scene on the island in front is by taking the reader into a chicken coup. Imagine the smells emanating from a thousand chickens; add to it the scent of rotting fish; bottle their fetuses, then boil and distill the mixture. You now have a cocktail as corrosive and pungent as hydrochloric acid. There wasn't a green leaf or breathing bark on the island. Every tree was topped by a cancerous growth of twigs, and stained white with shit. The smell hung over the island like an invisible barrier of rancid perfume and it would have taken a braver man than me to embrace it.

I was now engaged in a race against time. Limpets of rock and islands of sand were being left high and dry by the falling tide. I padded across the Outardes river estuary searching unsuccessfully for its current. I didn't like the idea of being left high and dry on a sandbar, but the thought of turning back up the bay into choppy seas looked no better. Suddenly - surprise, surprise - the wind died.

They say if you wait long enough in these parts you will experience all the climactic changes summer can offer in one day - sun, rain, fog, wind and calm - and now I had.

With time on my hands before sunset, I searched out a good campsite and it was well worth the effort. I camped next to a small brook and pitched my tent on a plateau of moss on top of a high dune, with a 180 degree view of the setting sun.

That night, I treated myself to a huge bonfire. The high tide mark on the river's estuary was knotted by trees uprooted by spring thaw. I spent a good hour collecting its driftwood and built myself a bonfire to be proud of, then cooked, ate and crashed.

I broke camp just before sunrise. It was a bleak hour, but I wanted to beat the certainty of a mid afternoon storm to Baie Comeau before it struck. The wind was already brisk and the sky's thick dark clouds looked ready to burst. It was cold, unusually cold for mid July, and already its penetrating dampness was searching out my body's weak spots, like a bully. I didn't exactly relish the thought of paddling in these threatening conditions, but Baie Comeau was only 32 kilometres away.

The Manicougan Peninsula curved into the wind with relentless monotony and already its shoreline corridor of shoal was awash in surf. I plugged away all morning at rounding its bend, sometimes paddling 2 kilometres out and sometimes nervously skirting its shoreline to make up for lost time. By noon the rain that had threatened and teased in isolated bursts of drizzle set in for the day, and by mid afternoon the wind had turned 90 degrees and was coming straight down the Gulf, towards me.

I was in a sorry state. My hands continually wet from

the surf and rain now looked like crumpled up parchment, and were just as pale. In fact my hands were so cold that the only life signs they registered were the shooting pains of needles every time I dug in my paddles. I was cursing myself for not practicing with angled blades before leaving on the trip, as every time I raised the paddle out of the water, the wind would catch its blade and push it back. I was now pushing against both the water and the wind, and the added effort was draining me fast. Sometimes the gusts were so strong it shaved off the tops of waves picking up heavy droplets that would then race towards me like clouds of rain. They would pepper my kayak and blind me, and the noise of the wind flapping in my hood was driving me insane. Thankfully the wind's direction remained constant as I rounded the peninsula. Had it turned and broadsided my progress into the shoal it would have been dangerous, but then it did.

I had just exposed myself to the Manicougan River, however when the wind shifted. Then, to make matters worse, it collided with the river valley's downdraft. Within minutes waves were forming on waves. The sea swell now carried with it a contrary flow of shallow waves that was making surfing dangerous. I was in no fit state for the constant bracings this way and that. The estuary was not a place for the faint hearted, or the foolhardy either. I waited between gusts; quickly pulled out my sea chart, and decided the best course of action was to paddle down the estuary and beach at the nearest house.

I phoned my friend Mark within sight of Baie Comeau's landmark pulp mill. It would have been crazy to have continued across the estuary, but I was disappointed. It would have been nice to have beached under Mark's house and surprised him, but that wasn't to be. We met at Pointe Lebel and sixty minutes later, my kayak was parked in his garden. With my clothes in the washer and his wife preparing an evening meal, I found myself soaking away the day's aches and pains in their bath tub.

Mark's name had come via a friend of a friend, during one of my infrequent visits to Toronto. Few people east of Quebec City, I had been told, owned kayaks and Mark was one of them. I had purposely put away all thoughts of contacting him before my trip. I don't like pre-planning anything if I can help it, especially when it involves travelling. It takes away the edge of a new experience and always saps out the energies generated by the fires of spontaneity and risk that drives my engines towards them. These are vital ingredients for success, but they comes a time in any trip, and today was one of those occasions when the picture of the unknown is too sharp and too colorful to ignore.

Mark turned into a veritable mother lode of information. He had not only visited the Lower North Shore, but he and his wife had kayaked the very section I knew nothing about. Until today, Quebec's Lower North Shore from Havre -Sainte- Pierre to Blanc Sablon had been a complete mystery. I had sea charts-a-plenty, but outside the occasional dot here and there which denoted settlements, I had no idea if these were year-round places of habitation, or summer communities lived in during the fishing season. The only thing I knew for certain was that they were all isolated from the outside world. The Lower North Shore's highway 138 abruptly ends just east of Havre-Sainte-Pierre, and from there on, the only connection with the outside world was a weekly ferry service between Sept Îles and Blanc Sablon.

For two days, Mark turned into my guru. I poured over his maps and listened with a keen ear to his stories, but one thing was missing......BAD WEATHER! He had made the trip between June and July. He had encountered calm conditions almost from start to finish. It sounded all to easy. Today was July 10th. The window of opportunity in the north is a small one, and it was getting smaller by the day.

I could have stayed much longer, but I could sense the winds of change were already in the air. Mark and his wife had spoiled me rotten, but like a migrating bird, I could no more stop myself from paddling away than I could have stopped breathing.

Before I left, Mark gave me an old translated article about life on the Lower North Shore. He had correctly read my mind, and I was glad of its cautionary note.

'The Basque Cord Nord (Lower North Shore) is a region where summers are too short and winters too long; a region of wild blowing snow, whipped by gusts of wind; a region where the sun rises and sets on the sea, colouring the foaming waves as they crash furiously on the shore.'
Jean O'Neal : La Presse

Once again the scenery rose to the occasion. I left Baie Comeau under a clear blue sky and was soon paddling alongside its vertical cliffs. This was by far the most impressive section of shoreline to date. All morning, my route hugged its impressive rock faces, with only the lapping noises of a tame sea swell tickling at their toes for company. At Pointe a la Perche, I disturbed a flock of nesting gannets who on seeing me, peeled away from their dizzying perches in a black and white cloud. Everything that morning was larger than life. The dark cliffs, the hazy grey blue horizon of the South Shore and the huge ocean-going vessels that steamed up and down the Gulf. I was in a meditative mood. The sea was at rest, and I was neither in the present or the future, then..........

Woooshhh.......I was thunderstruck. I watched in awe as first one, then three pale green objects surfaced. Their sounds were akin to some mystic yogic exercise, alternatively releasing huge gobs of air in geysers of fine mist to the time-delayed accompaniment of hissing noises like a gaggle of angry geese. They weren't sperm whales, but they were too big to be minkes. Twice all three rose and then tails turned to the sky, they sunk back vertically under the surface, and the next time I saw them they were a mile out to sea..........HUMPBACKS!

That night, I made camp on a small table of rock connected by a narrow causeway from shore to sea. I had left it a little late, but I'd been picky. The sun had already dropped below the cliffs. It was just one of those days. There hadn't been a hint of a breeze since first light, and it wasn't until the

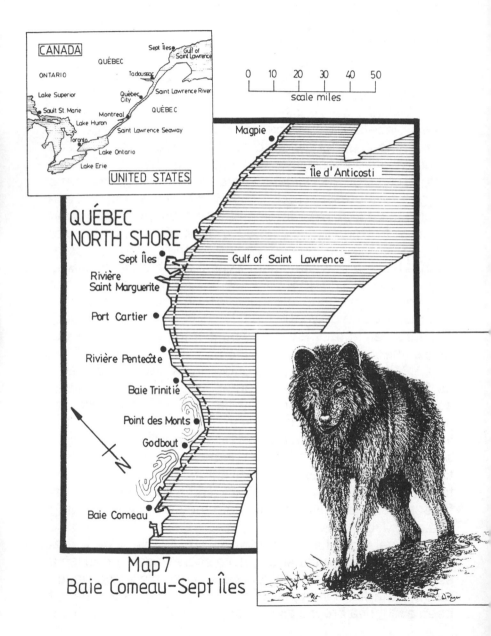

CANADA

ONTARIO

QUÉBEC

Sept Îles

Gulf of Saint Lawrence

Tadoussac

Lake Superior

Québec City

Saint Lawrence River

Sault St Marie

Montreal

QUÉBEC

Lake Huron

Saint Lawrence Seaway

Toronto

Lake Ontario

Lake Erie

UNITED STATES

0   10   20   30   40   50

scale miles

Magpie

Île d' Anticosti

QUÉBEC
NORTH SHORE

Sept Îles

Gulf of Saint Lawrence

Rivière
Saint Marguerite

Port Cartier

Rivière Pentecôte

Baie Trinitié

Point des Monts

Godbout

N

Baie Comeau

Map 7
Baie Comeau–Sept Îles

arrival of sunset's sobering chill, that I started to look in earnest for a campsite. Almost every night, I had fallen into the same trap - wanting to know what lay round the next bend and paddling too deep into the day - but this time, I was rewarded.

It was now after dark and the sea was sleeping. The moon had not yet risen and the Gulf's waters were pitch black. I was sitting on a knoll of rock, with my legs dangling two metres above a deep pool of water. I was bewitched. Below, small fish were shooting by like illuminated tracer bullets, but when their hunter suddenly surfaced in a huge mushroom of light, I was back into my kayak and on the water in a flash.

For me the best place to see whales is from land, but there are exceptions, and tonight was one of them. I love paddling at night. Invariably the nights are breathless and the seas calm, but it's not the action above water that seduces me stroke its surface,, but the action below.

A sea plankton's force field will illuminate any object it comes in contact with, and on a clear still night, as brightly as any moon. Tonight's conditions were ideal, and as all the action was close to shore, I knew that if tipped - whether by excitement or collision - I could easily swim my kayak back to the beach.

I can be fearless at night especially when no one can hear my cries of fear. I know its a contradiction in terms, but there is something familiar in danger when you can paint it in your own colours. Twice the whale swam directly under my kayak. Once, as if shot by a canon, it roared almost vertically out of the water. The whale was forever chasing a pale white ghostly cloud, whose pin-like shapes would dissolve, reform and sometimes, too close for comfort, shatter like white-hot shrapnel.

Eventually the scene played itself out. The moon had risen, and the shoreline turned into a magnificent lunar landscape of silver and grey. I now honed in on my beacon of fire and once ashore, I collected an armful of driftwood to feed its hunger. I was on cloud nine. My night paddle had only whet my appetite for more. I now sat for hours tracing out the night sky's constellations an the never-ending streams of satellites passing through its seas. It was a night to savour, and I didn't turn in until the fire had died away.

Today, I began another chapter, for once I had past the impressive white and red striped lighthouse at Pointe des Monts the Gulf opened, and its shoreline extended to infinity. It was like walking a tightrope. The view was dizzying. At any moment, I expected my nerves to crack. I had visions of free falling over the horizon. That morning, my eyes attached themselves to the land with the same intensity as a mountain climber's fingers cling to a crack. To say I was nervous was to put it mildly, and it wasn't until I had reached Baie Trinite, six hours into the day, that I felt sufficiently at ease with my new expanded horizon to embrace it.

Rain, rain and more rain. The next three days, from Baie Trinite to Sept-Îles, went by in slow motion. I had lost all my enthusiasm. I was waking later, finishing earlier, and my strokes during the day had lost their punch. Bad weather can do that to you, but it wasn't that. It was as if my trip had lost purpose and direction. It was now six weeks since I left Toronto, and Sept-Îles was only the half-way stage. Even the shoreline's surrealistic views in the rain and mist, its stunted rocky clefs, its twisted wind-bent pines and indented coves, could do little to inspire me. I had fallen into a depression of my own making, and that night when I made camp opposite the town of Sept-Îles, on Pointe Noire, I was ripe for the picking.

The sun on that fate-filled day rose and shone through the mist which enveloped the far side of the bay like a great glaring headlamp. My mood mirrored the environment. The air was stained and rusted by the smell of iron ore, and its waters had the consistency of olive oil. No one could have mistaken the port of Sept-Îles as a tourist attraction, but that morning neither could one have denied its vibrant spirit. It was not yet 7:00am, yet the bay was alive with the background hum of a buzzing economy. Mark had told me that Sept-Îles was the North Shore's crowning jewel. A worker's playground of near full employment. A place where men were men and women expensive. I had read somewhere that its harbour traffic was the second busiest in Canada, and being surrounded by seven islands, its deep water anchorage one of Canada's most sheltered. Sept-Îles, with its population of over 25,000, is by far the largest town on the North Shore. It boasts the biggest hospital east of Quebec City, was home to two of Canada's largest multinational companies, I.O.C. and Alouette, and with two bustling shopping centres and numerous businesses to its credit, was not only the last place I could replace equipment, but probably to make repairs also.

That morning, I broke camp to the sight and sound of a laker steaming towards me out of the sun's hallowed misty eye. At first, I could only make out one laker anchored in the bay, but as my eyes adjusted to the diffused light, and my ear to the sound of their idling engines, I ended up counting six. Sept-Îles appeared through the mist in bits and pieces. At first, I followed my ears. I attached myself to the sounds of a bulk carrier being loaded with iron ore pellets, then as it came in view, I turned into its wharf. I was now paddling slowly down into Sept-Îles bay, past another wharf, a fish plant, the ferry terminal, and before long I was facing its neat yacht club.

By now the sun had trail blazed its way through the fog. It was going to be a scorcher, but I knew it wouldn't last. It was the calm before the storm. The morning's long range weather forecast was calling for moderate southeasterlies in the evening with a gale warning posted for the weekend. I was in a strange mood, neither up nor down. I had almost forgotten I had a friend to meet, and a mail parcel to pick-up. Usually, I can't wait to get news from home or use the excuse of a friend to unwind, but today I wasn't in the mood

It was decision time. It was not yet 10:00 am. There

was still plenty of time left in the day to clock-up some good numbers. I could paddle onto Moisie, call my friend from there, then take it as it came. I took a walk on rue Arnaud, drank a cup of coffee then - just to be on the safe side - I visited the yacht club to ask permission to stay.

"Vous parlez Anglais?"

I had, without thinking, started the conversation in English, now I was trying to backtrack. It was like closing the stable door after the horse had bolted. I had asked for a shower, but had been offered a beer. I had mistaken the yacht club for the local sports bar, and now I was sure they had mistaken my need for *'une douche'* for *'une biere'.*

Looking back on the incident (Sept-Iles is now my home and its Sports Bar 'La Gage aux Spa' my local pub) it would have been laughable, but for the fact that I was suffering from a severe bout of heat exhaustion. The fermenting body odours bursting out of my wet suit smelled like rotting fish, and my head was in a tail spin. Then just as I was about to leave, a guiding angel descended on my troubled waters.

"Can I help you?"

Wow....I thought it, but kept it to myself.

"Yes!!!!" I could hear my sentences tapering off, but for the life of me couldn't understand a word I was saying. What the hell is it about me and Quebec women that makes me dumbstruck. I was beginning to think 'Les Femmes Quebecoises' had cornered the market on sex appeal. From the outset of our meeting, Lynne was like an itch I couldn't quite scratch. Petite, blond and athletic, with the cutest set of cheeks - encased in latex - that I had ever seen, Lynne was picture-perfect. Why this young woman accompanied me down to where I had left my kayak, or, for that matter, tried it out in the water, is beyond me. I must have acted like a child under a sugar attack. But it was when she sat in the kayak, and that confident air that bristled around her body fell as she put paddle to water, that, *'J'ai tombre amoureux.* It wasn't that long-lasting type that begs 'Have my children, and I will protect you forever'; the one based on the four corner stones of shared values of friendship, trust and commit-

ment. No, this was pure passion; the type your friends coun-
sel you to put down, yet every fibre of your body tells you to
pick up. I was caught hook, line and sinker, and I knew it.

The next few days passed in total confusion. After
meeting Lynne, I decided to stay. I had connected up with
my friend Hector Blake and was now staying in his home,
but there was only one thought on my mind......'Lynne'. I
knew it was crazy, but I am a risk-taker. I always have been,
and and although I didn't know it at the time, I had already
changed addresses, but that was in the future. As for the
present, Sept-Îles was in the grip of a full blown storm. I
stayed one more day, then against all signs to the contrary,
I decided to leave.

How blind was I? Completely. I set off in waves
whose reflective twins had turned Sept-Îles' harbour into a
mini roller-coaster. It was plain stupid. That morning, Hector
had accompanied me down to the wharf and his half dis-
guised brave face spoke volumes as to the conditions. I
couldn't even muster an excuse. His invitation to stay had
come open ended. It mattered little to him whether I stayed
an extra day or a week, and then there was Lynne. I just
wasn't concentrating on the job at hand. Even when I made
it to the mouth of the bay and saw the angry seas beyond
the shelter of its islands; even then, so deep in trouble, my
predicament didn't register. I had committed the cardinal sin
of looking over my shoulder to where I had just left, and
within the hour, I would pay the price.

I was some distance past Île petite Boule. I was
approaching the exposed rocks at Cayes de l'Est. I was
probably around 3 kilometres from shore, and somewhere
between the first and second page of my letter to Lynne. I
was searching for words not waves, and the only sounds I
heard that morning were the ones in my head.

BINGO!!!! A wave crested and slapped me.
Physically, I froze. Mentally, I was racing. My heart must
have been pumping ten to the dozen because the next few
moments felt like an eternity.

I remember noticing that my paddle's hand protective 'poggies' were on back to front, and having the time to calculate their distance between each other on my paddle's shaft. I remember seeing a sea rainbow, a prism of light through a developing wave. I remember wishing desperately to rise above it, seeing its deep blue pike turn green, then opal, then rush towards me in a wall of brilliant white bubbles. I remember watching the tip of my kayak disappear, the sensation of free-fall, then silence...........utter silence. Everything seemed disjointed. Noises fell in and out of my head like a faulty disc and my neck was burning. It didn't registered at first. The whole incident had happened that quickly it felt unreal, then it engulfed me. Water was everywhere - up my nose, down my throat, in my ears. I didn't know how to eskimo roll, but even if I did, I wouldn't have had a hope in hell under these conditions. I must have been paddling across some offshore shoal water, but that thought wouldn't occur to me until later.

My survival instincts had kicked in the moment I tasted water. I was trapped, sitting in my kayak upside down, and going nowhere. I couldn't find my cockpit skirt release chord. Twice waves rolled me over, and twice I curved my spine to get my head above them. I was now punching the cockpit skirt for all I was worth; trying to tear it, anything to let me out. I was screaming my head off, swallowing gallons of water and starting to think that was it. Then without warning, I popped out, like a cork under pressure.

This was not as it should be, I thought. I remember thinking how warm I felt, and watching the rise and fall of my equipment in the sea. Twice, I tried to reach out and grab my yellow boots, but twice the wind and surf took them away. I tried to scoop up my purple dry suit top, but each time a wave stole it. I even thought, for a split second, of letting go of my kayak and trying to swim ashore, but thought better of it. The waves were huge and the spit of surf was flying in the wind. I was now telling myself 'don't panic - be happy'. I was repeating it like a mantra as I held onto my kayak as if my life depended on it. The shoreline from my new vantage point in the water looked a long way away, but the wind, I knew, was in my favour. I never once gave into the thought of dying. I didn't see God, cry for my mother or have an out-of-body experience. I was back in the office, making decisions and keeping my fingers crossed that the tide was a rising one.

It took the wind and tide over an hour to carry me and my kayak ashore, but once on land the full weight of the incident hit me like a ton of bricks. I stood and fell, laughed and cried, then started to shiver. I am not a touchy-touchy-feely-feely kind of guy, but there is a time and place for everything and today was one of those rare occasions.

It probably took me thirty minutes to pull myself together, but once I had, all thoughts returned to the sea. I had to wade back in waist-deep water to retrieve my dry suit, and came across my sleeping bag's water-proof bag washed ashore and rolling in surf some distance away. My boots were lost to the waves, and as for this week's sea charts, my camera, thermos flask, flares, fiberglass repair kit and sandals - they were all lost and by now most certainly resting on the sea's bed. It was depressing, but I pushed the thought away. I still had plenty of money, still had Hector, and my kayak looked none the worse for wear.

Before leaving the beach, I emptied my kayak completely, sponged dried its interior, laid out its contents in the dunes to dry, put up my tent, then walked to the first signs of life.

If my body language - still dressed in my wet suit - didn't give me away, it didn't take long for my new hosts to fill in the blanks. They had an excellent view of the beach and the waves, if anything, looked even more threatening from their kitchen window than they had on the beach.

Getting into the house to warm up was one thing, explaining the whys and wherefores of my situation was a different ball game all together. I was suffering from lockjaw, trying my best to ask permission to use their phone, and shooting blanks. The poor couple had their hands full just trying to calm me down, but as soon as I spat out the name

Hector Blake their worried expressions immediately melted. Hector was my distress signal and thank Christ they knew him. I had been in no fit state to explain anything further than offering his name, and no sooner had it registered when the shakes kicked in, then I was sick. I had had too much excitement for one day, and by the time I heard Hector's welcoming voice, I was ready to cry with joy.

Ninety minutes later, I was in a restaurant, filling my empty stomach and off-loading the morning's events into Hector's lap. My trip was by no means over, but my confidence had taken a pounding. I now spent the rest of the day orbiting Hector's enthusiasm. He was my Man Friday. He taxied me here, there and everywhere, and while I chose the equipment and paid the bills, he did the translating.

That evening we called into the yacht club and got drunk, but afterwards I insisted he take me back to my tent. I knew if I returned to his house and put my feet under his table, it would spell the end. They say the best medicine for falling off a horse is to get right back into the saddle again, and come hell or high water, I wanted to be back in the saddle and paddling by morning.

When he dropped me off, Hector again wore his brave face, and I was grateful for it. Thankfully that night, I was tired. I offered up little resistance to my fatigue, falling asleep almost immediately without a care in the world, but the next day was a different story.

Everything looks darker, bleaker and without warmth when your heart isn't up to the task. That morning aided by alcohol and stirred by the sight of a wind blown sea, I woke up with a mega hangover. Every simple chore inside the tent seemed an uphill battle. I couldn't find any drive, and my usual checklist of things to do went unread. I had neither the guts to listen to the weather forecast, or the will to tune into its air waves. I was neither prepared to face the elements, nor felt I had the strength to paddle in them, but I did. God knows where the resources came from, but they only stayed with me as far as the Moisie river estuary. When I needed

1st June: Downtown Toronto, Lake Ontario
only 4500kms to go

Bernie's fibreglass sea kayak
Thank you Current Designs

Thousand Islands Bridge
Saint Lawrence River

Eisenhower Locks, USA
Saint Lawrence Seaway

Canada Geese: Once an endangered species
are now a nuisance

Signs like this one followed my progress down
the Saint Lawrence River, but never stopped me
from camping

Photo: Duplessis Tourism

Sept-Îles, Quebec; the Nordik Express connects the isolated settlements of Lower North Shore with Quebec and Highway 138

Photo: Duplessis Tourism

Sept-Îles is not only Canada's second largest port, and its most isolated, but also a playground for pleasure boats

Photo: Duplessis Tourism, Nick Gauthier
Natasquan, Quebec Lower North Shore

Photo: Newfoundland and Labrador Tourism
A tranquil morning on the Labrador coast
Isn't it great to be alive

Photo: Duplessis Tourism
Magpie, Quebec North Shore.
Meeting people as always been the name of the
game and especially fellow kayakers

Photo: Duplessis Tourism, Nick Gauthier
Riviere au Tonnerre, Quebec North Shore
somedays I owned the shoreline

The Quebec Lower North Shore is full of beautiful nooks and crannies

top: Ile Quarry

bottom: Mingan

Photo: Newfoundland and Labrador Tourism

top and bottom

**Minke whales are a common sight.
I like to see them at a distance,
but sometimes our paths would cross like the
one below**

Photo: Newfoundland and Labrador Tourism

top and bottom

I love seeing Humback Whales. Known both for their acrobatics and their haunting songs. I saw them both at play and in eating frenzies.

Photo: Newfoundland and Labrador Tourism
Razorbill, Labrador

Photo: Deplessis Tourism, Jean Guy Lavoie
Cormorants, Quebec North Shore

Photo: Newfoundland and Labrador Tourism
Ganets, Labrador

A colony of Puffins near Blanc Sablon,
Quebec Lower North Shore

Photo: Dupessis Tourism
**Petit Rigolet near Saint Augustin
Quebec Lower North Shore**

Photo: Duplessis Tourism
**Mutton Bay from the air
Quebec Lower North Shore**

Domino Run, Labrador
Fishing is still alive, but only just!!!
My heart goes out to the people who live on the
Labrador coast, but I know many a person who
would gladly exchange their well paying city jobs
for just a slice of coastal life

Black bear near Patridge Bay, Labrador
It seams that every time I make a portage,
encounter a bear

Photo: Newfoundland and Labrador Tourism
Iceburgs are a comon sight on the Labrador coast
The best times are from June - August

Seagulls playing in some bergy bits close to
shore - near Cape Charles, Labrador

Mud Lake, Labrador
It was almost mid september before I made it
back home.

I had paddled over 4500kms; lost 10 pounds to
the conditions, and my aging body felt like it had
gone 15 rounds with Mohamed Ali

If it's true that God looks over his chosen fools,
then I've had a blessed life.
Until the next time readers..\.......
"Beam me up Scotty or send me down the home
brew?"

them the most, they abandoned me.

Until then, the day had been relatively calm. I had paddled the Baie de la Boule with little incident. Today's waves were only the poor cousins to yesterday's monsters, but leaning on the side of caution, I had taken the long route around. I had paddled within a stone's throw of the beach all morning, but now felt confident enough to let go of its land. I had just passed the Moisie river, was less than half way across its bay to Pointe Saint-Charles when the weather turned. It was unfortunate that the wind and rain chose that moment to descend on me. The clouds had been threatening all morning, and anytime but now I could have handled it. The Baie de la Boule had been one long sandy beach. I could have turned and made it ashore before the momentum of the wind-blown waves had turned to surf. But to strike now, almost 10 kilometres into my crossing of the bay, and far from dry land, was just plain bad luck.

Common sense told me to keep on going. The beach I had left was unprotected while the shoreline ahead was full of indented coves that spelt shelter, but that day belonged to panic. I wanted to get ashore quickly. It had been overcast all day, but with a descending sun it had turned downright gloomy. I know I should have continued to cross, but I didn't. I turned with the wind and headed down into the throat of the bay.

I was within spitting distance of shore when the situation became ugly. There was a wicked undercurrent, and to make matters worse, what I thought was a sheltered harbor in Matemek, turned into a barrier of rocks. I was inching this way and that. I wasn't really in any danger. I had passed the worst, but my brain had a hard time reading its signals. Sure the swell was rising by the minute, but I was still in deep water. I was heading towards a gap between some rocks and under normal circumstances this obstacle would have posed no problem, but these weren't normal circumstances. My lack of confidence had shrunk the distance between them, pushed up its surf and turned the whole exercise into a test of nerves. I couldn't believe how tentative I was. I sat in the kayak letting wave after wave pass by. I was willing myself on, trying my best to reopen the gap and douse its surf. It's strange how your mind can play tricks on you when your nerves are shot. For no sooner had I gained the sheltered water behind the rocks, than the waves bottomed out, and the wind seemed to lose all its cut and thrust.

I wasn't exactly spoiled for choice camp sites. The beach was exposed and being close to houses it had been clear-cut of trees. By now, the rain was pelting down. I quickly put up my tent in some reed-filled dunes, cooked and ate as if there was no tomorrow, then put every stitch of clothing I had on, zipped up my sleeping bag and tried to sleep, but it was an impossible task. I was suffering from too much adrenaline. That night, my sleep mirrored the highs and lows of the storm, and it wasn't until the first light of the new dawn, when the wind and rain was at its peak, that I surrendered to sleep.

The storm pinned me to my tent for two whole days. I was miserable. I was full of self doubt and my inactivity only heightened it. I had lost all motivation and appetite. I was starting to feel sorry for myself and came within a whisker of calling Hector and jacking it all in. I would have, except for one small detail. I didn't want to get my feet wet.

I peeped outside the tent as apprehensively as a mouse. It was frigid and the noise caused by the breakers didn't need any further investigation. My confidence was still at a low ebb and it was just the excuse I needed. Once again, I stuck my head back down into my sleeping bag and started the slow count back into oblivion.

It was nearly noon before I stirred again. This time I'd been woken by the steady rap of rain on my tent. It was still bitterly cold, but the wind had died. I'd been in my tent for almost thirty six hours, and I was starting to get claustrophobic. I could see there was still a sea swell to contend with, but there were only a few white caps in the bay.

It was a case of the worse of two evils. I didn't like where I was camped and my hours in the sleeping bag had done little for my confidence. I took a quick walk along the shore, spotted a small outcrop of rocks, dragged my kayak over them, then broke camp.

The tide was falling and soon the outcrop exposed a channel. I now sat patiently in my kayak like a tortoise, with my hands in the sand waiting for an onrush of water to pick me up. Twice the surf rushed up the channel and twice I broadside onto its walls, but the third time the back eddy carried me out into the bay, and I broke free.

I didn't get far. At Pointe Saint Charles, eight kilometres down the coast, I lost my nerve. I misjudged some shoal water. A wave crested from nowhere. I was slapped sideways, and when it happened again, moments later, I dropped my tail like a frightened pup, and beat it for the shore.

That night, I was in a terrible state. One part of me wanted to walk up to the road, hitch a lift back to Hector's and jack-it all in, while the other was hell bent on finishing the job. I had begun this trip with few objectives in mind and even less passion. I'd never been able to muster much enthusiasm, and now it seemed the bottom had even fall on out of that.

I had not spoken to Lynne for more than thirty minutes, yet she had punctured a hole in my protective bubble. She had touched nerves I thought long since dead. As if woken from a deep sleep, I had felt with Lynne the same way a child with little gravity orbits his mother. I had not had a relationship in over a decade. I had pulled up the drawbridge on women twelve years before, while travelling in Africa; not because I don't like women, but because I like them too much. Women and travel just didn't seem to fit together. Since then, I had neither sought out a relationship or more importantly, been in a place long enough for one to gel.

I am neither naive or stupid. I had met women before, while travelling, but I had never asked for or received any commitments. My friends will tell you that I have a dark, selfish side to my personality. When I leave on a new trip, I cannot afford to look back over my shoulder. And depending on what your perspective, my selfishness is either a gift or a character flaw. I have always been able to telescope down past personal involvements to the end of a trip, and because of that, I have been able to concentrate one hundred and ten percent on the job at hand. I had put my capsize down in Sept-Îles to hormonal imbalance, but now I wasn't so sure. Was I getting soft ?

I fell asleep with this thought in mind and when I woke, it hadn't resolved itself, but at least I was able to put it on the back burner.

The North Shore was turning into a seductress in more ways than one. She could be calm and beautiful one moment, dark and passionate the next, It was like dancing with the devil, and today's conditions were typical. I broke camp at 5:00 a.m. I wanted to put in some good numbers before the afternoon winds set in, but that was not to be. A strong west wind picked up the moment I set off, then at mid-day dropped away completely. It was like a relationship that runs hot or cold, so I was always on edge. The beaches invariably looked soft and inviting, but once exposed, their soft underbellies were pitted with sharp rocks. Impressive points would announce clapping waves, and numerous rivers that emptied into the Gulf chopped up the seas at their mouths like a paper shredder.

By late afternoon, I was approaching the mouth of the Manitou river, and I could see clearly the river's current. Yesterday's rain had obviously been stronger inland that out. Silt and debris snaked out for about a kilometre, before tailing off east and diluting like milky coffee into the Gulf. For the whales it must have seemed heaven-sent. The rich silty residue would have attracted the caplin and the whales had just followed. Like a group of playful school children splashing about in a swimming pool, about halve a dozen or more pilot whales were in an eating frenzy. Some were rising vertically from the water, while others, like football players dove for the end zone.

I must have drifted amongst them for over an hour. Again the North Shore had teased me, and once again I was about to pay the price. The wind picked-up, the sea was becoming choppy, and I found myself rounding Pointe Manitou too close for comfort. I was searching for a small secluded sandy beach between the river and the point that I had seen from a distance whilst watching the whales, but now I couldn't find it.   I was in spitting distance from Manitou's vertical face of rock, and I could see clapping waves at its point. I knew from my map that there was a long beach just around the point, but it had dangerous breakers written all over it. I should have turned back to continue searching for that secluded beach, but retracing my path doesn't seem to be in my make-up.

I crept along slowly and then at the point, I stopped. I wanted to test the waters. The clapping waves were not steep, and as the reflective swells were taking off at 45 degrees from their point of impact, I judged them not dangerous.

I can't fully explain what happened next. I may have fallen into the trap of looking at danger too closely. I think I got sucked into the waves, and got caught in a back eddy without realizing it. I was now too close to the shore line of the beach as well as too close to the point's rock's face. I was just turning to head back out to the open sea. My rudder had just bit, and I was leaning into my stroke when a huge wave bounced off the point behind, reflected back, picked me up and slapped me straight into a wave heading directly for the beach. I was now pointing in the wrong direction, and before I could turn around, I began to surf.

I should have kept paddling but I didn't. When a powerful wave catches you like this and you start to surf your rudder is useless. But when you have been using it day after day, it becomes a knee-jerk reaction. I lost valuable seconds to my rudder, and by the time I started to paddle, the beach was racing up towards me.

I was now paddling like crazy, to keep my bow above water. I didn't want a repeat performance of Sept-Îles, and I knew if I lost sight of it, I was a goner. The wave I was surfing was starting to crest like a long pipe. White globs of water were being shaved off its top and it was becoming transparent. I was using everything: my paddle, my hips, my will. I had just given into the inevitable when suddenly the wave passed under me. I was now in the wave's back wake being sucked along, with my back to the beach, and could see another wall of water forming in front. My only chance was to make it back out to the open sea. I paddled with all my strength, but it was too late. No sooner had I broken loose, found purchase and movement when the wave crested on my kayak.

At that instant my world shut down. I was enveloped in a foaming mass of water, and the next thing I remember was a sharp pain in my hips and salt water down my throat. But, I was on the beach. I didn't make it out of the cockpit on the first attempt. It was full of water and sand, but I was in one piece. I was lucky, very lucky. Not only did the beach drop steeply into the sea, but the full force of the cresting waves stopped ten metres out from where I stood looking at them. I hadn't seen a better example of breakers anywhere. There was hardly any surf, and what made it up the beach drained back almost immediately. What you saw is what you got. The waves just beat the beach and nothing else. Breakers are called breakers for a reason. Just looking at them made me shiver, and today's conditions, believe it or not, were relatively calm.

I was now cursing my sea charts. Sea charts come in two sizes. 1:250,000 and their big brother 1:50,000. The former is devoid of detail, has few icons and is neither use, nor ornament to a sea kayaker. The latter comes with all the bells and whistles you could hope for. It has topography, shows the position of all coastal radio towers and high points of land, all sea buoys and lighthouses, and - most importantly for me - uses the shoreline icon that denotes dangerous breakers. I had purchase over fifty   Saint Lawrence Seaway charts and sea charts before leaving Toronto. All but six were charts scaled at 1:50,000. The six smaller scale charts covered the shoreline from Quebec City to Havre-Saint-Pierre - some one hundred kilometers east further down the coast. I had deemed it not worth the extra expense to buy the fourteen extra large scale maps of this section. I had, in fact, originally planned to use a Quebec provincial road map for this part of the coast, but in the end had bought the six 1:250,000 scale charts just to make up the set. Maybe it was the proximity of Highway 138 to the shoreline, or maybe it was the lack of islands and numerous beaches that influenced my decision not to purchase the larger scale maps. Right now it was of no consequence, but that night, I promised myself never again to save money at the expensive of sea charts.

The incident with the breakers had been a mixed blessing. Sometimes, a life-threatening incident can crush one's confidence. Today's incident was never life threatening, but my kayak could easily have been snapped in two. Lightning very rarely strikes in the same place twice, but if it does and you are still alive to talk about it, it's easy to start searching for answers from a higher being.

I fell asleep to the rhythmic sound of breakers, but woke to the pattering of rain. Once again, the gods were smiling at me. The wind had died and the tide was nearly full. I quickly took my tent down and packed, then sat and waited until the tide was at its highest.

It's always best to enter the sea at high tide. The waves tend to smooth out like the rumpled corners of a stretched out rug, and for some inexplicable reason, the wind normally takes a break. Nature gives you a one-hour window of calm, and that morning I didn't require a second invitation.

For the next two days it rained non stop. The coast had flattened out, and in places was half hidden behind a curtain of mist, looking like Labrador's Height of the Land. At the mouth of the Chaloupe river, I spotted a lone whale on the hunt, and at Sheldrake, a school of whales in an eating frenzy. I had seen people clam digging at low tide, and even two seadoo enthusiasts tearing about like jet-powered bugs, as if in some strange mating ritual.

I made camp the first night, tucked in behind Pointe-au-Tonnerre. It was my 38th since leaving Toronto, but my first camped so close to a road. All night traffic woke me and then came the thunder.

The next day, the steady down pour turned into a monsoon, and the sea started to bubble like a huge pan on the boil. I was now so wet that my skin was turning white. My hands looked as if I had immersed them for hours in hot water. All their colour had drained away, and they now had the wrinkled texture of a dried out raisin.

As I approached Magpie, I had stopped for a flask of coffee and was trying to roll a cigarette. I was probably ten metres from a face of rock in an armpit of sheltered water, when a whale surfaced directly between me and the rock face. I was gob-smacked. It seemed to rise in slow motion, let out a blast of air, then sunk back effortlessly with hardly a ripple or a wake.

I had heard that whales are the gentle giants of the sea, but until today would never have believe it. I am a Doubting Thomas, and believe strongly in the principle of 'seeing is believing', but the trip, until today, had been full of subtle hints. Just before Sept-Îles, I had been amazed to see a whale surface between two flocks of ducks with hardly a flutter of acknowledgement. At Tadoussac, I saw two kayakers paddling right down in the path a school of whales, only to witness the whales change direction. Until today, I had leaned towards caution, like a small child skating in rink surrounded by a team of adult hockey players. I had always watched them from a distance and if I spotted a school coming towards me, had always given them a wide berth. The odds of a whale unknowingly surfacing directly in the middle of a ten-metre space between a kayak and rock face, seemed to me no different than those of winning a lottery. I now felt immune. Like a cripple who bathes in the holy waters and finds he can walk, I threw away my crutches and started to paddle. When the whale returned, I found myself sharing its space with pleasure.

From Magpie, I cut straight across the bay towards Riviere Saint-Jean, but as soon as I glimpsed the river, the rain stopped and the fog - aided by an onshore light breeze - obliterated it. I was now paddling in a no man's land with only a wall of white humid clouds to follow. It was a strange time. I could only hear the sound of traffic crossing the river's bridge, but not see them. Then the sun came out, the sea turned a silvery blue and I found myself travelling through a beautiful golden triangle of calm. I stopped paddling and drifted. Four dolphins came calling, then a lone seal. When the sea is at rest, your eyes can latch onto the least movement, and even the flotsam and jetsam of sea garbage are easy to spot. A long piece of driftwood, maybe the top half of a submerged tree, glistened and winked at me in the sun. Then I saw a plastic supermarket bag caught on a twig, waving at me in the light breeze. Even a small gas slick, one of the sea's great polluters, now under the influence of the sun's rays burst into a rainbow of colour. These were moments to savour. Once again the North Shore had raised her skirt and was purring. For thirty minutes, I was spellbound, but once the shoreline fog evaporated, the breeze picked up, the sea's surface began to ripple, and the clear pictures melted away, like wax under the sun.

It had been my original intention to camp within sight of the small settlement at Longue-Pointe. I was hoping for an invitation. I had heard that a couple of anglophone families lived there, and I knew people on the coast were aware of my trip. I was starting to crave company. It had been six days since I'd left Sept-Îles and much had happened. I was bursting with stories, but the sight of a pack of wild dogs, snarling and growling at me from the beach, forced me to change my plan.

That night, I camped down in a bed of high reeds, hidden from the view of man or beast, way down at the bottom of a long stretch of treeless beach, probably 4 kilometres from Longue-Pointe. For once, I dragged my kayak off the beach, over the sandy bank and into the reeds next to my tent. The golden sand was full of RV tracks, and the thought of some high-spirited driver hitting my kayak during the night was too much to contemplate. The beach had been vacuum-cleaned of driftwood, but as I was keen to light a fire, I walked almost to the road in search of dead-wood.

    I cooked a lovely evening meal. At Magpie, I had beached and bought some fresh carrots, onions and a few potatoes. I boiled them all together, then added half a pack-et of my favourite Big Bills Beans and Rice. I now sat back in the crook of a natural back rest, at the foot of a steep bank, smothered in reeds. My beach fire was crackling and the wood was spitting out the sand in its pores like explosive sparklers. In the fading light the outstretched arms of Chenal du Mingan were turning into a live amphitheater, as first one group of ducks then another - either by species or by size - landed, pooled, then paddled to their nightly parking spots. It was turning cool but it was tranquil, and a perfect end-of-the-day experience.

    The mist returned as the sun set and as soon as the stars appeared, they were blotted out. The mist now hung above my camp like a canvas canopy, reflecting the light from the fire, and as I walked along the beach, it beaconed my return like a lantern in a halo of light

    There is nothing more irritating or, for that matter more embarrassing than to be watched by a lone spectator. I can handle a group, simply by playing the crowd, but to be peered at by a lone spectator is more than a little disarming. He'd arrived on the beach in his RV as I was breaking camp, and was now sitting on the bank, within a stone's throw of my kayak, waiting for me leave. He'd no doubt seen me beach last night, taken one look at the early morning break-ers, and happily left his cosy quarters in hope of bearing wit-ness to a disaster. In all honesty, the breakers weren't that bad, but with his beady eyes burning into the back of my neck, and Pointe Manitou still fresh in my mind, everything that morning was under the microscope.

Technically, I know what I am doing in breakers. I set off in conditions like this on scores of occasions, and I didn't expect today to be any different. I had pulled my kayak down to the beach until I was just above the line of surf. I sat in it, secured my cockpit skirt to its frame, tightened the neck and wrist straps on my dry suit and then waited for the surf to pick me up. I had followed this procedure hundreds of times. The surf would come, roar up the beach, pick me up, and I would follow its backwash into the sea, using my hands to walk on. Then it was just a matter of keeping myself at right angles to the breakers and paddling.

The secret doesn't lie in one's upper body strength, but in timing - and being able to keep your kayak pointing directly at the onrushing surf. The first few seconds are critical. You cannot allow the backwash to turn the kayak. Even if you get caught high and dry on your first attempt, you can still brace yourself for the next onrush of surf if you meet it head on. It sounds technical, but it's just plain common sense.

My first attempt was pathetic. The wave broke, rushed up the beach and picked me up, but my hands sunk in the sand, anchoring me where I was. The second split as it was cresting, tapered off in opposite directions and slapped me sideways, whilst the third caught me half in and half out of my kayak, and I got wet. The cockpit filled with water and sand, and I had to retreat back up the beach, turn it upside down and sponge it dry.

I tried again. This time everything worked perfectly, until I became caught in the back wake of the line of surf I had just crested. I misjudged the depth, my paddle hit bottom and my kayak turned into my stroke; not much but just enough, and before I could straighten out and start paddling again, I was slapped and flipped by the next rush of surf. Now, I was not only completely soaked from head to foot, but embarrassed. Once again, I had to turn my kayak upside down, drain out my cockpit and sponge it dry. All this time my lone spectator had been watching me, with an air of detachment, but this time, on catching my eye, he waved me over. I sat down besides him and accepted his offer of a cigarette.

It's strange how men bond. Maybe he had similar experiences - pushing off his speedboat in just such seas, being watched by curious neighbours, and now the roles were reversed. We smoked in silence, and the longer I lingered, the more I felt at ease. The smoke had cleared my brain, his kind smile had taken away my stage fright, and I made it through the breakers as if I had been doing it all my life. I was now in a good mood. I surfed with the wind, cut out Mingan, then noticed a pair of hands waving like an excited windmill from the shore.

I was approaching Butler's Point. The male figure looked vaguely familiar, and when his pale stubbly legs came into focus, the rest of his stout frame fell into place.
"How's it going, boy ?"
Hector was a sight for sore eyes. He'd taken a time out from his work in Sept-Îles, motored down the coast on the off chance he would spot me, and now wouldn't take no for an answer.
"Fancy a pizza ?"
Hector is the type of guy all travellers dream about - a back-slapping optimist who likes to follow rainbows -and today it was mine. It was not even noon, but I dropped anchor for the day and while Hector went for a six-pack of beer and a pizza, I made camp.

I woke bright and early. Meeting Hector had helped enormously. His enthusiasm for my trip, his promises of help, and his unexpected arrival, along with food was just the tonic I needed. I'd had nothing but bad or indifferent weather since leaving Sept-Îles, and had been like a spring under tension, ready to snap. I had needed to let my hair down, shoot the shit, get grounded and drunk, and he had been a willing participant. He'd put me back on track, smoothed down some of my sharp edges, and put my trip into a much needed light hearted perspective. It was as if I had a blood transfusion during the night. His promise to buy two 1:50,000 scale sea charts of the route ahead in Labrador and mail to me in Red Bay, was like money in the bank, and his list of coastal contacts on the Lower North Shore provided much-needed escape routes in case I hit bad weather. That morning the colours were brilliant, and even the morning news of an imminent coastal storm didn't effect me. I was chomping on the bit, and made Havre-Saint-Pierre without a break.

The day turned into a beauty. The wind died and the threatening clouds encroached no further than the horizon. I could now relax, take in the tourist route and give into one of the North Shore's most spectacular sights. Every region has its picture postcard scene, its sexy underskirt that seduces travellers into visiting and the North Shore is no different. Simply put, Havre-Saint-Pierre sells rock; not any kind of rock, but giant mushrooms of rock. The whole area is both a testament to the forces of nature, and a huge visual reminder that time always wins.

Like the leaning tower of Pisa, some of these eroded outcrops will fall prey to gravity sooner or later, and obviously the municipality of Havre-Saint-Pierre decided to make hay while the sun was out. Some of these rocks rise out of the water, like huge phallic symbols, while others, high and dry on beaches, look like lone sentries on guard. The area is festooned with them, and from a distance these rusty-looking sandstone-like formations could easily be taken for a wrecker's yard of rusty axles and wheel bearings. Having said all that, there was one thing missing, fog!

Just as the twisted and hunchback gargoyles of Notre Dame Cathedral in Paris loom up through the River Seine's early morning mist, the natural rock formations in Havre-Saint-Pierre glare out from the fog. If only the provincial government in Quebec City had vision, and sprung for one of those 'Phantom of the Opera' fog-making machines, this tiny off-the-beaten-track place could, in a few year's surpass Monument Valley as Hollywood's premier film location. It has it all: a community centre, abundant electrical power, an airport, a couple of stores, a bar, and a willing work force.

GOOD MORNING AMERICA

You don't have to be a student of English literature to understand. I was in a good mood that day, and as I don't take drugs, evidently suffer from a vivid imagination. I had taken Havre- Saint-Pierre as it had taken me, with a pinch of touristic salt and good humour.

That evening, I made it to the island of Saint-Charles. I'd logged in some good miles and still felt fresh, but the clear skies above promised a sparkling sunset. It was my first island campsite since Quebec City. For three weeks I had paddled down a mostly unprotected and unbroken shoreline with little change, but from here on in, for the next 250 kilometres to Blanc-Sablon, I could expect deep cuts and an almost unbroken chain of islands.

I chose the seaward side of the island and camped on an elevated plateau above the beach. There was hardly a table of rock or carpet of moss that didn't bear witness to a feast. Broken conch shells and split open mussels littered my camp site like the leftover peanut shells you find on the floors of sports bars. I ate early, built a huge pyramid like fire of driftwood, then sat back in its glow to watch the colors change.

The sunset in a low haze, and the clouds it fell through were turning orange. High overhead, long wisps of purple-tinted vapour tailed eastwards, then lost themselves in a dark blue sky. I was in my element. Hector had started my unwinding process and the sunset was completing the job. Slowly the colours melted into one. As the night sky darkened, some thirty minutes later, and as the stars started to shimmer, I called it a day.

I woke to the flapping of a loose chord beating on my tent.The morning sky was grey and the sea did not look friendly. I had been hoping to pass the islands ahead on their seaward side, then cut diagonally across 16 kilometres of open water from Pointe de l'Est on Île Sainte-Genevieve to the settlement at Baie-Johan-Beetz, but now I wasn't too sure. This was not a time to be tentative. My 1:50,000 scale sea chart of this section looked like an underwater mountain range close to shore and, once started, there would be no turning back from my alternative route across the open sea at the mouth of the bay. A kilometre offshore, sea levels rose and fell like steep mountain ridges. I knew that tide currents would rise to the surface as sure as air currents rounding a bend, and that once the storm arrived the whole coast would chop up and foam. Could I trust my nerves in the open bay? I couldn't decide whether to take the inside passage on the leeward side of the islands, or to cross the mouth of the bay. I was camped in a beautiful little cove, and I could easily reposition my tent and wait out the storm, but at that moment, it didn't seem like an option. I knew I hadn't pushed the envelope since Sept-Îles, but to capsize here, in the open sea, miles from shore, with not a soul in sight, would be folly. To do it twice in one trip would be unforgivable. I put the decision on hold, broke camp and took off, but two hours later the decision resurfaced. The storm had arrived. The winds were beginning to chop up the surface swell, and a fermenting mass of foam was beginning to form in the channel ahead.

I beached on Île-de-la-Chasse, and climbed to the top of a rocky knoll. I now had a clear view of the two channels I would have to traverse and the open sea ahead. My first hurdle was Chenal-des-Saints west; between where I stood and Île-Sainte-Genevieve. The choppy sea swell seemed only a few hundred metres across, where the main stream of tide was rushing out against the wind, but how deep and choppy was its big brother on the eastern side, between Île-Sainte-Genevieve and Rochers Bowen was anyone's guess. Actually, it didn't look that bad and the view of the open sea swells across the bay, even in this strong wind, looked like plain sailing.

I came down from my perch and was in the water before any second thoughts about an inside passage behind the islands and along the shore could gain momentum. Within minutes, I was soaked, and by the time I reached Point-de-l'Est on the seaward side of Île-Sainte-

Genevieve, I was already shivering from cold.

I had got my second wind after crossing the first channel, but now it was draining fast. Once I passed the point, turned to my left and saw the land drop away from me, I lost my nerve. I froze. I was probably 4 kilometres out from the shore, but I might as well have been twenty. I now felt like a tightrope walker who had lost his safety net.

For two hours, I struggled with my nerves. The sea swells were building, and I was angling, very slowly, for the shore. I was in no real danger, but I have never found that delicate touch that you need, to surf well. When a sea swell picks you up from behind, it's important to surf it at right angle. If you're too shallow it will either pass under your kayak or slap you, and if you're too steep, you'll end up speeding down to its trough with your bow lost in water. Every now and then, I misjudged my angle, and either got slapped or ended up in a free-fall. Then the inevitable happened.

I must have been passing over one of those subterranean mountains my sea charts had warned me of. A sea swell suddenly turned into a cresting wave. It slapped and spun me around so quickly, I wrenched my back. A jolt of pain shot through my shoulder blades like an electric shock. I was still a long way from shore, but once I had gained a foothold some forty-five minutes later, I beached at the first opportunity. Without thought of food, I pitched my tent, pulled out my sleeping bag and crawled into it.

I woke up stiff and sore, but hot pain had gone. I applied half a tube of 'hot rub' athletic ointment - packed away for such an occasion - and thirty minutes later was as right as rain. That morning, I broke camp in a heavy fog, unable to see the group of small islands just off shore or the imposing arm of rock at the end of the beach, but I didn't care. The air was full of the perfumes of exposed kelp rotting on the rocks, and there wasn't a hint of a breeze to transport them away. For two hours I picked my way round a small chain of islands. It was like paddling through a seascape in a silent film, viewed through frosted glasses, with only the sound of your own breath. Visibility was cut down to the nearest rock and except for the small cove before Point-Tanguay, I never let go of the land. Even the few nesting birds I paddled past hardly stirred in my presence, and a lone seal talking to himself between great gulps of air didn't even give me a second glance.

I pulled into Baie-Johan-Beetz, not out of any need to socialize, but to give me back a much-needed rest and stretch. Mission accomplished, I was back in the water.

The fog rolled back and forth all day, sometimes offering glimpses of open water, but never for too long. I stayed in the saddle for eight hours. I found a rhythm, and the time flew by. I revisited old loved ones and replayed my favourite songs until they were worn out. It was one of those days when your mind takes over, and you can visit the cinema of your choice. A multiplex of stages where you can change seats and performances without interruption.

It was the time of a new moon. The tide was at its lowest ebb and just past Pointe-Pashashibou, I beached, sat back near a late afternoon fire of driftwood, and watched a group of clam diggers. The night came quickly. The fog soaked up the setting sun and I retreated from its penetrating dampness into my tent.

I broke camp before sunrise. The fog was still thick, but I had no problem packing, and by the time I was finished the sun was forcing its way through. The sea was still calm, but as I pushed-off ripples were starting to form. Once I crossed the bay ahead, the light breeze turned into a bone chilling northeasterly.

It didn't take long for the rain to set in and all morning, it alternated between steady downpours and drizzle. On the few occasions it stopped and gave way to the sun, it carried no heat. For two weeks, the sun had been playing hide-and-seek, and I was beginning to wonder if it would ever put in a full appearance. I was suffering from 'Newfie blush'. My face and hands - the only exposed parts of my body to catch any rays recently - were reasonably tanned, but the rest of my body was ashen. Any excess layer of fat I'd put on in Sept-Îles had long since peeled away. My body was turning from the 'mean lean machine' of Quebec City into something more akin to an advertisement for famine relief. I could easily count my ribs and, if shaken, I'd swear their cage would rattle. Even my usual bottomless appetite had gone the way of the dodo. I could no longer muster any enthusiasm at supper time, and my weight began to play on my mind as much as the weather. I've never been a breakfast person. A Mars bar, a couple of breaks for coffee and a smoke can easily keep me going during the day. I had always made up for it in the evening. I ate till I dropped, crashed out early with a full stomach, and always woke refreshed.

I once read a dietary book, written by a a fellow explorer about eating habits. I didn't fit into any of his categories. In fact, I seemed to have broken all his rules. I have travelled for over twenty years, and I surmised after finishing his book, why change old habits if they work? Today, however, I was beginning to wonder if he was right. Maybe my stomach was getting the equivalent of the seven-year-itch, and today felt as good a time as any to break with tradition, and have a fling.

I had just traversed a rather boring stretch of water. From Pointe-Nabisipi the shoreline had flattened out like a pancake. The wind had picked up and the rain was slating. There was nothing much to see, and to make matters worse, sea swells were forming into waves and cresting, far out to sea. I was just passing the small community of Aguanish. I could just see the tops of its houses tucked in behind some sand dunes when my stomach grumbled, then it grumbled again. As taking the advice of a complaining wife who's only telling you the truth is the best thing to do, I knew that as soon as I turned my kayak towards the shore, it was the right decision.

I beached at the headwaters of Riviere Aganus, nipped in behind a line of large sand dunes and put up my tent. I fried up some garlic, added some curry powder then, using the same pan, boiled up maybe half a litre of water, added one packet of 'Big Bill's Beans and Rice', stewed it all up together, and ate the lot. It was as if some one had told me I had just won first prize in a lottery.

The rain stopped, the wind died, and the sun came out. The day changed from a miserable reality into a real afternoon dream-come-true. Islands grew in size and beauty, and after leaving Aguanish the shoreline rose with my spirits. Once again, the shoreline chipped and broke and this time I traced its contours, not out of any need for my safety, but to explore its diverse rock formations and colours. Even the early afternoon downpour worked in my favour. The rain stopped as abruptly as it had started, and no sooner had the sun popped out than the sea began to steam and halo everything in its wake. I was now passing through a cluster of islands around a point of land just past Baie Washtawouka. The sea was calm, the quickly-forming mist soaked up all sounds, and the road - my constant companion for the last two months - now disappeared from view for the last time. The umbilical cord of the North Shore's Highway route 138 had been severed. I was now entering an isolated part of Quebec called the Lower North Shore. A tremendous feeling of freedom swept over me. From Natashquan to Goose Bay, Labrador some 1200 kilometres away by sea kayak, there would be no road contact with the outside world, and with the exception of the 120 kilometres of paved highway from Blanc-Sablon, Quebec to Red Bay, Labrador, none of any length.

I was now on my own, which is how I like it. I'm a risk-taker at heart, and the road had given me a false sense of security. It had coloured my judgements on more than one occasion, and although it had been a life-saver in Sept-Îles, it had also proved an unreliable safety net. From now on, if I made a mistake, the trip would be over. I had neither the finances to fly equipment in, or the time to anchor myself in a community to wait for its ferry service. Before I started this trip, I knew little about Quebec's Lower

North Shore, and it wasn't until I met Hector Blake in Sept-Îles that I found out about this unique piece of Newfoundland tucked away in Quebec, and I was looking forward to experiencing it.

That night, I camped on the seaward side of an island opposite the Petite-Riviere Natashquan. It was an eerie place. Although my map showed a village close by, I could have been on the moon. The low-lying fog had cut everything down below its knee caps, while overhead the early evening stars were pale and remote. The flickering light of my campfire brought me little solace and when the crescented moon rose above the gloom, I turned in for the night.

Chapter 5
The Quebec Lower North Shore

I woke to a fog so thick, it took a leap of faith to trust my compass, although once I crossed the 1000 meters of open sea and caught site of the mainland beach near Natashquan, I hugged it as if my life depended on it. The sea was so calm, I was able to kayak within a stone's throw from the beach and with the exception of a few gulls, had it all to myself. The morning drifted by in a beautiful haze. The sea had turned into a vivid shade of green, and the beach a shiny gold. The fog had burnt off as the sun rose and now it looked like a bleached curtain. For ninety minutes the scene tapered out to the mouth of the Natashquan river. At Point-Parent, I turned into the river and was about to beach when the whirring sound of mosquitoes drove me back out again.

I eventually beached close to some sand dunes, on the west side of the river. I climbed to the top of a point of land, turned to the east and was immediately slapped by a burst of wind. I couldn't believe my eyes. I had just paddled through thick fog which still had a strangle hold on the view behind. But in front, influenced by moderate breeze with only a trace of fog, and stretching into infinity was the longest unbroken stretch of beach on the Lower North Shore.

At first the view didn't quite sink in. Reading something on a chart and seeing it firsthand are two different experiences, and it wasn't until I'd passed the fog sign at Pointe-de-Natashquan and started the long haul up the coast, that the full weight of my predicament hit home. Breakers were pounding the beach and surf swept up and down in never ending patterns of motion. I now cursed myself for not stopping at the Indian Reserve at Pointe-Parent. I had little drinking water, had drunk most of my flask of coffee, and I knew I would have to make it almost to Kegaska before I would find a safe camp site.

Map 8 : Sept Îles–Blanc Sablon

I was already a seasoned surfer. I had the confidence to ride a wave in, and I knew - from watching a wave develop - which one to take, and more importantly, the safest spots on the beach to come in on. Today, a landing would pose little problem. The waves were starting to crest far out, and although the surf looked powerful, it didn't look dangerous. But take-off would be a different ball game. The whole coast for the next 30 kilometres looked like it had been drawn with a ruler. There wasn't a nipple of exposed land, or a brook or stream with a deep enough cut in the beach to follow. Without a doubt, if I made camp on this section and the weather turned ugly tomorrow, I would be stranded.

For four hours, I paddled non stop, then at high tide the bottom fell out of the breakers. The sea turned calm and I beached. I was on land for less than an hour. I took a walk to get my blood circulating, got some water from a brook and ate a chocolate bar, but once the tide turned, the breakers returned, and I was back in the sea within minutes.

By early evening the wind turned ugly. I had been paddling in a coastal rip tide since my early afternoon break. Sometimes it had worked in my favour and sometimes against, but now the choppy surface forced me to head for deeper waters. I was now paddling some 1000 meters from shore. The yardsticks that I'd use to judge speed and distance were gone, and the point of land I'd been heading towards all day now slipped away from me, like an illusive cat. The wind was unrelenting and when it changed in the early afternoon from southeast to northeast, I felt like throwing in the towel.

The sun was just starting to redden, when I finally gained a foothold on the point of land I had been concentrating on all day. I was absolutely exhausted. My back was as rigid as a plank, and my rear end had lost all sense of feeling. I put up my tent, lit a blazing fire, cooked, ate and fell into a deep, dreamless sleep.

I woke into gale force winds. Breakers were pounding the long beach down the coast in a monotonous rhythm. My decision to bite the bullet yesterday, and paddle to the end of the beach was justified. It would have been suicide to have attempted leaving through these thundering breakers. They were huge, but the water besides my present camp-site, which was sheltered between a large tidal dune and a rocky point of land, was almost still.

I skirted the point with ease, found a sheltered route behind some islands, then sixty minutes into my paddle, almost lost it. I'd just tucked in behind a point of land at the headwaters of the Kegaska river, and I was taking a breather. The wind was very strong and the sea down the bay was full of surf. I should have known better, but the sight of Kegaska's radio mast only 8 kilometres away was too much to resist. I had just pushed off, leaving the shelter of the point, when a burst of wind broadsided my kayak.

The next moment ice cold water was pouring down my neck. I'd flipped. Instinctively I slapped down my paddle. I was leaning into the water, twisting and pushing. Not again! All I could think of was Sept-Îles. Then, just as suddenly, I popped up. It wasn't an eskimo roll, it was Bernie. I'd just braced, used the blade of the paddle and pushed off against it with all my might. I was elated and crushed at the same time. What ever confidence I had built-up since Sept-Îles instantly evaporated. The seas now looked huge, and surf-ing an impossible technique to master. I gave in to my fears, angled into shore, and called it a day. It wasn't even noon, and although the wind dropped a few hours later, I had nei-ther the will nor energy to break camp and continue.

That night, my brain was racked in sleepless thought. Not only did I seem to have lost my daily rhythm, but - more than that - the high level of concentration I pride myself on. I often daydream when I'm travelling; a beautiful girl, my favourite tunes and always food. When I day-dream, I know I have hit a rhythm. I can relax into my strokes and the kilo-metres just fly by. But I couldn't remember a day when I had been relaxed, and as for concentration, I seemed to have lost it. I live by the old credo *'when times are tough the tough get tougher'*. I used to be able to shut down the least distraction, but now all kinds of negative thoughts were creeping into my head.

I reached Kegaska the following day under a heavy cloud of my own making, and although I immediately accepted a wharf side invitation to stay the night, my mind was never quite in the present. I tried to unwind. My hosts had a VCR and I never stirred far from their television. I ate meals with the family and played the dutiful guest, but my heart wasn't in it.

The next day the fog was like pea soup. I should have stayed another day in Kegaska, but the dark cloud hovering above me was starting to show. I was beginning to become irritable, and the last thing I wanted was to pass it on to my hosts, but I was in luck.

"If you want to take a break, use my cabin at the other end of the bay."

"Where ?"

"Over there, son."

I was following his finger, but couldn't stop laughing. He might as well have been pointing to a needle in a hay stack. The fog was so thick I couldn't imagine anything in it, but an invitation is an invitation.

You can never truly understand the disorientation that fog causes until you've left sight of land. Your world immediately shrinks, all plains, vertical and horizontal, dissolve and you become trapped in a bobble. I never did find out if I stayed in the correct cabin. I was so relieved to find land where it should have been that I stopped at the first cabin I came to.I was still within spitting distance of Kegaska, but light years away in my mind. I stayed two full days, but never saw Kegaska again. I slept and slept and slept, and it was just the tonic I needed.

The sun began to make inroads through the fog on the third day. I still couldn't see Kegaska, but I had enough. I got itchy feet and decided to leave, but still, it wasn't easy. The whole bay seemed to be reefed in a semi circle of shoal

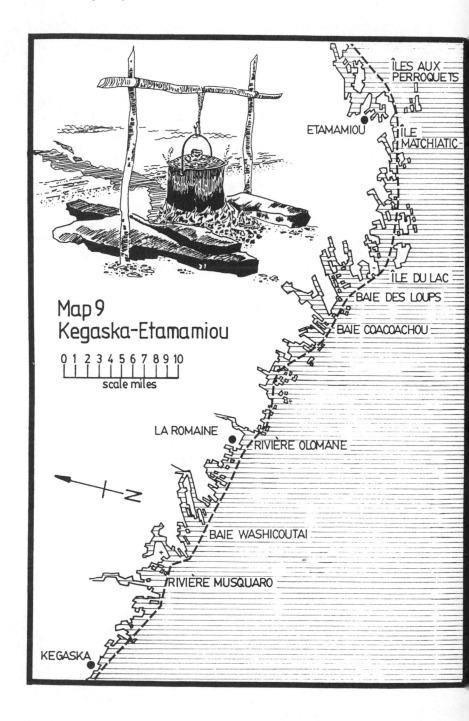

ÎLES AUX
PERROQUETS

ETAMAMIOU

ÎLE
MATCHIATIC

ÎLE DU LAC

BAIE DES LOUPS

BAIE COACOACHOU

Map 9
Kegaska-Etamamiou

0 1 2 3 4 5 6 7 8 9 10
scale miles

LA ROMAINE

RIVIÈRE OLOMANE

N

BAIE WASHICOUTAI

RIVIÈRE MUSQUARO

KEGASKA

water and exposed rock. There was no wind and hardly a sea swell worth mentioning, and after an hour of detours and back paddles, my nerves were wrecked. At Pointe-Curlen, I decided to take the inside route across Havre Mistassini. The fog was still thick and I didn't want to let go of the land. I did the same thing at Pointe-du-Cap-Rouge, and by the time I reached Pointe-Musquaro, I had become so tentative, that I paddled all the way down to its throat. I doubt if I strayed more than 500 meters from land all day. I could have probably recited every nook and cranny on that stretch of coast. As the crow flies, I doubt if I covered 16 kilometres in the fog, yet I must have paddled close to 30. But still, every day has its silver lining, and mine saved itself till the end.

It was one of my easier decisions. The morning fog had turned into a late afternoon drizzle, and I started to search for a campsite. I had just turned into a cove for a closer look when, quite suddenly, the heavens opened and the rain peppered down. The rain made the decision for me, and as soon as I beached, it stopped. I chose a small clearing between two large trees, erected my tent, broke off some dry wood branches and had a blazing fire going before sunset.

This is my favourite time of day - when the sun is down, when the sea starts to darken against the sky, and the still waters close to shore glimmer like molten metal. Its the twilight zone between day and night, when an evening meal tastes the best and when I can walk off the daily stresses in solitude, on a deserted beach. That night the glow from my fire of dead branches and driftwood illuminated the cove, and the fermenting stars offered me beams of light on which to dream. I stripped naked and went for a walk. After eight hours in a wet suit, the freedom of a cool drying breeze on my moist wet skin was intoxicating. For thirty minutes I walked up and down the beach, and had it not been for the evening chill, I would have willingly slept outside.

It was a beautiful morning. Beams of light shafted

through the trees and rainbowed in the early morning steam that surrounded my camp. The sea was turning honey-coloured and a gaggle of geese, oblivious to my presence - their heads tucked at angles under their wings - were still resting where I'd last seen them, grazing in a patch of red berries. The faint plume of smoke now fanned by the morning breeze was starting to re-ignite the embers of last night's fire, and I was tempted to aid it. It was one of those mornings when it felt great to be alive. I didn't want to stir. I knew that as soon as I rose, the picture would shatter. The geese would fly, the fire would have to be tended or extinguished, and the natural bowl of honey would lose its attraction.

Sure enough, my movements disturbed the geese. They rose like a disjointed squadron of jets from the bank, reconnected over the sea and flew overhead in long wavy threads, rising and falling in unison. I was more curious than amazed. I had never seen geese flock so early, and I had not seen any nesting on the coast since Quebec City. It's not as if there was an abundance of berries or grain to feed on around here. I watched them disappear west and wondered if, like me, they had homes to go to.

For the first time in weeks, I relaxed into a rhythm. There was a moderate head wind from the east, but the sea was calm. The islands were easy to negotiate, and the broken mainland full of seductive headlands and coves, a pleasure to paddle through.

At Havre-Fraser, I let go of the land and cut right across the open body of water. I was a little nervous. I had meant to call in La Romaine, but the day was splendid and by the look of the puffy clouds above, it would remain so. I was probably over three kilometres out and eight from the nearest point of land. I was just approaching the leeward side of Îles-Triples, angling back to the mainland, heading towards the mouth of the Olomane river, when an immense mass rose in front of me. It was a whale. A silver-green monster with all kinds of barnacle-like pigmentation studded in its flesh. I'd never seen anything like it. It was huge, and as it had broken surface, was attended by tremendous gurglings and rumblings as water cascaded off its sides, back into the sea. It let out a huge blast of steam, glided for what seemed forever, then dropped effortlessly below the surface like a submarine. I was amazed. I've seen scores of whales, from humpback to pilot, from their playful cousin the dolphin to the albino beluga. I've seen them during eating frenzies, roar out of the water, and I've seen them in schools rising and falling in graceful arcs, en route to their next meal, but never one as huge as this, or that stayed on the surface quite so long.

Sighting the whale had boosted my confidence, and I followed it out to sea. I was now a long way from land, heading for an isolated group of islands called Îles-de-la-Brume. The sea swells were uniform and although dark clouds were queuing up over the horizon, the wind died completely, and then I got scared.

Maybe it was the sudden drizzle, but I knew it wasn't. Sometimes I feel like a tight rope walker who suffers from vertigo. Ninety-nine times out of a hundred, I can let go of the land in conditions like today's, but now I lost my grip. I had looked over my shoulder at the infinite horizon, and was free-falling towards it. The drizzle had nourished my fears and they had taken root quickly. My capsize had obviously cut much deeper than I thought. I panicked, turned towards the mainland, and paddled like crazy.

The storm never did materialize, but the dark clouds hung around for the rest of the day. I was now hanging onto the coast like a frightened child clutches his mother's hand. For two hours I crawled along the shoreline, and it wasn't until I reached the mouth of Havre-Bluff, found shelter within its numerous islands, that I could once again relax into my surroundings.

The sun was close to setting before I called it quits, but no sooner had I beached, pulled out my tent and laid out my equipment, when the clouds opened and there was a tremendous and sustained downpour. Everything got wet. I had opened the watertight seal on my sleeping bag's plastic sac, and in my haste to put up my tent, forgot to close it. I was now determined to light a fire. I wanted to salvage something from the day, and an evening fire seemed just the tonic.

I love everything about fires, the wood collection, the lighting, its smell, its look and, especially, toasting my buns after a long day. The St. Lawrence Seaway had offered few secluded spots, and the Gulf of St. Lawrence far too few opportunities. But now, on the Lower North Shore, I was spoiled for choice. I was now looking forward to this end of the day ritual like some people look forward to sex, and topped off with a mug of tea was the icing on the cake.

Tea, as I was finding out quickly on the Lower North Shore, is something akin to a religious experience. Just consider a piping hot stove, the humid hiss of boiling water and the chatter of friendly voices. Coming from England, I've always been an addict, but tea stewed in a smoke stained pot, balanced on a twig over an open fire, sugar by the spoons-full, and drunk on a deserted beach, is the best tea of all. There are not many advantages to being single, but this experience is one of them.

The sun was starting to set before the rain stopped. I had cooked the evening meal on my gas stove inside the tent's vestibule, but once finished, I set about my fire. I scoured the undergrowth beneath the trees for dry wood, broke off some dead branches, and hurriedly collected as much driftwood as I could carry before the night set in.

It was hours after dark before the fire finally took hold. The early evening clouds had dispersed and stars were beginning to dance. I had boiled my water, stewed my tea, and was now relaxing into the night. For once, I slept half in and half out of my tent. The fire was dying and its smoke kept the mosquitoes away. Flames extinguished and fell inward with soft cindery sounds, and yellow sparks illuminated the beach. It was time to close my lids. CBC radio wavered in and out, then stuck, and the last I remember was a tale as told by Fireside Al.

As soon as the sun was up it vanished. The storm

clouds that threatened yesterday's calm had returned with a vengeance. They now swept over the horizon like a tidal wave and the calm sea that heralded the day was soon boiling, but this morning it didn't matter. Since Havre-Saint-Pierre, the coast had splintered like a pane of glass and I was spoiled with choice sheltered routes. I was still tentative in the windy conditions, but island-hopping was turning into a frustrating exercise. The maze of islands in this section of coast offered up little daylight, and sometimes it was hard to differentiate from a distance between a craggy point of mainland and overlapping islands. I still hadn't the courage to let go of the land and take the quicker routes on the seaward side of the islands, although I knew I would have to try, someday.

The wind's force increased as the day passed, but I was reluctant to beach. I had already lost two-and-a-half days to fog since Natashquan, and two afternoons to wind. On one occasion, I had been forced ashore by a sudden but prolonged squall. It hadn't even been midday and by early afternoon, I had found myself frustratingly anchored to a meal while looking out on a ripless sea, but the weather was too unpredictable.

Breaking camp is always a chore. I don't like it, and the thought of doing it twice in a day unbearable. In fact, I'd only done that once so far, and it was only because I had been too tired to pitch my tent in a more secluded spot and had found myself surrounded by pedestrians in a tourist village, that I had broken camp after the wind had died and continued. My problem is; once I start unpacking, I carn't help but finish the job.

The wind now blew through my wet suit like a net stocking. I was freezing. I should have been wearing my protective windbreaker, but for some stupid reason that morning, I had jammed it down by my sleeping bag at the bottom of the cockpit. I'm not double jointed, and in calmer conditions it would have been fairly easy to reach down into my cockpit and retrieve it. Today, however, that would have been foolish, and dangerous. It wasn't just that the waves were too steep or the surf that continually broke over my gunnel threatening to capsize me, it was the sudden unannounced gusts of wind. A strong down draft, waves would flatten, shave into spray, then take off like fast-moving bands of fog. The first time one caught me, I lost my paddle. It hit me like the back draft of a passing truck. One moment the paddle was firmly in my grip, the next ripped from it, and had it not been for the chord that secured my paddle to the kayak, I would have been in a right pickle.

I'm a stubborn bugger, and this incident only riled me. There were still plenty of escape routes, as islands and sheltered inlets were everywhere. I wanted to get some miles under my belt. But, when I finally reached the open water across Baie-Coacoachu, I choked, surfed the next two kilometres down its throat as if under sail and beached just behind Pointe-Milne. I was pissed off. Where had the summer gone? June had been brilliant. Even July had started with a mini-heat wave, but now it was ending with a fizzle.

I went for a walk to calm down. I needed to unwind, and my legs needed the exercise. I was in no fit state to make camp yet, or to risk a bay crossing for that matter. When you are tired, it's not one bad decision that catches you out, but the sum total of all those smaller decisions made under haste or fatigue that add up to disaster. Somewhere along the line, you have to take time out, take stock and own up to your weaknesses. Patience is not a virtue I have in abundance, or until recently, one I have valued. I am your stereotypical action man who sets goals through blinkers of narrow vision, and then guns it.

I knew I had been playing catch-up since Sept-Îles. I'd added a few more hours to my day; rising earlier, logging in extra mileage and forcing myself to reach the next point. It was all logical. Canada's summers are short, and as you go north, the window of opportunity diminishes. I was caught between caution and haste. I have always prided myself on being a safe paddler. If a trip looks like taking four months, I allow for six. If a point of land looks too dangerous to traverse on water, I'll portage over it. I don't have an ego when it comes to danger, but this trip had been different. I had commitments. I had wanted to start from Lake Ontario at the beginning of May, but couldn't. I had already lost my four-week cushion by starting in June. I hated playing catch-up, but if I wanted to round the bend at Red Bay, Labrador before the easterlies arrived, I couldn't afford to drop further behind.

My mind was racing. Like Einstein and his formulas, I had mine. Point to point, outside passages, and even paddling at night when the sea was usually at its calmest. I didn't have to play catch up every day. I still had, I judged, six weeks of reasonable weather, but every half day lost from now on would be very difficult to make up. I still needed a daily minimum of six hours paddling, and I was very sure that I had the endurance to put in some back-to-back, ten-hour days if the weather allowed it, but I didn't want the trip to turn into one long endurance test.

By the time I returned to the kayak, I had another piece of the jigsaw puzzle in place. I put up my tent, cat-napped for three hours, then - under much calmer conditions - crossed the bay. From now on, if necessary, I would put up my tent during the day and wait out storms. They had certainly come more frequent of late, but had not settled into any real pattern.

I made the east point of Baie-Coconipi by late afternoon, and by early evening, I found myself tucked away between clean sheets. I had spotted a summer cottage whilst crossing the bay, dropped in for a chin wag and, for once, fell asleep on my hosts. Maybe it was the heat inside their home, maybe my compounded fatigue or just plain lack of sleep. No sooner had I accepted their invitation to lie down, than I crashed out.

I woke to a brilliant sunrise. The extended sleep had done me a power of good. I felt on top of the world, and I was raring to go. During breakfast, my hosts, Tom and Harry, invited me along to check their salmon nets. I was of two minds. It would be nice, for once, to shut the door on travel, be chauffeur-driven around and watch someone else at work, but the sea was too inviting. There was not a breath of wind, and apart from the last trails of vapour above the shoreline rocks, everything was still. Even so, it was a hard decision to make.

Isolated as Tom and Harry were from the outside world - probably 24 kilometres from Etamamiou to the east, and more than double that distance from La Romaine in the west, they had all the comforts of home. A small portable diesel generator supplied their power, and tonight the Blue Jays were in town. There was a promise of fish steaks for lunch, and a potluck supper with oven fresh bread for supper. They were working men with appetites to match and they probably had enough food in the fridge, or in tins, to last until freeze-up. While all this appealled to my stomach, their surroundings tugged at my heart string. Their summer home - a kind of after-thought of add-ons, freshly painted in an off-white with red trim - looked almost too picture perfect for words, and the granite hills, that only yesterday looked bleak and uninviting with their stubble of trees, now looked spectacular against an ice-blue sea. The whole coast had sprung to life. The bare rock, streaked in greys, blues and light browns, provided contrast to the pine green fern that sprouted out between its cracks. Even their boat, bobbing in and out of the sea swells and winking at me in the sunlight, looked too good to be true. Then, splash ! ! !

Tom had tossed some of yesterday's waste into the sea and almost immediately a frenzied pack of gulls appeared from nowhere. I couldn't help but laugh aloud. I'd almost slipped into a world of retreats and monasteries, but their pail of fish heads had brought me back to earth with a bump, and before the sun set, it happened again.

For once, the inside passage between the islands was in my favour. The coastline turned northeast. The islands grew bigger, and it wasn't until I reached the tail end of Île-de-Ouapitagone that I had to consult my map. I had planned to call in at Etamamiou, but the weather was too good to pass up and my sea companions just too entertaining to miss.

Like a wolf pack of submarine telescopes, curious seals were popping up everywhere. They would rise, watch my progress with those sad puppy dog eyes, then sink back under the surface without a sound. Only once did a seal slap his tail down, and only then because I'd snuck up behind him. Then, I paddled through probably one of the most unusual sights I'd ever seen.

Picture the silhouette of a low-flying Concord, the haunting cries of a love-sick duck and a black velvet, after-dinner jacket pattern in brilliant white spots, and what do you get ? The loon, to me, is the aristocrat of the duck world. To see a loon in these parts is not unusual. In fact, I had been seeing and hearing them almost daily since Natashquan, but to come across a colony of them - now, that's unusual. Loons are not very sociable as ducks go. They don't gather in huge flocks like their migratory cousins, or dance in groups during courtship. They say that once a loon mates, it mates for life, so it's not as if they have to go cruising. I had been spotting them in bunches all morning, but always from a distance. They are not exactly timid, and as ducks go, are not worth the hunt. They rarely take off - choosing to dive and swim away - and if you've ever seen one warming up for take off, you can understand why. They may be graceful flyers and powerful swimmers, but their take offs and landings leave much to be desired.

I had just paddled through a narrow tickle, when my eye was caught by a black smudge ahead, and bingo ! Not a bunch, but at least twenty adult loons with a whole flotilla of young in tow. I couldn't believe my eyes.

The saw me almost at the same instant, as I'd noticed them, and were now beating a hasty retreat towards a protected shoal of exposed rock, but I was one step ahead. I dug in, sprinted for the rock, cut off their retreat, and within minutes, I had herded them back out into deep water. I know some readers will be up in arms. How dare he ! Well, it's not that I beat them with my paddle. I just like watching how the adult loons play the old ' broken wing routine' to protect their young, and I love watching their young scatter like pellets in water when they are excited. I only tormented them for about fifteen minutes. I just had to turn in their direction and they'd scatter. Some, like mini-torpedoes actually shot right under my kayak and a couple more, to their horror, even surfaced directly besides me. But the adults soon had me pegged. After only ten minutes, one brazenly swam right up to me and soon after, all had corralled their young. I was now judged no threat. Slowly, normality returned, as one after another - their young now attached to their mothers like chinese dragon streamers went on their merry way.

The weather stayed relatively calm until midday, then a sea breeze picked up. I was just passing by Île Matchiatic, when I paddled into a flock of ducks resting in the sea swell.

If I could have a dollar for every duck that couldn't take off, I would be a rich man. The poor ducks must have been dead to the world. From a distance they looked a bit like a colourful oil slick. There were probably about a hundred or more. Maybe they hadn't expected a yellow kayak, or maybe they were still asleep, but, I was almost on top of them before they stirred. The first couple took off against the wind with no problem, but the rest left it far too late.

I was now parallel with them, but up-wind. They all turned en masse, rose, then fell, then rose and fell again. They couldn't find purchase in the wind. Some angled out, and after lengthy attempts, made it. But the majority were reduced to beating wings and treading on water. It was utter confusion. Some gave up in less than a minute, while others bounced off the tops of waves and either made it on their first attempt or ended up somersaulting back to the sea, time and time again. I was totally at a loss. Not at what I was seeing, but how I could have got so close to them in the first place, then ....

Bang ! Bang !

A speedboat shot past, not one hundred meters away.

Bang ! Bang ! Bang ! Bang !

Then another one, they were both in tandem, both wheeling

around as if in a dog fight, both glued under their prey and spraying pellets everywhere. Just as suddenly they stopped, threw out a couple grappling hooks, pulled in a few birds, then took off behind an island. It all happened so quickly it took my breath away.

Call me an old romantic, but I still like the idea of man against nature. I'll stand up anytime and fight for the right to put food on the table, but when the chase repeated itself thirty minutes later in a blaze of action, I began to question not their motives, but their technique.

I'm normally a vegetarian, but when I travel, I listen very closely to my own body. It's my vehicle, and I want to get the best performance out of it that I possibly can. In fact, I am so dependent on it, I only offer it the best. And when I travel it seems to crave all kinds of game. Whether it be caribou, moose, seal or duck, its seems to have a bottomless appetite. But there's only one problem with natural foods, and that is it's quality depends mostly on the harvester who harvests it. A good farmer will not sell his milk after a violent thunderstorm, because he knows the cows have been terrified and the milk they carry will probably be sour. Just as a good hunter, having spotted an exhausted moose, chased and harassed by a pack of wolves, will pass it by, because he knows its meat will most certainly be bitter. For sure these ducks were both frightened and exhausted. I said my piece, albeit to myself, scowled in the boats' direction and continued on.

I was now aided by a southwest tail wind, and the shore line ahead was opening up like the leaves of a book. Pages were turning quickly and each page revealed a different story. Once again, I saw a school of seals and just after, what looked like a moose on the mainland's shore. The jagged shoreline was smoothing out and when I saw a low flying plane disappear in the bush, I knew Chevery was just around the corner. The miles had flown by, and had it not been for the steady drizzle that had settled in, I would have pushed on to Harrington Harbour.

What a difference a day makes. My elevated campsite, sheltered in the crook of a natural arm of rock with a
glorious view over a waterfall below, was all gone. It was as
if someone had turned off the light. I had to strain my eyes
just to see the water's edge. Not another day fog-bound! I
couldn't bear thinking about it. Only five kilometres of open
water lay between me and Harrington Harbour. It was the
only place on the Lower North Shore I didn't want to miss. It
had everything - boardwalks, tiered fishing stations, the only
island community on the coast as yet unspoiled with an
active fishery. I could expect something akin to a hero's welcome. I was in fact expected. It was only yesterday that I
spoke of my impending visit to a couple of fishermen from
Harrington Harbour. If I bypassed the island and, took an
alternative route without telling anyone, I know people would
not only be disappointed, but worried. It wasn't beyond the
bounds of possibility that someone may even be in the fog
searching for me right now. Communities are like that on the
coast. They have an 'all for one and one for all' mentality,
which crystallizes in times of emergency.

I knew for certain I would be missed. Maybe it has
something to do with the way I travel. Meeting people has
always been the name of the game for me. To outsiders it
may look like I sponge off people, relying too much on hospitality, but I truly believe I give as much as I get. I know that
many wilderness junkies search for isolated areas to get
away from people. Well, I am the opposite. I like the thought
of being public property. I respect the extended family greet-
ings, the *'don't bother with your boots, come straight in ta'
kitchen me'boy'* attitude I receive at the door, and the way
that these people embrace my character and my story.
When I travel, I like to get my hands dirty - taste, touch and
smell my surroundings - but with that comes responsibility,
not only for my own well-being, but for the safety of others
who may needlessly endanger themselves, looking for me.

It was important that I got a second opinion on the
weather. My radio batteries had died, and my present campsite didn't offer a true reflection of coastal conditions. I left

my camp, followed the narrow path back down to the beach, and sniffed the air.

On this stretch of coast the only certainty is that the weather can change rapidly. There was a light southerly breeze. The sun was just starting to make inroads through the fog, but that may have been an illusion. I could hear nothing. The sea was still and even though Chevery was only 500 meters away on the other side of the river, I may as well have been on the moon. Whatever life existed this early in the morning had been chocked by the fog. Then as if by a miracle that only a traveller would take for granted, Harrington Harbour's tall red and white radio mast appeared above the mist.

I was packed and on the water in a flash, but no sooner had I checked my compass bearings, plotted a route and started to paddle, than it sunk back into the fog again. At first, I wasn't worried. I was confident I was on the correct heading, but when the mast reappeared to my right and a little behind where it should have been, I was confused. Once again, I checked my compass, but as soon as I turned on a new heading, it disappeared again. This time the fog carried a chill. It was so thick, and heavy with moisture, that it condensed like rain in my hair.

I'd now been paddling for over an hour. Again I checked my compass. For all intents and purposes I should have been paddling up someone's back garden, but there was neither sight nor sound coming through the fog ahead. I began to worry. The first signs of alarm were percolating in my head. What if I had missed the island completely? Maybe I was heading out to sea ? There were the beginnings of a sea swell. Either I was passing over shallow water, or in an exposed area that was influenced by yesterday's wind or by a deep sea current. Neither possibility felt inviting. Although I have used a compass before, I've always put more faith in my own instincts and being able to read the lay of the land. I had never used my compass in fog before, because I'd never needed to. I had always kept land in sight and when I judged it too thick, as in Kegaska, I had stayed

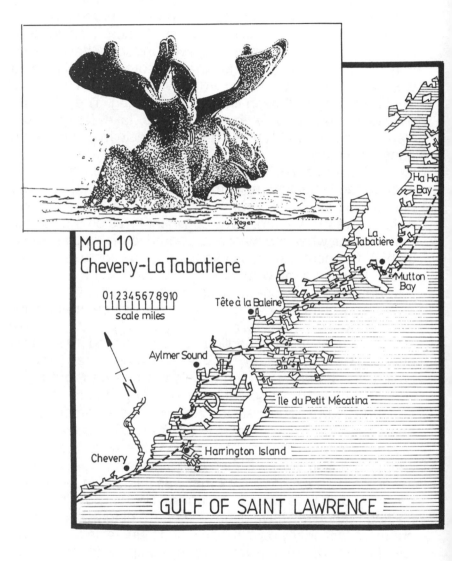

Map 10
Chevery-La Tabatiere

0 1 2 3 4 5 6 7 8 9 10
scale miles

N

Ha Ha Bay

La Tabatière

Mutton Bay

Tête à la Baleine

Aylmer Sound

Île du Petit Mécatina

Chevery

Harrington Island

GULF OF SAINT LAWRENCE

put for the day. I was now paddling in uncharted waters, and I didn't like it.

Suddenly a wave picked me up and crested. What the hell ! The waves were travelling in the wrong direction. Then another wave crested. Then I turned to face a third, rode its crest, dropped into its wake, and hit a rock. I was in shoal water where none should have existed. I could see rocks spouting up everywhere. Where the hell was I ?

For ten minutes I battled just to stay up right. Waves would suddenly puncture through the fog, crest and slap me, then the inevitable happened. I bottomed out. The kayak cracked so loud I thought for sure it had split in two. I was caught in a deep trough, trapped like a ship in dry dock between three large rocks, and had I not instinctively dug my paddle and shoulder into the wall of angry water that proceeded the noise, I would certainly have lost my kayak, if not my head, on the rocks. I began to panic. To my left and in front I could hear the distinctive sounds of beach breakers, but that escape route was barred by rocks. To my right was the echoing clap of waves slapping against a large face of rock. The only way out was to go back, but I couldn't turn around.

There comes a time when your brain skips onto a different plain. Your heart starts to pump like the pistons of a steam engine, and you get what I call an adrenaline rush. It happens so quickly and with such force that it quite literally separates mind from body. At times like these, I've been able to spot objects on the horizon that only a person using binoculars would see. Colours become brighter, sounds sharper, and your brain telescopes through the chaos to a clarity that only mystics and yogis attain. Its like you've been there before; seen it, done it, and really its a piece of cake. For some reason, at that instant, I turned with a wave. I hadn't a care in the world. I rose with it, surfed it and then rushed between two rocks. I squirted past a couple more, then glided into a still lagoon, hit the bottom with my paddle, and then stopped. I was in a state of shock. I turned, looked back at where I'd come, and froze. Good God! Rocks rose out of the surf like tree stumps in a clear cut. The surf must have not only pushed me forward, but cushioned my route through and over them like a protective bumper. Was I ever lucky! I pulled out my cigarettes, pondered on my-out-of-body experience, and tried to relax. It took a long time. First I got the shakes, then I started to cry. It took an enforced cat-nap to pull myself together, and when I woke, the fog had lifted. Harrington's radio mast had reappeared and the slab of rock, that I had been aware of jutted out into the sea like a huge knuckle.

I was now high and dry, buried in mud. I dug out my map, and took a walk on the bank. I lined up the cliff to my left with the radio mast in front and then visually checked my new position. I was at the entrance to a shallow bay at the back side of a tidal island. I checked the map again. I had pencilled in a short note 'only to use if the tide was in'. The note jogged my memory of an alternate route that I'd been told about. It was my plan B. I had been advised against it because it was full of mud banks, but it was sheltered.

The fog had almost cleared, but I had neither the enthusiasm nor strength to wade back through the mud and rocks to the sea. Harrington Harbour was now like the fish that got away. I would change my plans and visit Aylmer Sound instead. Tonight I would call my contact in Harrington and make my apologies. I now turned my attention to the compass. It had failed me. Either it was broken, or the whole area was one huge depository of iron ore. Whatever the reason, I now didn't trust it anymore and with one quick move-ment, I dispatched into the mud. Good riddance!

I was not, as I soon found out, exchanging a difficult route for an easier one. The path down the bay, as I remem-bered being told, was only navigable by boat when the tide was in, and the narrow cut at its base - that connected the bay I was paddling down to Aylmer Sound - was probably only navigable during that short window of opportunity dur-ing high tide, but I was banking on the fact that a kayak draws less than six inches of water, and that the advice I had been given was based on a speed boat's clearance.

Wrong!

I should have guessed from the maps liberal use of the icon that denotes marshes, that I'd get stuck. But I'm a stubborn son of a gun, and when I get my teeth into something suffer tunnel vision.

The channel in which the kayak now floated opened out, raising my hopes giving that it would become more navigable, but they were short lived. The tide was still dropping and my predicament went from bad to worse when the channel dead-ended and my kayak became totally stuck. It was as if it was glued to the bottom. There was nothing to do but get out, unpack and pull it over the muddy bank to the next channel. I repeated this time consuming-portage twice more, before running out of water. I had only made it half way down the bay and now there was nothing I could do but wait until the tide returned. I buried my paddle in the mud, tide up the kayak to it, took tent, sleeping bag, sea charts, and some food, and headed across the mud flats to dry land.

I pitch my tent on top of one of the nearby hills with a magnificent view of the basin below. The carpet of pale green marsh reeds that marked the shallow valley between bays at the backside of Île-Cresent was clearly visible, and the light brown cut that I would have to paddle in zig-zagged and forked through the reeds from bay to bay, just as the map showed. I put it all to memory, and even climbing to the top of an adjacent hill to see if I could spot Aylmer Sound. I couldn't, but I did see that the bay I was heading for was a twin to its neighbour. It was festooned with mud banks, shallow channels, lagoons and rocks. I could only hope that once the tide returned, I could cut point to point and make it to Aylmer Sound before nightfall without getting stuck.

Twice, I woke to the false alarm of worry, but on the third occasion my kayak was already straining at the bit and threatening to leave me marooned.

I found the cut with no problem. A large pole had been erected and it was decorated with all kinds of objects, like a Christmas tree. It turned into an interesting detour.

The whole area was a huge daycare centre for ducks. They clogged up the cut I paddle in, and blanketed the lagoons it opened into. I was an intruder and they weren't shy to tell me. Once I took a wrong fork, bottomed out and found myself having to pull my kayak, calf deep in mud, through thick neck high-reeds like Humphrey Bogart in the African Queen, while being dived bombed incessantly by scores of angry nesting birds.

The tide was now rushing in. In places it seethed like a pot of brown soup on the boil, pushing its froth in all directions. And in the longer, wider stretches - where the silt had as yet been disturbed -the water, was a brilliant shade of turquoise. The shallow hills that bordered this scene were bathed in lush green and in places the plateaus of land, long since elevated above the sea, were still rich and lush with plant life, and blazed with late summer colours. It was a little piece of heaven and I owned it. I doubted if half a dozen people a year used this route each summer. The narrow cut I was paddling in was probably only open for an hour a day. A speed boat would have to gun it. In winter, I have no doubt it would turn into a six-lane freeway for snowmobiles, but right now I could probably have died and no one would have been the wiser.

It was early evening before I made camp. I was in sight of Aylmer Sound, but the sun was dropping quickly, and I was too tired to put in a sprint. I had just erected my tent and was about to start cooking, when I saw a brilliant streak of white cutting across the bay. It was a small speed boat. Suddenly its engine cut, glided almost to a stop, then reared up, turned and came in my direction.

"How's it going,Boy ?" What a stroke of luck. The only contact name I had outside Harrington Harbour and Saint Augustin further down the coast was in Aylmer Sound, and it had just fallen into my lap. Within minutes, I was being sped down the bay, and within the hour into a welcoming committee of friends and relatives that would not only feed me, but insist I stay the night.

After supper, I went for a walk. An early evening mist

was just starting to form and the night air was unusually humid and warm. I had wanted to explore Aylmer Sound's small cluster of houses and its unique elevated boardwalk that connects them, but I had company and not the type to take no for an answer. I have travel many times in Canada's northern wilderness. I have seen it documented, packaged in glossy brochures, and on the news, referring to its rich mineral depositories, but never have I heard anyone show or talk about its mosquitoes. Surely the mosquitoes are Canada's last line of defence in case of attack. If the defence of Stalingrad saved Russia from the overwhelming forces of the German military during the bitter winter of '42, then the same argument could be put forward for our mosquito. That night they didn't so much bite me as suck me dry. They came in waves, like a chinese army on a suicidal mission, and you knew with certainty there were more of your enemy than you had bullets, and that they would just keep on coming. That night they literally drove me crazy. I had been seduced by the warm breeze to put on my shorts and now I was paying the price.

I hadn't even made the first house before the whirling noise that had accompanied my walk had crescendoed into the film score from 'The chainsaw massacre'. These bloody coastal mosquitoes don't take prisoners. I beat a hasty retreat, if not a humiliating one, and that night my ankles, thighs and crotch itched so much, I hardly managed a couple of hours of good sleep.

I woke into a thick fog, but during a delicious breakfast it suddenly lifted, leaving long tattered remnants of vapour trailing above the water. It was like the aftermath of an artillery barrage. Pockets of steam floated in the light breeze and diluted as they rose. I had entered Aylmer Sound after the sun had set. The tide had been in and the only visible signs in the early evening gloom had come from Aylmer Sound's dozen or more houses that dotted its shoreline. Now I could clearly see what the sea charts had forwarned me about. The bay was full of mud banks, large rocks, the flotsam and jetsam of village life and a couple of grounded boats stuck out like sore thumbs in an otherwise polished surface. The falling tide had sucked the very life from the shallow bay and exposed its ugly underbelly.

Within the hour the early morning fog was in full retreat. The heat was building and soon the sun shone down without hindrance. The tide had now visibly changed, and the lagoons were beginning to overflow and connect like mercury droplets. David, ever the bouncing bean of the household and requiring only the hint of an excuse to escape the family chores had me down the bay in his father's speedboat within minutes of me asking him. We found my tent as I'd left it and with his help, I quickly had everything packed away and was soon back in the water.

The day drifted by at a leisurely pace. I found the headwaters of the Mecatina river with ease, but lingered too long in its still waters. By the time I had traversed the shallow passage behind Île-du-Petit Mecatina and had reached Baie-des-Rochers, the tide had turned. The shoal rocks now rose like dangerous spikes down the bay, and slowly Tete-a-la-Baleine sunk behind them. I was disappointed as Tete-a-la-Baleine is one of the few settlements between Kegaska and Blanc-Sablon that is truly French, and I had wanted to capture some of its flavour before leaving Quebec.

I now took a diagonal course inland to pass Tete-a-la Baleine's ferry terminal on Îles-du-Grand-Rigolet-Ouest. I still had one more question to be answered before Mutton Bay, and I was hoping I could find it at the ferry terminal.
"Bonjour, comment ca va ?"
"It's o.k. You can speak in english !"
Well so much for my book of French phrases. Actually, it was a stroke of luck. I'd spotted three men about to leave on a speedboat, waved, caught their attention on the wharf, then paddled over to meet them.

Have you ever tried to referee a family dispute? Don't. I should have bitten into the first bit of information, buttoned my lip and paddled off, but for some God only knows reason, something inside me compelled asking for a second opinion, and now I felt more confused than ever about the route ahead.

It's not as if what I was asking was a matter of life or death. It mattered neither here nor there whether I took the portage route behind Cape-du-Gros-Mecatina, or rounded its cape. The weather was gorgeous. It's just that the story surrounding the man-built portage of logs at the backside of the cape to Mutton Bay intrigued me. I'd only heard of it the night before in Aylmer Sound and it sounded unique. I had been told that the fishermen in Mutton Bay had built it so that they could cut out the cape during stormy seas and get to their fishing grounds further up the coast, using the sheltered island waterways from here to Harrington Harbour. Until now, I had taken exactly the same route from Aylmer Sound, and although today it looked like it would be probably quicker to round the cape, I didn't want to take it.

On the coast, the most mundane questions about distance, directions, time and weather have a habit, if posed to a group of men, of ending up in an argument. There maybe two answers to every question, maybe five, a dozen depending on the crowd. The only thing that is certain is that everybody's opinion has to be vented and that all could be different. Once the process is started, there's no easy escape route and all one can do is relax into its chaos, and wait the arguments out.

It's not that people on the coast are stupid, far from it. Local information has saved my bacon on many occasion: 'turn left at the bleached tree; between those two hills; behind the old cabin at the bottom of the bay, and those romantic old man of the sea rock formations. These are the expressions I know the best, but today I wanted it to be pinpointed on the Government of Canada's chart 4469.

Imagine giving a New York subway route map to a street walker who's only terms of reference, until that day had been visual ones, and then ask him, what train to catch to get to Time Square?

Sea charts are read from above. You can't visualize the vertical plane if you don't understand its language of contour lines and icons. There's no 3D, and they do not offer the reader silhouettes to guide you. In short, they weren't made for me. Really, I'm not that bad, but today the map offered two obvious routes, both close to each other and both at the bottom of deep cuts of water. I'd already got lost once this week, due more to bad weather than anything, but to get lost today, to take the wrong portage, to have to back-track, to add both distance and time to my day when the weather was in my favour would be unforgivable.

I had just about given up, and made up my mind to round the cape when the blatantly obvious hit me. *"Didn't you say the portage crossed a large pond"*? Sometimes the obvious routes are the hardest to spot. And there, in bold black and white letters on the map, the name Baie du Portage marked the pond and the portage route to Mutton Bay. It had been written so big, I'd discounted it immediately. And starting with Baie (french for Bay), I had taken it for tidal waters. In fact, if I had been listening more closely to my friends on the wharf, it wasn't the route that they had been arguing over, but the French use of the term Baie, which was clearly a pond.

I was now back on track, with time in the bank and a clear sky above, and more importantly a new contact with a promise of another night between clean sheets in Mutton Bay, if I wanted.

The early afternoon turned into a procession of small rocky islands that opened up like doors along a long corridor, until they finally dead-ended in front of a huge slab of rock. I now followed the deep cut in the cape, clearly visible from the sea and on my chart, paddled to its end, beached, and then found without problem the start of the elevated wooden portage walkway just above the high tide mark.

I didn't even have to unpack a thing, and although my kayak seems to weigh a ton out of water, once I had pulled and then pushed it up onto the walkway, it slipped forward with ease. But the portage turned out to be more difficult than I imagined. The logs, stripped and polished from years of usage gave my feet little purchase, and twice I fell through some gaps, the last time almost shattering my ankle. I should have gone for a walk first, to get my blood circulating and put some life back into my legs, but it's always easier to judge these things after the event. It probably took me an hour to get from the beach to the first small pond, and thirty minutes to the Baie-du-Portage, but then I did the unforgivable. Capsize in still water.

I just became lazy. Having crossed the small pond sitting astride my kayak, I tried the same trick crossing the second pond. It couldn't have happened in a worse spot. I was probably smack dab in the middle. I'd turned to watch a flock of ducks take off, followed their flight pattern, turned too much, and followed them into the water, but my spirits weren't dampened for long.

Sometimes a sudden view, like that of a raised skirt in the wind, can rocket your passion to heights that the slow sensual striptease can never attain. I had just crested a hill. My head, like that of a tired donkey, was staring at the ground. A breeze tickled my neck. I looked up, then it hit me.

Mutton Bay stretched around a small cove in a semi circle. Its reflection in the still waters seemed to turn upon itself like a hall of mirrors. Those typical Newfoundland house colours of green, blue, red and white jumped out from land and sea like a multi-coloured sparkler. After weeks of green, shades of blue and the occasional pocket of colour, Mutton Bay was dazzling. Boat jetties spread out like painted fingernails and fishing stations tiered down over rocks to the sea like wooden staircases.

If in doubt head to the nearest variety store, is one of my golden rules. In small communities, the name variety store or depanneur stand for a multitude of sins. It's usually the home of the gossip mill, dispenser of everything from Aunty Maud's herbal remedies to the exotic guava fruit flown in specially for the foreign doctor down the coast. They dub as post office and freelance advertisers, and hold the keys to the lost-and-found village notice board. In fact, besides the church and community centre, they are probably the most used and abused facilities on the coast, and for the few lucky enough to own a liquor license, it's a legal right to print money. I love 'em, in fact, they are usually my first port-of-call, and today was no different.

"Do you know where the flying vicar lives ?"

I'd been practicing the question in my head ever since this morning, when I heard there was a vicar in Mutton Bay who flew an ultralite plane. I'm just old enough to remember the Flying Doctor series on BBC radio that ran all through the mid '50s and '60s in England. The story line was based in the Australian outback, and revolved around a doctor who not only made house calls by plane, but also dispensed advice on everything from birth to kitchen surgery from his home radio transmitter. So you could imagine my excitement, when I heard Mutton Bay had its own 'Flying Vicar'. It's not that he flew-up and down the coast raising the dead, or for that matter converting the multitude of sinners. It was that an outsider, a vicar - and a young one at that - would not only have a flying license, but could want to live on the coast, love it, and couldn't think of living anywhere else.

There is a common misconception held by many city folk that anyone who lives in a place not connected by road, whose closest high school is a boarding distance away, and whose water and electrical supply can sometimes be dodgy at best, requires not only their help, but needs educating into the 21st century. It wasn't too long ago that New York, the epiphany of high tech, got struck down with a mega thirty-six hour power failure. Suicides skyrocketed, riots and looting became the norm and the federal guard roamed the streets, so who's kidding who? Most people on the coast own a TV, and I've even seen a few satellite dishes. Washers, dryers and microwaves are the norm, and even the smallest communities seem to have their share of cars. In all my years of travel in Canada's north, I've never seen a malnourished child, a village beggar, heard of a homeless or wanton vandalism that couldn't be policed from within.

The Flying Vicar was just the tip of the iceberg, when it came to lifestyles on the coast. Some people have built summer cottages with views that your average lawyer could only dream of owning, and as for hunting and fishing - most people I've met on the coast treat it no differently than a trip to the supermarket. Almost everyone is a handy man of sorts and what can't be baked, pickled or smoked isn't worth mentioning. It was with that thought in mind, and with an empty stomach to fill, that I turned tail, headed back down the hill and to the vicarage where for one night I could relax into a philosophical discussion on the pros and cons of the ultralite versus the twin otter.

     I left early, probably too early, but I was being driven by forces outside my control. Yet another storm was brewing over the Atlantic. It wasn't forecast to arrive today, or for that matter tomorrow, but I wanted to take the inside passage to St. Augustine, visit a friend of a friend, and then paddle past the dangerous exposed shoreline around the Graves and into the shelter of islands near Old Fort before it struck.

     That morning, I woke to the sweet smells of Columbian coffee. I drank in haste. Outside the view was amazing and I didn't want to miss it. If I had thought Mutton Bay looked too good to be true, under a clear blue sky, its deep harbour, bordered by cliffs, looked absolutely spellbinding in fog. The heavy mist hung like a fluffy duvet just above the roof tops. It compressed the harbour, pushed objects together, and pulled in the narrow inlet like two falling arches of the Parthenon.

     Under normal circumstances, I would have waited for the sun to burn its way through the fog, but the sea was still, and I would have no problem hugging the cliffs until it cleared. Unfortunetely I forgot to ask about the shipping lanes before leaving, and as soon as I exited the harbour and turned left, I heard the deep-throated drone of the ferry.

     I was paddling between a red and a green buoy, and I couldn't remember what they stood for. Any moment, I expected the ferry would loom out of the mist and devour me, then the buoys disappeared, and then the cliff. If it wasn't so frightening, it would have been laughable. Only minutes before, I could pinpoint my position to the metre, now I didn't have a hook to hang my eyes on. I had no way of telling if I had drifted into the shipping lane. I gazed in one direction for several minutes, then the other. The noise was tailing away - at least that problem had solved itself - but where was I? My compass was somewhere between Harrington Harbour and Aylmer Sound, deep in a mud bank, and my instincts, had deserted me.

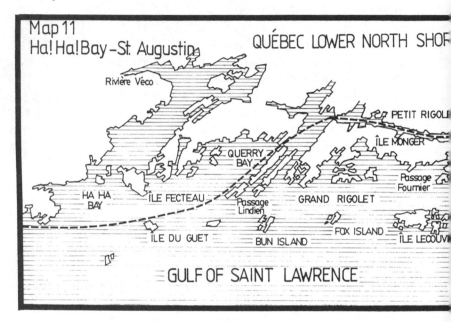

Map 11
Ha! Ha! Bay - St. Augustin   QUÉBEC LOWER NORTH SHOF

Rivière Véco

PETIT RIGOLE

ÎLE MONGER

QUERRY BAY

Passage Fournier

HA HA BAY   ÎLE FECTEAU   Passage Lindien   GRAND RIGOLET

ÎLE DU GUET   BUN ISLAND   FOX ISLAND   ÎLE LECOUVI

GULF OF SAINT LAWRENCE

I stopped paddling. Shapes were forming; they'd twist and melt into my imagination, then fall into the sea. Being alone is one sure way of summoning up phantoms, as anyone who has stood sentry in a lonely place at night can testify. However, I was far from being scared, and in fact was beginning to enjoy myself. I probably occupied this state for only five minutes, but it felt like an hour, and when the entrance to the harbour reappeared, I was disappointed.

    For ninety minutes, I slowly paddled through the fog, hugging the contours of land until the cliffs tiered down and announced with its chimes the entrance to La Tabatiere

Harbour. The fog was now in full retreat and by the time I reached Île-Caribou, everything was bathed in a brilliant eleven o'clock light. The early morning mist had evaporated and a slight breeze had soaked up the humidity. It was turning into a lovely day. Overhead, infinitely remote in a pale blue sky, delicate white wisps of clouds were being blown to tatters in a wind too high to have any effect on my progress. Although my map had advise me against it, I was hugging

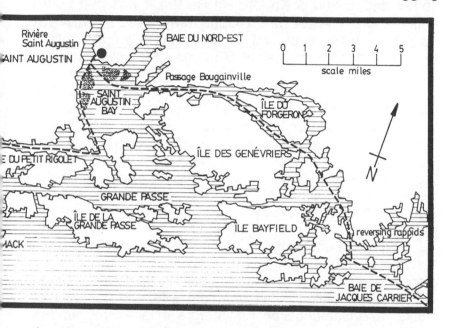

the shore. The tide was in and the sea was as calm and as clear as glass. Paddling over shoal in these conditions is akin to low level flying and the pictures that were unfolding below were just as riveting as those above. Underwater rocks rise up to greet you like mountains, and crevices drop away like deep bottomless canyons. Sea life viewed through clear salt water only magnifies its inhabitants. Small fish look like trophy salmon and salmon like huge monsters from the deep. For thirty minutes, I drifted through this scene, aided by a slight coastal current and abetted by a light tail wind, when suddenly the whole scene flipped channels, and the curtain dropped. It was caplin, thousands of them. A liquid pool of black on silver. I was amazed. They were so thick I could feel them brush my paddle. Then they started jumping. A school of seals appeared and no sooner had they started their attack when the caplin were gone.

It was now past noon, the late morning breeze had turned into moderate winds, and the waters around the point were clapping. I gave them a wide berth, and as I turned the corner and looked down into Ha Ha Bay, I was met by an amazing site. The sea just dropped away. Miles and miles of opal blue water stretched inland, topped by the rolling foothills of Labrador's Height of the Land. It was a sight for sore eyes.

I was now spoiled for choice. I could skip point to point across Ha Ha Bay and take the outside ferry passage to Saint Augustin, or I could paddle directly down to the throat of Baie Querry to the beginning of the inside passage. Or, my route of choice - to cut diagonally down the bay, make my way through its maze of islands cutting into the inside passage, some 10 kilometres along from where it started. They were all scenic routes and they all held the promise of shelter if the wind picked up.

It's amazing, but no matter how extensive my experience of solo travel, of its highs and lows, I manage to summon up the devil inside me, to spoil an unblemished day. An old friend called it my phantom wife, the needle that pricks my inflated ballon just before it takes off to the clouds.

Until now my day had been, without question, my best since entering the Lower North Shore. I had turned every hurdle to my advantage, from getting lost in the fog to the magical journey over the shoal. Now, just as the gods were smiling on me, out came the needle.

It started with a lone mosquito. It had taken a liking to my kayak, was hitching a lift and was now stareing me down from the far side of my cockpit. It seemed to have an in-built antenna that told it within a fraction of a second when my paddle would strike. Each time it evaded my feeble attempts to swat it, only to land back in exactly the same spot, and stayed with me for the next hour. Was it male or female ? Was it just visiting or waiting for its lunch ? It was driving my crazy. The wind changed direction, then it changed back again. Then what I had mistakenly taken to be smoke coming from a cabin on one of the islands turned into a pale, barkless dead tree behind a large jet black rock. Where were people when you needed them?

By mid afternoon I had reached the junction at the bottom of the bay and found little visually to excite my attention. The adrenaline high of the morning had slowly seeped out of me like a leaky cup. It was time to stop, brew some tea and regenerate myself before I gave into permanent fatigue, but where ? The Inside Channel, was in places, like a long green tunnel. Trees grew to its very edge, some angling out, threatening to bridge at its narrowest points. The heat was oppressive. The humidity was suffocating, and to make matters worse, the flies returned. On one occa sion I got bush-whacked by a swarming cloud of black flies, when I was enticed by the shade of a collapsing tree with the promise of a natural armchair of undergrowth to rest on. I was in a Catch 22 standoff: should I stay on the water and fry, or seek shade and be eaten alive by blackflies?

Twice more I beached only to find small cabins that were locked and deserted, then I spotted a third.
"Fine day for a paddle".
The voice was laying out a large net on some rocks. I didn't require a second invitation. Soon I was inside his cabin with a large home made cheese and spam sandwich in one hand, and a mug of tea in the other. He'd just returned from visiting relatives in La Tabatiere. He'd put his net down the night before, en route down the coast, and had just taken it up that morning.
"Caught anything ?" I asked.
"Just the scattered one, but the bloody loons ate the best of 'em."
I knew what was going to come next. I am no stranger to coastal life. We all have to get by with what we have, and

make sense out of the sometimes confusing and conflicting forces that govern us, and this man was no different.

"But you won't tell anyone?" he said with a laugh.

Being a traveller and a rootless outsider most of my life has allowed me a unique insight into life's grey matter. The pearls of normality that are called everyday life. We've all, at one time or another, danced with the devil or skirted a law or two. There is a rebel inside all of us, ready and waiting to flare up at the least hint of breeze. It's one of the main reasons we have rules and regulations, but the fish moratorium, as it's played out on this stretch of coast, and how it now acted on this man, was a hard act to follow.

I was half way through my second cup when he picked up the conversation again.

"Did you see the fisheries plane ?"

"What ?" I didn't know they had one, and before I could say another word, he jumped back in.

"Must cost the fisheries a bloody fortune. It's as if I haven't enough to worry about, I have to worry about them spotting me."

It's not that his fishing nets weren't the correct mesh size, he was fishing illegally. I knew it the moment I saw his nets, but I wasn't about to pass up on an opportunity for a natter.

"I only lay the nets down when I visit my relatives down the coast," he said, without a hint of malice.*"Its not as if I could make a living out of it even if I wanted too, but it pays for the gas."*

I know it was all said tongue in cheek. I knew also the fisheries tend to turn a blind eye towards the scattered few. They're after bigger fish, so to speak. But still, knowing that Big Brother knows is a bit uncomfortable. He seemed generally at ease in my presence. It wasn't as if my gossiping about his poaching habits to the wrong people down the coast would carry any weight, but I felt grateful that he had trusted me enough to explain his nets. I had already happened on two people shooting ducks out of season, who had beaten a hasty retreat on seeing me, and two brothers, trying their hand at some illicit lobster fishing, had been all red-faced and embarrassed when I'd changed course and paddled over to watch them haul up their traps. But what else is one to do on the coast but fish? Thirty to forty boats are hardly going to sway the balance between abundance and extinction. They weren't the main reason for lack of fish, and they certainly weren't the reason that the eider duck is on the endangered species list, either. The fish moratorium had painted everyone with the same brush, a prime example of regulation overplay. A judgement passed down from above with little thought given to detail, and this man, trapped somewhere between its fine print and its enforcement, was having to look over his shoulder.

I left before the third cup of tea could be brewed. It was late afternoon, and I could probably make Saint Augustin before night fall, but the flies were terrible.

Over the years, I have immunized myself against the mosquito, but I have never got accustomed to the black fly. Once in northern Manitoba, I got bitten so badly that the following morning I suffered the shakes. Another time, my ears - red with blood - ballooned up like two cauliflowers on a prize fighter, and on yet another occasion, while covered from head to foot in repellent, they somehow found my eyelids to their liking. They chewed them up so badly, that one even closed. In fact, I would rather walk into a pack of snarling wolves than paddle through a swarm of hungry black fly. With that thought in mind, I made my camp early. I found a small point of land across from an island at the junction of another channel, beached and put up my tent on a natural springy bedding of red berry bushes. Black flies got everywhere.They got sucked down my throat, crawled up my nose and got caught in my eyelids. Even my wet suit was crawling with them. They were like a second skin, for no sooner had they landed and folded their wings away than they had regrouped and headed straight for the hot spots. They must have been two deep around my wrists and three deep around my neck. My armpits were a literal breeding ground, and God knows, how many were trying to crawl in through the worn-out tear on the back of my wet suit. I was wearing a wool toque, but they had already penetrated its seams and were now probably, at this very instant, sliding down my hair to my scalp. They must be the most perfect eating machine on the planet. Under a microscope, I've been told by a botanist friend they look like winged mouths, and believe you me, they don't talk much.

Thank God, they are all claustrophobic. It's their Achilles heel, and once inside the tent, they immediately shot straight for my mosquito net, trying to get out. They were now at my mercy, and when the sun eventually set, the only evidence inside the tent that they had been there, were three rather large streaky smudges of red.

I woke twice during the night. The first time to damp and cold. I had been sleeping on top of my sleeping bag and the night mist had forced its way in. The second time it was to a clap of thunder, followed by heavy rain.

I woke into a dark gloom. The fog had returned and I immediately got lost rounding the small island ahead. I was going round in circles, then I heard the sound of a motor boat.

I watched the speedboat materialize out of the fog. I'd snuck-in behind an outcrop of rocks, as I hadn't wanted my trip to end sliced in two by a speedboat, but it was travelling much slower than I had imagined. I still hadn't been spotted. The man was half standing. He leaned forward, sniffing the water through a ragged moustache, like a clever bloodhound on the scent. Then he turned, gave me a surprised look and cut his engine to idle.

"I thought you'd still be here. So you're the kayaker I've heard so much about. My brother saw your camp last night. The fog's even worse down the bay. And I reckon' you're gonna have problems."

His face broke in two.

"Ay mate. Even I had a problem getting here."

We bantered a little, shooting the breeze then....

"Have you eaten yet ?"

What a piece of luck. Not only was I to be fed and taken for a ride in his speedboat, but he also turned into a living dictionary of coastal information. He told me about a short cut from St. Augustine to Baie de Jaques Carrier, the 'reversing rapids', a section called the Graves and about a storm that was supposed to set in by the evening. Then as a topper, he offered his cabin in the bay (baie) if the storm turned ugly.

"If I was you, I'd wait out the storm in my cabin. There's plenty of wood, but I don't think there's any food left. Haven't used it this summer so probably mice 'ave all eaten it all up. Just drop the lock back in place when you leave. It's broken, but I put it back on the latch to keep bears out."

The fog had already lifted by the time he'd dropped me back at my kayak. It had settled in the tree tops, but true to his word, once the channel entered the bay, the fog seemed to fall as if the cords that held it had been cut. The tide was out and by the look of my sea chart, that meant trouble.

It's a total mystery to me why someone would build a community at the headwaters of a river that is guarded by mud banks, but then who in their right mind would try and paddle down a bay chocked in fog, knowing that the tide had turned against him? Knowing that if he ventured out of the river's current he would certainly get stuck? Unless of course his name is Bernie and he's too stubborn for his own good.

I was actually being driven on by pride. The person I was heading to see held the key to another adventure. He was a traveller of sorts, and I wanted to make a good impression. One of my dreams was to walk up the Saint Augustin river in winter to Goose Bay, Labrador, and this guy not only knew the route, but had snowmobiled it with friends the year before. Unfortunately, my swollen pride was much bigger than my directional nose. I got hopelessly lost. I couldn't find the sea buoys that marked the deep channel down the bay, as I had somehow wandered off course. In fact, I had assumed that a half opening in a mud bank ahead was the river's entrance, and the surge of water from the falling tide as its current. Soon I was stuck at the bottom of a cul-de-sac with only a colony of agitated gulls for company.

There's nothing like wasting a morning to weigh your spirits down - having spent ninety minutes battling through the fog, mistaking the Indian Reserve on the west bank of the river for the community of St. Augustine, and then missing the person I had detoured to see by only minutes. I was now paddling back down the bay against a rising tide - that did nothing to raise my spirits or cover the mud banks ahead - and a strong head wind - that had somehow sprouted wings the instant my paddle hit the water.

Thank God, my paddle across the bay was uneventful. The wind blew the fog inland. It rode the hills, filled in the shallow valleys and ended up resting on the peaks, but as soon as I found the narrow channel that led to the reversing rapids at the other side of the bay, the wind died, the fog rolled back, and my view vanished.

Once again, I was paddling in an eerie silence boarded by twisted trees that seemed to snapp at me like medieval monsters. It was play time. I knew I wasn't going to reach the reversing rapids by nightfall, and the pot-belled stove in my friend's cabin would have to wait until another day. I now sat back, drifted and let the fog's dark humour unfold.

Ahead, a sweeping cliff topped by a majestic tower of evil appeared out of the gloom. It was an abandoned cabin. Roofless and doorless, it glared at me through the lifeless eyes of two jet black openings. Two trees, supported as if on a tidal wave, tilted lazily across the water. Another, almost horizontal, like a swimmer frozen in the act of diving. All these scenes were living on borrowed time. Spring thaw ice had created deep gouges in the bank. Trees were leaning, roots were exposed, and gravity and time would do the rest. Suddenly there was an explosion of noise. Twenty, thirty. Perhaps a hundred geese took off in a huge thunderous wave of black on white. Later, I followed two muskrats home, then the piece-de-resistance, I spotted a moose crossing the channel. At first, she didn't spot me, but when she did, it was awesome. I thought the channel deep, but on seeing me, the moose rose to its full height, pushed its way through the water with powerful ease, climbed the bank, and disappeared.

That night, I made camp on a postage stamp of an island. It offered neither sheltered, as it had no trees, nor any fuel in the form of drift wood of running water. It was of no consequence. I had ample supplies of water and gas, and ten freeze-dried meals stored away in my kayak. I had good reason to choose the island. I'd seen a bear, not any bear, but a big miserable bugger, who, on seeing me reared up to his full height and damn near fell into the water. I am not scared of bears, but to see one so close to civilization, where I know they are shot on site, begs the question. Is he stupid ? Plain lazy ? Or has he a death wish ? I don't carry a gun, so I couldn't oblige him on the third account, and he certainly didn't look lazy, but a stupid bear is a dangerous bear, because stupid bears have lost their fear of man, and it was with that thought in mind that I chose to sleep on the island.

I woke to the sound of wind whistling through the tree tops. The storm had arrived on cue, but it would be some time before I felt it. I was paddling in a narrow protected channel which kept out everything, including the rain that was now being blown horizontally through the tree tops.

By the time I reached the reversing rapids on the seaward side of the channel, they had been lost to the tide, but it didn't matter anyway, because the only thing that held my attention was the sea. Whipped by the wind and lashed by the sheets of rain, it had become a boiling cauldron of water. The picture was so sudden, that my situation didn't immediately sink in. It wasn't until I was rounding a point of land that guarded Anse du Portage that my plight hit me.

I had not even paddled three kilometres, but already my tanks were empty. I was so chilled from the wind, so fatigued from fighting the waves, that making the last few metres into the sheltered cove became almost impossible. I

was paddling like a maniac, but my strokes had little purchase and no rhythm. The wind was so strong, so full in my
face, that my eyelids hurt. My shoulders felt like red hot pok-
ers, and the pain at the base of my neck was excruciating,
but what frightened me most was that I couldn't feel my fingers. For lack of a better word, I was cooked.

If you met me in a bar, you'd never believe that I
kayak for a living. I don't possess the upper body strength
associated with kayakers, and I certainly don't have an arse-
nal of strokes, braces and eskimo roll techniques at my dis-
posal, but by God, I'm a survivor. I'm like a pit bull when
called upon, and this was one of those occasions........And
there but for the grace of God go I......

Don't ask me how I made it, I just did. Don't ask me
how big the waves were, because that is irrelevant - most of
it is in your head anyway. I finished the business and that is
all that counts. The rest is bravado. But God, was I ever
lucky!

I found David's cabin although it looked more derelict
than lived in. Home Sweet Home. It was as damp and
cheerless as a grotto. The musky smell of rot was almost
overpowering, and from the shadowy gloom came the
sounds of insects. It was time for a spring clean. The storm
had really set in. I would be spending one night in the cabin
at least, probably two, and possibility three. I lit a fire, got out
a garbage bag and filled it with empty beer cans, mangy biscuits, old tins and anything else that was neither nailed
down or in drawers. I cleaned the cabin from floor to table
top. Boiled some water, washed the dishes, cleaned the
windows and did everything except vacuum.

By night fall, I had transformed the cabin into something more akin to the cosy living room of Sherlock Homes.
I had wired my radio up to the CB antenna on the roof and
was listening to violin music. The kerosene lamp illuminated
my writing table in an orange glow, and the crackling of the
pot-bellied stove spread warmth throughout the room. I was
as cosy as a pig in shit and didn't give two hoots for the
weather outside, but by the end of the second day, my mood

changed. That forever closing window of opportunity was playing on my mind, big time.

The weather was changing fast and it worried me. The sun didn't hang in the sky as long and at night the temperatures were plummeting. It was only the begining of August, yet outside, autumn was knocking at the door. The early morning damp now penetrated to the bone and when a cloud obscured the sun, even a blind man could tell. The weather was pulling me down and I knew it. Outside I could hear the breakers pounding away at the point and the wind, my constant companion for the last two days, peppered the window with rain. I'd just about had it. I'd lost two days to the wind this week, and it sounded very much like I was about to loose a third. I can take cold, adjust well in heat, give me as much rain as you like and fog. Well at least the fish moratorium had cut down my chances of being sliced in two. But, wind is a different matter.

Wind affects the sea just as black ice and freezing rain does the roads. It changes the surface on which you travel. It becomes less predictable, cuts down your control and if you lose it, you're in the lap of the gods. I hadn't slept well last night, or for that matter, for the best part of a week. I had been reliving capsizes recently and they had sealed my nights like messengers of doom.

I didn't have to look far to see my first hurdle. The cove was streaked from one end to the other in surf and the point was lost in spray. It was time to get back in the saddle and today was as a good a time as any. I had been trapped in the cabin for three days and the thought of a fourth felt worse than leaving.

I wasn't totally stupid. The morning forecast on CBC radio called for moderate winds in the morning and fair to moderate in the afternoon. The sky was clear to the south, and I gauged these strong squalls to be the tail end of the storm. My idea was to paddle out to the point, check the sea conditions and then make up my mind whether to continue or not. I hadn't purposely paddled into a storm since Sept-

Îles, and then I put down my capsize more to lack of concentration than to turbulent waters. It was a calculated risk.
I knew the dangers that lay ahead but I was confident I could
handle them.

I was just about to enter the Straits of Belle Îles and
this wasn't the time to pussy-foot around. From Blanc-
Sablon to Red Bay, I could expect cliffs, rip tides, strong sea
currents and plenty of surf. The deep bays at Lanse-aux-
Claire and Forteau were boarded by vertical cliffs that could
germinate gale force winds. There was a good reason for
building a lighthouse on the extended arm of rock at Lanse
Amour. Throw in a strong easterly like today, and you have
a cocktail for disaster. I hadn't even turned the corner up the
Labrador coast and over the last two nights, my imagination
had built a wall of possible dangers that seemed insur-
mountable. I know I was exaggerating my position, but I had
been too cautious of late. I'd not gone point to point since Ha
Ha Bay. Sometimes it's faster and safer to take the shorter
route, but what you save physically in distance covered can
drain your mental banks. The Gulf of St. Lawrence had
offered all kinds of protection. I'd hugged its shoreline far too
often, rounded its bays at the least sign of wind and always
taken the sheltered inside passages. All this sounds reasonable except that it comes down to distance versus time.
Clapping waves, my worst enemy after the wind, thrive
close to shore. They love cliffs, strong currents and points of
land seem to attract them like bees too honey. At least out
at sea everything becomes more uniform. The waves are
less steep, rarely clap and are infinitely more consistent. It's
just a matter of letting go of the land.

A 'sea was on'. The swells were now enormous, but
the wind had died. I was parallel to the point, which was still
lost to spray, and the breakers; now more curved than ever,
cracked and echoed like the rythmic report of cannon fire on
its exposed rock.

My plan was to paddle south-east into the Gulf, away
from the clapping waves, and pass the islands in front on

their seaward side. No sooner had I broken contact with the land, however when the wind and rain picked up. For twenty minutes, I had to literally force myself to go on. My plan to give the islands a wide berth looked fine, but the traverse of the tickle between mainland and the open sea was another question. The tail end of this tickle had a sting like a scorpion.

I couldn't believe what I was seeing. Obviously the point I was now passing dropped vertically into deep water. Incoming waves would smack its face, climb to its summit, fall, depress, then reflect back with such force, they would crash into their incoming twin, shooting up spray like powerful geysers. That, in itself, wasn't a problem. I was nowhere close to the shore. The problem was that these reflected waves kept right on coming. I could trace their reflected flow right across the water I was about to paddle through, and thank God I could. Twice my head dropped into my stomach. A reflected wave, now three hundred meters from its original point of impact on the point, collided with an incoming swell directly underneath me. I swear it lifted the kayak in the air. Then another slapped me with such force I skidded sideways into another. It was like being passed about under a basket net whilst all the time bracing yourself for the all important dunk-shot.

There's nothing quite like the adrenaline rush you get from seeing a huge wall of water bearing down on you, with no way to go except up and over it. Maybe if I was close to a sandy beach, a car, a cellular phone or had friends close by in case of accident, I could appreciate the feelings that were pumping through my body at that very moment, but I didn't have that safety net. I was frightened shitless, and it's always during these times that David meets Goliath.

Now about a mile out, I turned my bow into the waves, dug out my flask of coffee, had a well earned cigarette, and let my hips do the balancing. I wanted a breather, but it wouldn't last long. Life has blessed me with many gifts, but the one that fuels my journeys the most is my insatiable curiosity, and it was this appetite for new experiences that propelled me into my next challenge.

I was now approaching the aptly named mini fiord, that locals call the Graves. Newfies, and there are many on the Lower North Shore who can trace their family tree back to the Rock, have an uncanny ability when it comes to name people and places. It seemed only yesterday that I had snowshoed up the Labrador coast, from Red Bay to Goose Bay. During the trip, CBC radio had interviewed me on numerous occasions. The interviews were always courteous and polite. I was always called Bernie and although these interviews were always lighthearted and humorous, they lacked that unique *'come into my kitchen, me' boy and leave your boots on'* quality that Newfies have for their own. Then one day, I tuned into the Bas Jamerson Show on CVHO.

"Where's the Walking Man ?"

I knew immediately who he was talking about.

"The last I heard he'd left Cartwright. If he doesn't fall through the ice or get eaten by that polar bear uncle Chubb saw the other day in Black Tickle, he'll be alright."

From that moment on, I knew my trip up the Labrador coast had been accepted. Somehow my new name, the Walking Man, made me feel special. They had captured the essence of my trip and, in their own way, they had added a special ingredient, a splash of colour that until then had been missing.

The same could be said of the Graves. The name was vivid and as black as the ace of spades. It's always these throw-away names, coined during a kitchen conversation or in a bar, that give me a clearer picture of the places I pass through. Now I was about to add the Graves to my ever growing list. The word was a dead giveaway, but I had to find out if it was as bad as its name suggested, and now my piqued curiosity was pulling me far too close to it for my own good.

When I got there I began to wonder what all the fuss was about. Why the Graves ? But just as I was beginning the slow traverse from point to point across its open water, I saw it...across the Graves ran a narrow band of white turbulence, probably the river current rising to the surface, and it was now at odds with the tide and an early afternoon wind.

I can't remember it being that bad, but I do remember getting tired, very very tired. Maybe if I had come from the opposite direction, from Blanc-Sablon, I would have appreciate its name more, because what was to take place further down the coast put everything else that had happened since leaving Toronto into perspective. You have to remember, I was on a high. Not only had I reached new thresholds of pain during my paddle three days earlier, but that morning I had conquered the largest and strongest waves to date, and I had just tamed the Graves.

The next stretch of coastline, in today's conditions, didn't offer up much in the form of escape routes. To make matters worse the wind was coming from the south, and getting stronger by the minute. All the conditions were against me. I stopped just past the Graves, and took a time out to check my map. Just at that very moment, a low-flying plane banked directly in front of me, turned at right angles, bellied as if to land in the sea, then disappeared up an inlet.

I was stunned. The last thing you expect on a trip is to see some kind of page one incident land in your lap. 'PLANE CRASHES AT SEA'. I was totally confused. Tired and hungry, I forgot about the map I was checking, the coffee that I had poured from my flask, and the Mars bar that, in my excitement, had been lost to the sea. I was now focused on someone else's problem.

Immediately the wind died, the sea calmed and I got a sugar high of energy you wouldn't believe. Of course, all this was illusionary. The storm had, in fact, returned. The sea driven by a southerly wind, was pounding the sheer line of cliffs ahead. I was in deep shit, but I doubt if you could have woken me up to this fact with a megaphone.

I set off in overdrive, my eyes rivetted to the rock face that the plane had disappeared behind. I was surfing the incoming swells, gaining speed and distance. I was too focused on the job at hand to notice that they were increasing in size and force, in direct proportion to my fatigue. I was on automatic pilot, and when I eventually reached the inlet, I was frantic. There just didn't seem any way out and I couldn't see any wreckage. I didn't know what I was searching for, and something inside me didn't want to find out. I've seen dismembered bodies before and they aren't a pretty sight, and what could I do if I found someone alive in the water? I stopped, tried to take stock of the situation, but before my fatigue registered, I had turned back and was sprinting out to the sea.

The deep rhythmic drones of a sea vessel, heralded the appearance of a bright red hull. I was now on an angled course to rendezvous with the Nordik Express from Blanc-Sablon, en route to Sept-Îles. I had some important information to share. There were lives at stake and I was paddling like crazy to get there.

My French, at the best of times isn't up to much, and when excited, not worth a nickel. The ferry stopped. It didn't have a choice. I'd arrived early and I'd put myself between it and its set course. To give the captain credit, he didn't lose his temper, but he just couldn't understand my message. By now, any passenger with a camera was pointing it in my direction. The tables had turned. They could see me as front page news 'KAYAKER SAVED AT SEA'. It wasn't until the pursuer was called, who translated my garbled message and the captain had replied, that the dime dropped.

It had been the fisheries plane that I'd seen. It was flying low so that they could read the license numbers of any boats poaching fish down the inlet. I wanted to crawl into the nearest hole and hide. Even the captain's offer to winch my kayak aboard fell on deaf ears, and when the ferry left, my heart, my energy and my will to go on left with it. It was, without a doubt, the low point of my trip, but I still had over 8 kilometres of mountainous seas between me and the sheltered islands ahead. If the morning's paddle had tested my metal, this stretch of open sea would test the very depths of my physical endurance.

I covered the distance one step at a time, latching onto imaginary spots on the sea and points of land, literally willing myself on. For two hours, I kept up a steady rhythm, but no sooner had I tucked myself in behind Île-Bilodeau when my whole body crashed like an overloaded computer, as first one function then another, ceased until my whole body shut down and the only life sign left was the flickering of my eye lids. I quite simply fell asleep.

Now and then a good lie is better than the boring truth, but sometimes life is stranger than fiction. I was woken by a group of children hailing me from the shore. I followed their shouts, turned into a sheltered shangri-la of sandy beaches and shallow coves, and found two summer cottages, all topped with smoke, tailed with multi-coloured flags of washing, and one - the one I was now gingerly walking towards, the one whose door was wide open, whose smells now pulled me towards it like a magnet with a promise of fresh oven bread - that was going to offer me, I knew with the certainty that I know my own name, a night to remember.

There are many reasons why I choose to travel the physical way, why I choose kayak over speedboat, snow shoe over snowmobile, and bicycle over the car. It keeps me young in heart and spirit and offers me a chance to meet new people on their own turf, but the main reason is that it gives me a healthy appetite..... and boy, do I love to eat.

I entered the kitchen like a starved lion and once the oven-fresh bread hit the table, all thoughts except food existed my head. I only had eyes for the smoke salmon fillets, and by the time the freshly fried rock cod had disappeared, I was ready for the main course. The keys to the kitchen were now mine. I was on a help-yourself basis, and it wasn't until I had finished my second helping of caribou stew, drunk my fourth cup of tea, and was just starting into a fresh supply of flap jacks that my stomach cried stop.

I am a damn good story teller and even better when I am dressed in the suit of a traveller en route. That night, I had a captive audience - the three children who had hailed me, their parents, one uncle and the young couple whose smoked salmon I had eaten, who lived on the far side of the cove. It was a night to remember. I had a full stomach and energy to burn. Sometimes I truly believe in Peter Pan and in his gift of transportation, and the way he can weave fantasy into reality. Life's a journey and, like Peter, I've been there. I gave them volcanoes in Hawaii, a hurricane in Fiji and then took them on a whirlwind safari from the steaming jungles of equatorial Africa to the snowcapped peaks of the Himalayas. For three hours, I held them in the palm of my hand. From sunset to bedtime, I kept on talking and it wasn't until the youngest fell asleep that I stopped. I too eventually hit the sack, but the day's events didn't quite hit me until the first rays of morning.

I am not as young as I used to be. It's not that I haven't the strength or endurance anymore - yesterday's storm had proved that - but I just can't bounce back like I used to. I had to drag myself out of bed that morning, as my whole body felt like it had been hit by a mack truck. From toe to temple it ached. The sun burned more deeply into my eyes, and every movement was closely followed by an accompanying jab of pain. For the first time in my life, I had to stretch and twist my body into action. Blood that only a few years before seemed to pump at will, on just such occasions as this one, couldn't even answer the bell. My neck was stuck somewhere deep down between my shoulder blades, and my knees gave way under me on my first step. I had the beginnings of tennis elbow and both my wrists grated like sandpaper. I wasn't really fit to continue, but the sun was out, the wind nonexistent, and the haze enveloping the islands was disappearing fast. Most of all, I didn't want to outstay my welcome.

I had been treated royally, but royalty has its day and mine had come and gone. I ate breakfast with the family, answered all the questions they had forgotten to ask the night before, then left.

The scene unfolding ahead was gradually rising. The jagged coastline swept up more steeply and its pale purple backdrop of foothills were deepening in colour. I had purposely set a course across the open sea to Blanc-Sablon. I was paddling miles from shore. I had time to make up and distances to cover and today offered the right conditions to do both. The early morning haze had condensed and its slight drizzle had long since been dispatched inland by a southwesterly breeze. I was now locked onto Blanc-Sablon's small cluster of colour, on a point of land some 24 kilometres away. With time on my hands, for the first time in a week I could relax into a paddle.

The whole crossing was like a walk in the prairies. Golden wheat was replaced by an opal green sea and the grain elevator I now pulled myself towards had changed into a church's white steeple. Everything else was the same. The endless horizon, the clarity of vision and that unique sense of freedom that comes with it. Still there was much to see. Three whales, nose to tail, heading east crossed my path only metres away. Then a school of dolphins followed my progress, sometimes abreast, sometimes circling, but always in graceful arcs of motion. It was a lazy day and it wasn't until I was rudely visited by a flock of angry dive-bombing puffins, that I snapped out of my idle mood and realized that I still had kilometres to go.

My initial plan was to camp on a point of land near L'anse-Aux-Claire that I knew offered a glorious view of the cliffs ahead, but the sight of a huge winged albatross, spi-ralling in a shoreline updraft and the sudden remembrance that my tobacco stocks were low (Newfoundland hammer the vice ridden smoker with high taxes), made me decide to spend one more night in Quebec.

I chose a beautiful sheltered outcrop of land to the east of Blanc-Sablon, with a view of the bay I'd just crossed. I pitched my tent looking east, lit a fire, ate, washed up, then walked into the village for supplies.

Have you ever eavesdropped into a conversation between a pet and its owner? Try it some day. I returned from shopping to find a dog curled up by the dying embers of my fire. It wasn't that I was starved for company, I'd done enough talking the night before to carry me all the way back home, but I did have a few problems on my chest and he did look more than a little receptive for a bit of gossip. I am really no different than your average Joe, but living somewhat of a hermit's life style, I offload my problems when a bout of depression sets in, onto whoever is around, and right now, the dog looked as good a candidate as any.

Thank God, no one was around with a tape recorder. Scruffy, for the sake of a better name, took it all in his stride. He was a proper little trooper. He never interrupted my flow of complaints, didn't judge, sighed at all the appropriate moments, wagged his tail when called upon, and tilted his head occasionally, as only a good sympathetic dog can do. He was cheap at half the price. Two biscuits and half a Kit-Kat. He was just what the doctor ordered and after my thirty-minute session, I was as right as rain. By the time I turned in for the night, it was as if a huge weight had been lifted off my shoulders.

It seemed as if dawn would never come. The moon, a pale hemisphere in comparison to last night's brilliant white disk, now churned its way through a sea of clouds. There was no wind, and from my exposed camp on the hill, the sea cut like black sheets of glass between the cluster of distant islands. The psychiatric dog that had listened patiently to my problems was still there, but the fire he had curled up around was out. Blanc-Sablon was still asleep. Even its hospital, (the only four storey building on the coast) the region's major employer with its 24 hour ER, and its numerous beds was at rest. Not a bark, crow or squealing tire could be heard. Complete silence, but I knew it wouldn't last. The sky to the east was faintly red and, as I broke camp, it began to flame. Last night's forecast warned of an impending storm. Another easterly front was on its way and I wanted to set off early. My plan was to make Capstan Island before it struck. Yesterday's brilliant sunshine had been my Quebec send-off. Maybe summer's last hurrah. Today's forecast called for imminent showers and heavy squalls, and tomorrow's for moderate to strong winds. It was supposed to blow itself out in a few days, leaving overcast conditions for the remainder of the week. I am no stranger to CBC's Marine Weather Forecast. It tucks me in at night, but I tend to take their predictions with a pinch of salt.

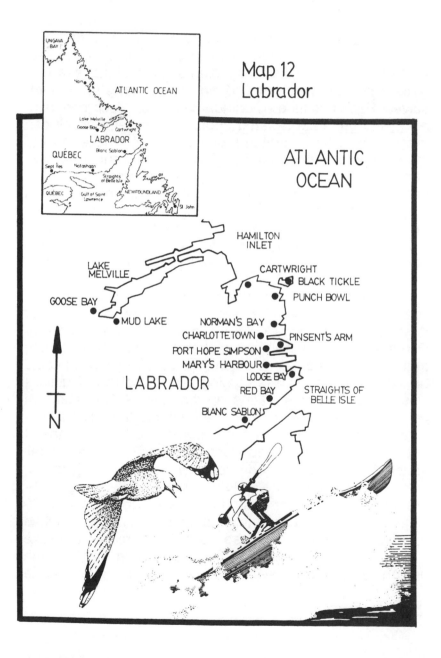

Map 12
Labrador

Chapter 6
Labrador

The Marine Weather Forecast is geared towards sea vessels, not kayaks, and focus shipping lanes miles out to sea. Conditions on the coast vary dramatically. Tides, sea currents, cliffs, exposed arms of land are all laws unto themselves. Each has its own unique character. Each can influence and generate isolated spots of weather, and all can magnify or puncture patterns of weather and make fools of the forecaster. Only when I hear of an imminent storm do I prick up my ears, but this morning I wasn't particularly worried. My spirits were high. I was going home. Today, I would be paddling in Labrador. I had a long list of friends and contacts. There was hardly a settlement on the coast where I didn't know someone. I knew I could ride out storms between clean sheets with a filled belly if I wanted. In fact, I was spoiled for choice.

I struck an early rhythm almost immediately and made it to L'anse-au-Claire just before the bad weather descended. The huge columns of cliffs round Pointe-du-Paresseux were peeling away. Ahead, houses were starting to appear on the opposite side of the bay, and above I could hear the distinctive calls coming from a colony of gulls. I wasn't exactly concentrating on the view. A fine mist had appeared. It seemed to stall, then darken, then, like a runaway express train, everything blurred into the inevitable. I got drenched. It came and went within minutes, then its tail struck. First, I heard a high-pitched whistling noise. It rounded the cliff, scattering the gulls - some almost vertically, others weaving and banking like ricocheted bullets from the cliff's face. It was a squall. It tore up the sea in the bay, picked up spray and slapped me so hard, I was forced to brace myself almost horizontally to the sea, but that was only the beginning. The promised rain set in and the moderate headwind that accompanied it, churned up the sea. It was like paddling in porridge. The picturesque scene of L'anse-au-Claire which had first captivated my attention soon crawled by in a monotonous series of tentacle-like utility houses. It took me forever to cross the six kilometre bay, and by the time I reached the huge grey cliffs in front of Forteau, I was very tired.

The tide was now falling, and conflict with the onshore winds made for a rough ride. I had been hugging the cliffs to save some and was now a little to close to them for comfort. As I was turning away from some clapping waves and just as Pointe Amour lighthouse came into view, things turned serious. Two dolphins suddenly crashed right out through the middle of a wave, the very wave I was surfing. Bloody road hogs! If they had been two seconds earlier I would have taken their heads off. I almost flipped, and before I could gather myself, another popped out in exactly the same spot, then another pair, almost vertical, using the back wake of a wave like an armchair. It seemed as if they were laughing at me.

I was in no mood for games. They were like children playing on railway tracks, oblivious to the adult's view of danger. But this was their playground, not mine. Here I was with white tops spraying me, back eddies and clapping waves tossing me around, and all they wanted was to play. By the time they had swam away, I had rounded the point and was now drifting in the wind, caught in a back eddy and heading down Forteau Bay.

Oh, what a fortuitous incident this turned out to be. Having found myself in calm waters, within hailing distance of its shores, I decided to beach and take a break.

"Going to a fancy dress are we?'

"What!" I could think of a few choice words, but I let it pass.

"You'll be the lad with the flashy yellow kayak."

I'd just entered this man's store, smelling of last week's washing, with bites, sores and scratches from head to foot and this man wanted chit-chat.

"Yep, that's me mate."

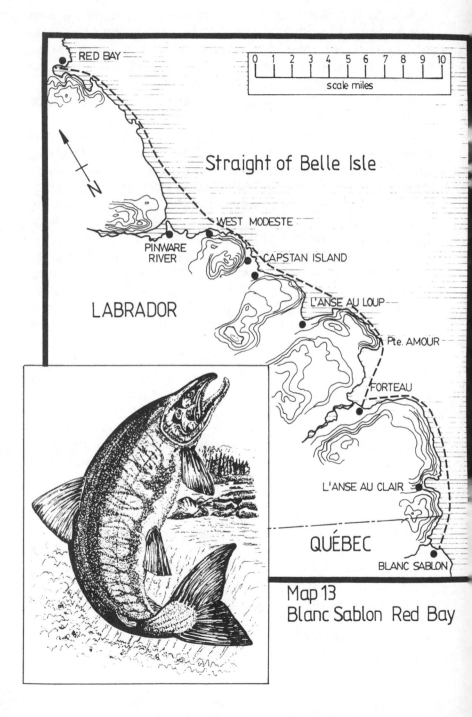

RED BAY

0 1 2 3 4 5 6 7 8 9 10
scale miles

Straight of Belle Isle

WEST MODESTE

PINWARE
RIVER

CAPSTAN ISLAND

L'ANSE AU LOUP

Pte. AMOUR

LABRADOR

FORTEAU

L'ANSE AU CLAIR

QUÉBEC

BLANC SABLON

Map 13
Blanc Sablon Red Bay

He obviously didn't like my reply or was it my emphasis on the word 'mate'? Whatever it was, we immediately crossed swords. For my part, I wasn't exactly in a good mood. Sarcastic, yes; egotistical, probably; but this man obviously had a position in Forteau, and now he seemed hell bent on bringing me - the new kid on the block - down a peg or two. I know whenever I travel, I'm just a side show - a blip in other people's lives, here today, gone tomorrow - but this side show has its off-days like everyone else. It wasn't until his eyes had adjusted to my blaze of colour, spotted the rips and homemade patches in my skintight wet suit that he let go his grip and relaxed into my presence.

The conversation that followed weaved its inevitable path from Toronto to his doorstep, but it wasn't until my story reached the Lower North Shore that he warmed to my trip. *"Did you see my cousin in Saint Paul's River?"* he asked. *"My brother's cabin was just round the point... my wife's family is from there.... I have another uncle who runs a fish camp up the Saint Augustine River, and a cousin who teaches in Romaine. My father worked there years ago..."* He went on and on. It seemed as if this man's family sperm had spawned up every river community on the Lower North Shore. By now the store, for all intents and purposes, had pulled down its blinds. Gossip overtook commerce, and soon my presence had turned into everybody's excuse within earshot to do the same. The owner now snapped open a couple of Cokes, then to everybody's approval, I sat down behind the counter and while the owner adjudicated on the subjects to be talked about, I answered everybody's question in turn. The more in number we became, the more in stature the store owner grew. Then that all important open-ended invitation came my way.

"You must visit my brother in Capstan Island." It was proposed more as a demand than an offer of hospitality. If the store owner's brother had lived in Forteau, I could have deflected it, and if further up the coast, then answered with an if, but I had already told everyone that I hoped to make Capstan Island before sunset, and that's

where his brother lived.

I had learned from past experience that, on the Labrador coast, it was better to accept these offers of hospitality without question. Failure to do so would almost certainly cause acute discomfort, not only to the person offering it, but also to people you've never met. On this coast everybody is either related or is known by his neighbour, and one's name and social standing in these communities is worth its weight in gold. To embarrass someone by turning down an invitation like the one being offered by the store manager, especially in front of witnesses, is an insult. People here have the memories of elephants. At the very least, a refusal - no matter how polite - could spoil it for the next man who passed through, and in the worst case scenario, the very mention of your name and impending arrival in another community would be treated like that of a carrier of the plague. And I am not joking.

I hadn't taken his invitation lightly, and already had thought up an excuse, but before I could respond, he'd picked up the phone and was forewarning his brother's wife of my arrival. I now found myself in a right pickle. His invitation had been witnessed in triplicate. I was trapped, but then I had a brilliant idea, and before he dug an even deeper hole for me to fall into, I jumped in.

"Can you show me the lighthouse at Pointe Amour? I've always wanted to see the view from the top."

I had caught him offguard, mid sentence, and before he'd gained his sister-in-law's approval.

"Sure, if you want."

My idea not only turned into a face-saver for the store manager and a golden opportunity for him to climb one more step up the ladder of prestige in front of his friends, but also provided me with all the information I needed to round the intimidating slab of rock, called Pointe Amour.

I've said it before, but it's worth mentioning again. 'Seeing is believing', and the spoken word -when attached to local knowledge - is infinitely more reliable than the written one. The view atop Pointe Amour Lighthouse was not only spectacular, but also informative. The most direct route close to shore, round its point, looked almost impossible. A rip tide was roaring out and the windblown swell coming across the Straight of Belle Isle was exposing numerous rocks in its shallows. Even from offshore, it looked no better. The sea was boiling at the bay's mouth and the shoal guarding its point was cross-hatched by the lines of two opposing currents. Wretched as these conditions looked, they were all localized, and elsewhere the seas looked tame. My visit to the lighthouse had turned into a stroke of luck. Sometimes you can be too close to the picture to see the best course of action, and with my reconnaisance over, the store manager returned me to my kayak.

I now took full advantage of what I'd seen. I paddled over a kilometre out from the point, rounded the shoal, then slowly angled back to the cliffs at the tail end of the rip tide.The Straight of Belle Isle's buttresses of cliff looked as awesome offshore as in, but it was when the sun had set and their vertical faces of rock, as if cut by a butter knife, had turned pitch black against a star-filled sky, that I will remember the most. I had just traversed the deep bay at L'anse-au-Loup, and the point's granite colours had been lost to the setting sun. Attaching myself to its easterly arm, I was paddling at its feet, unable to see the top. I was lost somewhere within the lapping of its shallow waves and the warm glow of its sun-heated surface when I heard the hum of chatter. It was a colony of nesting birds. I stopped, and was letting my eyes adjust to the darkness before continuing when an impish thought entered my head.

I clapped my hands. Seconds ticked away like a time bomb. Slowly, the chatter turned to cries, then suddenly the rock face exploded. Dark waves of motion peeled away high above me, then within minutes were spiralling above my head like a swarm of angry bees. It was amazing, and they didn't leave until I had paddled away.

I beached below a small cluster of brightly lit houses just before Capstan Island's flashing green harbour light. I'd been paddling too close to shore, and lost it behind a jet black island. I would have turned back had it not been for a vehicle, stopped on the road above. Its headlight acted like a beacon, and I followed its beam ashore.

My first night in Labrador was surrounded by friendly voices. Its bush telegraph system was greased and working, and when the store manager from Forteau turned up and said he was heading east to Red Bay, I knew I would be expected there, as well.

Every trip has its lucky charm. A person or persons who stand head and shoulders above the rest; who can pick up your spirit, medicate your wounds and ease your fears - and the Laydens in Red Bay are my Labrador charm. I first met them four years before when I was preparing to leave on a three month snow shoeing trek up the Labrador coast. They had taken me under their wing, cured my fears of falling through the sea ice, given my trip a much needed boost, lined my stomach with traditional foods and open my eyes to a way of community living that's long since been forgotten by Canada's mainstream. But most of all they had been themselves, and given me the space to be Bernie.

'The grass is always greener', so the saying goes, 'on the other side'. I have always been a misplaced traveller, with cravings for stability, and the Laydens are my alter ego. Too many sentences have been written and too many images sold in the pursuit of adventure, when the greatest adventure is family life. I know that many men envy my lifestyle. The universal wheeler; a girl in every port. If only they knew. A root transplanted can be stunted at birth. Stability, constant food and care are their staple diets. I am just a dream machine for the masses. A root in constant motion. 'But for the grace of God, go I'. With the Laydens, as with Jean and his family, I could live the normal life. Close the door on travel and be just one of the family - another body to fight over the TV remote, and another mouth to feed. It was with that thought in mind that I telephoned Phylis Layden in Red Bay, before leaving that morning.

At this time of year her family could be anywhere.

School was still out. They could be staying in their summer cabin in Barge Bay, visiting relatives in Newfoundland or out hunting, but I was in luck. Phylis recognized my distinct British accent immediately.

"Where are you calling from me'boy?'

"Capstan Island. If the weather holds out, I'll be there tomorrow." Then I went straight to the bone of the matter and the main reason why I called. *"Have you any bake apples in the freezer?"*

I could hear her laughing down the phone. She might not know my dark secrets, but she knew my stomach as well as my mother.

"Don't worry me'boy. I'll have a bake apple cheesecake ready for you by the time you get here."

I was in heaven. My favourite pie.

I stayed with the Laydens in Red Bay for two days. I had planned to stay longer, but the weather broke and the window of opportunity that morning was too good to ignore. The sea was glassy calm and the sun's rays had turned the ocean into a speckled wonderland of reflected light. Any other day, and I don't think my nerves could have taken it. I knew the section from Red Bay to Lewis Harbor was a daunting one. I only had to read the names of its coves and points of land to appreciate the undercurrent of danger, and that is why, although the conditions were ideal, I left under caution.

To fully understand the passions that pump through the veins of the coastal people of Newfoundland and Labrador, and the forces that govern them, one only has to check its sea charts. Just as Quebec's distinct culture can be understood through its expressive language, so it's equally true that the distinct culture of the peoples of Newfoundland and Labrador can be read through their gift for picking vivid, original and forever appropriate to the circumstances place names.

What other province in Canada can boast of places named after a death at sea, of a mother's love or a failed love affair. Take for instance Mary's Harbour. I wonder what she did to deserve a place named after her? And what of L'anse Amour, Paradise Sound, Ha! Ha! Bay and Heart's Desire. None of these names owe anything to tradition. These were the creations of men ruled by emotion, with strong ties to the sea and to their relationships on land. But not all place names reflected life's brighter side. Take today, for instance. I only had to check the route ahead to read into its darker passions as well as its grim humour. I would have to paddle past Wrecks Cove, Man of War Rock and Wise Man Head. It wasn't so much these names that worried me, or the sight of the jagged coastline ahead that spurned them, but the invisible forces that at that very moment were colliding under the surface of the sea.

From Red Bay, the coastline of Labrador starts its slow turn into the embrace of the Atlantic Ocean. From this point to Lewis Harbour, I would be contending with two opposing currents. For the first time, my paddle would fall under the direct influence of the Atlantic Ocean, and just for today, under the Straight of Belle Isle's strong current, squeezed in by the neck of the Northern Peninsula's arm on the island of Newfoundland and pushed along by a falling tide. Just the hint of wind or an Atlantic sea swell would make these colliding forces rise to the surface and that would spell mayhem.

Since entering the Gulf, I had not passed one completely relaxing day, without having its spell broken by the sight of a distant cloud or the whiff of a breeze. Just like a repentant sinner who sees temptation round every corner and doesn't go out, I too had sacrificed many a good morning's calm condition to the distinct possibility of an afternoon wind. I had always been on edge, but today the gods owed me one.

When the sea is at rest and the air is crisp and clear, you can spot objects on its surface with the clarity of a magnifying glass. After six weeks on water, anything out of the ordinary now registered with me immediately.

By this time I had seen lots of whales and, to tell the truth, I was more or less saturated with them - as indeed, the reader probably is if he or she has got this far, but today's sightings were well worth the price of admission.

I was not five minutes past the mouth of Red Bay harbour when I spotted a school of whales. They were pilot whales, probably a dozen, and no sooner had I joined their tail when scores of dolphins lit up the surrounding sea in fast moving arcs of light, breaking its surface in sharp hisses, then flipping back under its surface like rubber bands of speedy motion. But it wasn't until I started to rap the sides of my kayak that the fun started. The noise attracted them like bees to honey. Within five minutes I was surrounded, then they started to jump.

Wow!!!!!!! They spiralled out of the water, sometimes two abreast - like boys showing off their athleticism to a bunch of girls in a playground. They stayed with me until Barge Bay Point, then like winged bullets taking one more pass under my kayak for good measure, left.

Shortly after, another sight caught my eye. I had just paddled past the soiled and down-feathered remains of a flock of ducks. I was taking a break to watch - for the umpteen time - a wavering cloud of terns dropping like sprayed shot on a shoal of unseen bait. I was about to take a picture with my borrowed camera, and had the terns in focus. One had just folded its wings. He just about to drop when a wall of noise from the cliffs above distracted me. Brightly coloured puffins were disgorging by the dozen from their clifftop nesting holes. They were swarming, banking this way and that, then before - my eyes had time to adjust to their colourful beaks - they'd shot past my ears like a hail of bullets.

I took a break at Man of War Rock. I was resting against a small knob awash with the rising tide, and medi-tating. Even if I had not seen anything that day, it would have been one to remember. The lemon grey and orange streaked cliffs, rising from the deep water were awesome, and the lapping of the sea rubbing up against the cliff's toes had turned into the theme music of my day. 'But nothing lasts for long on the Labrador coast, especially the weather'.

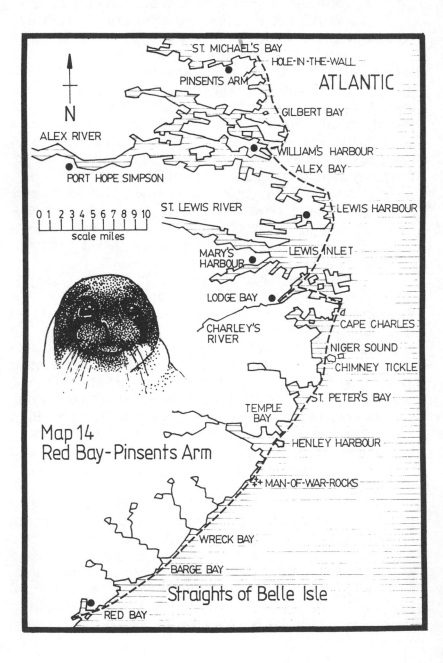

ST. MICHAEL'S BAY
HOLE-IN-THE-WALL
PINSENTS ARM
ATLANTIC
GILBERT BAY
ALEX RIVER
WILLIAM'S HARBOUR
ALEX BAY
PORT HOPE SIMPSON
ST. LEWIS RIVER
LEWIS HARBOUR
0 1 2 3 4 5 6 7 8 9 10
scale miles
LEWIS INLET
MARY'S
HARBOUR
LODGE BAY
CAPE CHARLES
NIGER SOUND
CHARLEY'S
RIVER
CHIMNEY TICKLE
ST. PETER'S BAY
TEMPLE
BAY
Map 14
Red Bay-Pinsents Arm
HENLEY HARBOUR
MAN-OF-WAR-ROCKS
WRECK BAY
BARGE BAY
Straights of Belle Isle
RED BAY

I know I said the gods owed me one, but there is something about familiarity that eases the pain. Like a junkie who has taken to opium's nectar and has forgotten the reason he started, I was beginning to think that my day would not be complete without one short burst of clapping waves, one blast of cold air and now this feeling had got the better of me. If I wasn't such an atheist, I would have believed that it was God's punishment. A slap in the face for the unbeliever, but I knew better. I had spent too long drifting and not enough time paddling. I was within sight of Henley Harbour's Table Top Mountain and the cluster of houses at its base were less than 8 kilometres away. Uptil then, there hadn't been a hint of a breeze, but all that changed in the blink of an eye.

Coastal inhabitants know that the sea has a simple genius for concocting exasperating situations which, no matter how much you've been exposed to it over the years, burst on the victim without any warning. Here I was, paddling along without a care in the world, an open sky above, a tame sea to paddle on, when along comes a quick tide change, a sudden downdraft of wind, and within five minutes I was surrounded by surging waves.

I was, to say the least pissedoff. I had checked my map that morning, and knew there was no river of any note until Lewis Inlet. I wasn't rounding a huge exposed point or behind an island where currents can be deceptive. I was half a kilometre from shore with only the open sea in Chateau Bay to cross, but I must have been above some outcrop. Some subterranean hill was causing the current to rise to the surface and encouraged by a strong offshore wind, it had the sea boiling in no time. In the five minutes it had taken the waves to form, my paddle had turned from a pleasant sunday afternoon stroll into 'I can't wait until I get home'. There was nothing I could do except concentrate on the day's end, keep paddling and wait for the waves to flatten out, but I only have so much patience.

If only I had not dawdled I would have been on dry land, counting my blessings and patting myself on the back at spending one whole day in the saddle without getting my seat wet - but when I eventually beached under the shadow of Table Mountain, I was soaked.

Before I describe Henley Harbour and the night I spent within its boundaries, I would like to give the reader a brief history on why most of the houses were abandoned and where the term 'resettlement' comes from, because Henley Harbour is a resettled community.

The word resettlement conjures up different meanings for different people. To your average student of Canadian history it simple means 'Joey Smallwood' and the Province of Newfoundland. It was a time when families were uprooted and forced by the 'carrot and stick' of government legislation to abandon their island homes for the mainland. It was, if you believe all you read, a time of cruel poverty, of malnutrition, rickets and blight. For the people of Newfoundland and Labrador, the sixties were not only a time of peace and love, but also the parting of the ways for two distinct lifestyles. Resettlement spelt the beginning of the end for a coastal people who, until then, were still influenced more by the powers of nature than by their government. Depending on what side of the fence you stand on the issue of resettlement, it was either a life saver or a slow sentence to death. I am sure the reader has by now worked out, that I am a 'Survival of the Fittest' kind of guy who would like to turn back the clock. I fully understand the advantages of a universal healthcare system, of free education, and of the advantages of living in a home that has central heating, electricity and running water, but what of the human spirit? I know these resettled places have been romanticized to death. Battle Harbour, for instance, which is just round the corner is a prime example. Resettled about the same time as Henley Harbour, its wharf, school house, church and many of its abandoned houses have been renovated with government grants, circled as a heritage sight, and is now a world renowned tourist attraction. But why is it so popular, and why do Newfoundlanders and Labradorians flock home in their thousands every summer instead of vacationing under a more dependable sun, for half the price, in Florida. Why??? Because it fills a vacuum. That space inside all of us. The one that cries out to return to a time when people were interdependent. When one person's weakness was another person's strength. A time when you were who you are, and within a community where the pressure releasing valve of gossip was a way of life, not a modern industry for the social worker and psychiatrist. In short, peace of mind. A tranquility that today's money-driven, profit-motivated way of life has relegated to nostalgia, and I will leave it at that.

For once, I landed in empty space. Although I had seen smoke and movement from the bay, no one had seen my arrival. I was in my end-of-the-day relaxed mode, one hundred percent certain that whatever the smoke's fires were cooking would end up in my stomach. 'This after all is Labrador', I told myself. 'My home.' I had changed on the beach, pulled my kayak up onto a fishing stage, had just turned towards the church when a familiar face appeared.
"Eh, it's Bernie isn't it, Bernie Howgate from Mud Lake, the Walking Man, remember me?"
There are maybe only eight thousand plus people living on the coast of Labrador, but there's only been one crazy enough, within Calvin Stone's lifetime, to have walked up its coastline on snow shoes in the dead of winter, and that was me.

My mother used to say, 'It is better to be talked about than be ignored', and today I fully agreed with her. I had immediately relaxed into Calvin's easy manner and soon fell into step with him as we returned to his house. He told me that the salmon fishing season had finished. He'd caught his quota, and last week his wife and children had joined him from their home in Charlottown, by speed boat. That morning he had dropped them off near Bad Bay. They were spending the day bake apple berry picking and if I wanted to come along for the ride, he would gladly give me a guided tour of tomorrow's paddle when he left to pick them up. I instantly knew I was not only welcome for supper, but also that he would be downright insulted if I didn't stay the night.

It's this tradition of hospitality, of opening doors and breaking bread with travellers that I like the best about Labrador.
But first things first.
"Do you want a cup of tea?"
Calvin left to pick up his family while I took a walk round his
home. Henley Harbour may be a mixture of old and new, of
abundance and waste, but this abandoned settlement over-
flows with character. Built close to the foot of Table Mountain
amidst some spectacular scenery, it's easy to see why the
memory of spending a childhood here would pull at your
heart strings. Only a quick glance would be needed to trig-
ger many a flashback. Take, for instance, the echoes of time
spent with your childhood friends in its one-room school; of
dreaming away during a sermon in its neat little church with
eyes fixed on your sweetheart; of playing in streets of grass;
of doors that open without a knock; and of knowing your
neighbours almost as well as you know yourself.

For some time, I walked through a script of my own
making. I watched a group of fishermen walk by, like a
bedraggled group of soldiers beaten and weary from forces
greater than their own. I heard a mother cry out and watched
as three-imp like children with eyes bigger than their bellies
raced home with a bragger's rights bet on their faces. I now
stopped walking to look at a group of houses that had obviously seen better days. One, its paint scarred by salt born
on the wind, now looked out to sea through eyeless windows while the others had obviously been lived in till recently, and were locked and boarded against the elements.
Here, a door left ajar or a broken pane of glass soon turned
into an open invitation that would not be ignored by nature.
Some homes on the perimeter, more exposed than most
and probably built during the settlement's zenith, seemed as
if forever closed and forgotten. At one point curiosity got the
better of me. I prized open a nailed shut door. Inside it was
so dark that after the glare of sun, it was difficult to make out
anything except for the overpowering stench of decay. Every
wall was covered with eruptions of dark green lichens and
what posters had survived these living growths peeled away

under their own damp weight as soon as I tore away at their corners.

But not all was gloom and doom, far from it. Henley Harbour's one-room school - although not used as a teaching establishment in over thirty years - was under renovation. It was bright and airy and by the looks of a freshly repaired fishing net stretched across its room, had found a new use. As for the church, it still had the look of a place more used than not, and going by the stack of bibles in one corner, with more than just a little life left in its old bones. Some houses, freshly painted in bright red and green, looked more like holiday homes than summer residences for workers, and it was obvious from the small cluster of orange buoys bobbing about just offshore, that more than Calvin's speed boat had anchorages here.

I must have legged it for over sixty minutes. I was more than a little tired and I was getting hungry. It wasn't until I crested a small humpback of land, spotted a group of children walking on the beach and a line of clothes attached to a house topped in smoke waving in the wind, that I realized I had come full circle and that Calvin had returned.

That night I earned my supper. Over the years, and especially on the Labrador coast, I had cultivated a reputation of being both a good eater and story teller, and that evening I didn't disappoint. I gave full justice to Calvin's wife's cooking, stuffing away ample portions of fried caribou steaks and polishing off her partridge berry pie in no time. After supper it was the children's turn, and I had no problem keeping them in stitches, always one step ahead of their questions and always ready and willing to drop down to their level and join in the fun.

Revelry came at the crack of dawn. In the excitement of seeing me off, the children beat me to the breakfast table. It had just turned 5:30 a.m. and there was still a deceptive embrace of heat from the stove, but immediately when the door opened, it disappeared. That morning it was bitterly cold. Just a few degrees less and we would have had ground frost. I lingered in the kitchen longer than I should have, well into my third cup of tea and was sinking my teeth into my second baloney steak - pressed between two thick slices of home made bread - when the dark curtain of clouds that had hidden the early morning's eastern horizon struck. Rain poured down, but stopped as quickly as it started, and by the time I'd pushed off in my kayak, the bay was arced by a beautiful sunrise rainbow.

It wasn't until the morning was more advanced and the skies empty of clouds that the air heated up. As as is the case almost everywhere on the east coast, when the surface temperature of rock and the ambient air temperature differ greatly, it heralds an off-shore breeze, and as soon as the sun put some colour in my cheeks, the cold wind blew it away.

At Saint Peter's Head, I was passed by a yacht under full sail. It was a magnificent sight. It didn't so much ride the waves as cut a course straight through them. It was obviously thriving in the conditions, which was more than could be said for me. I was getting caught by one too many rough waves. They'd pick me up without warning and had me free falling into their troughs. Then, as if to throw salt onto my wounds, within minutes of the wind dying it changed ninety degrees.

I was now paddling in a full blown squall. It came in pulsating gusts, killing my rhythm and taking away the only company I had. My yacht peeled away from the coast with the new wind. It turned, emptied its canvasses, almost kissed the sea with its mast, then angled out to sea on a northeast heading.

FromTable Head there wasn't a smooth or rounded corner in sight. The whole shoreline looked as if it had been cut on a precision lathe. Even the cliff's face had sharp edges. Obviously the rock had cracked under its own pressure and its hard granite surfaces had, over time, withstood the grinding forces of the waves.It wasn't until I had turned into Kennedy Blight, and started my slow traverse over its waters to the aptly named Chimney Tickle, that the unusual picture was broken.

Another bloody downdraft. Once again the wind had changed direction and was blowing offshore. I had been paddling into a steady head wind for the last two hours. It had been a hard slog, but over time I'd been able to shut down its surf and bite the bullet, even to the point of enjoying the scenery, now it was destroying me. The down draft was so strong it was like leaning into an open door. I had visions of being blown to Ireland. I had my rudder fully turned towards land and was only paddling on the seaward side.

Physically there is nothing worse than to be side-swiped half way across a bay when your tanks are low. You can't even take a break. Now the only thing that kept me from letting go of the tickle, and letting the wind carry me out to sea, was the sight of three cabins.

From this distance they could have been a bleached rock formation, but when you're falling, even the devil's hand looks inviting. I was almost two-thirds across before I got my second wind. Whether it was the distraction of the cabins, or maybe because my adrenalin was pumping so much that I was now on a different plain, but trouble strikes when least expected.

I had just got a toe-hold on land, having turned directly into the wind, and was within what I thought was wading distance from the beach. I had just passed a rock, when the rock suddenly rose, bent double, then - striking its tail on the water - disappeared under the surface like a whiplash. It was a seal. I immediately followed it into the water. Not all the way - I had smacked my paddle down and pushed up on its blade, but now my side felt like a red hot poker. I was doubled up in pain, and although I was spotted and warmly welcomed when I beached, the pinched nerve didn't loosen its grip until I had warmed up in their cabin, cosily heated by a wood-fired stove.

By now it was 4:00 pm. I had eaten, dried out and was ready to leave, but I felt guilty. Two cooked meals in one day. 'My cup runneth over.' My new friends - an old couple from Pinsent's Arm - had not only shared their supper with me, but had promised to make sure their son's cabin at the bottom of Nimrod Tickle in Lodge Bay would be open and stocked with food, in case I needed to use it. What a stroke of luck.

The rest of the day passed with little incident. The off-shore winds had fallen away with the sun. I had cut a direct course across Niger Sound to the high hump of land called The Soldier, then I rounded the most impressive knuckle of rock I'd ever seen in my life. Everything the day offered paled to the sight of Cape Charles. Huge, smoothed and shaped by centuries of gale-driven mountainous waves, Cape Charles falls in four huge waterfalls of rock.

I was thunderstruck. One can only imagine what forces had shaped this cape, and how the seas would look during a fall hurricane. Sights like this, with no escape routes and dizzying heights towering above are what first seduced me onto the water. Had it not been for the setting sun and a speed boat disappearing down the tickle ahead, I would have replayed the whole cape again. Still, Cape Charles wasn't finished with me, and when my eyes latched onto its small summer community of freshly painted cabins, it was icing on the cake.

I expected to finds signs of life in Saint Charles but found none. Built on either side of a narrow tickle that split Wall Island from the cape, its twenty-odd summer homes and fishing stages were all well maintained and in good repair. Huge neat stacks of freshly cut firewood piled up besides some of the houses indicated winter usage, and two diesel generators, were a sure sign that some homes had modern conveniences as well. In all my years in Labrador, this settlement appeared to be by far the most compact, and, set at the tip of Cape Charles near the headwaters of Lewis Sound, in the narrows of Saint Charles Channel, the most picturesque.

Until yesterday's conversation with Calvin, I didn't even know of its existence. Ignorance of it is one thing, but knowing and locating it on a map is another. The whole coastline of southern Labrador is a maze of sounds, channels, narrows and tickles, and from here to Hamilton Inlet some 400 kilometres to the north - with the exception of the exposed Strand - I could expect much of the same. If the weather turned ugly, there were plenty of escape routes, and if I wanted solitude and time to commune with nature, my options would also be virtually limitless.

That night it was cold and clear. The August moon was in the last quarter. It shone down on the water, filling the channel like molten metal. A flock of ducks rose, gleaming in the moonlight, but were soon lost in the dark folds of the hills on Battle Island. I'd surprised my only neighbours. Now, the only sounds - apart from the rhythmic bubbling of pebbles washed up on the shore -was that of my own breath....SOLITUDE

My next decision was an all important one. September was closing in fast and autumn colours were just starting to crisp around the edges. I had friends both in Lodge Bay and Mary's Harbour; should I visit them or push-on? That morning the wavering radio forecast mirrored the static noises it gave out. A low pressure system coming off the Atlantic was expected to strike anytime.

I made it to Lodge Bay just before noon, only hours before the wind and rain came knocking. I had not been expected, but within minutes of beaching, my old friend Margaret Pye and her husband had laid out the red carpet of welcome.

A point of interest to the reader: as I write there is a road under construction that will unite most, if not all the isolated communities on the Labrador coast. It is being built to unite the communities on the Straight of Belle Isle with their neighbours both in the north and the interior. It will start in Red Bay and end in Goose Bay, at the bottom of Lake Melville. In 1996, when I started this trip, its route was still on the drawing board. At that time only one road existed between the coastal communities and that was the summer road between Lodge Bay and Mary's Harbour.

*This new road may detract from the romantic image of set-
tlements cut off from the outside world, but, take it from me,
it's only a smoke screen. Nothing can change the isolation
of Henley Harbour or unite the pretty settlement at Cape
Saint Charles to the mainland, or for that matter, the numerous hamlets of summer fishing cabins up the coast. For
sure, the road will initially carry away more than it brings to
the people on the coast, but that's progress. The construction of the new road will ultimately prove that old saying -
what goes around comes around - as it will make the route
I follow more accessible to you, the reader.*

      The thought of having to spend a week in Lodge Bay
due to the weather was too much to bear. The wind, rain,
and cloud patterns had changed little since my arrival, but
my stomach had been stretched to its limit. I didn't think I
could bite into one more slice of Margaret's homemade
bread, or swallow one more spoonful of her caribou stew.
Denley Rumbolt's partner, Sheila, in Mary's Harbour force-
fed me the last few pieces of cheese cake by way of a guilt
trip, and during last night's potluck-supper, I had almost
burst a blood vessel. I must have put on six pounds and
hadn't yet scratched the surface of my committed invitations. I still hadn't visited Mary's Harbour's nursing station,
its fish plant or had supper with its school principled. There
are only so many hours in the day and so many courses of
food I can sit through. That morning it was a toss-up
between collapsing onto Margaret's sofa under my own
weight or being blown along by a strong cold damp wind,
and I chose the latter.
      You don't get anything out of a place you don't bring
to it and, today I offered up to the coast more than an ounce
or two of nervous sweat. The weather was brutal. Pushed
along by a funnelling wind, I made Nimrod Tickle in no time,
but stopped once I saw the cabin I'd been told about. Once
again, I was of two minds. The offered cabin, walled-in by
high rocks and overlooking the becalmed waters of the tickle, was tempting. Another time and I would have bit into its

bait of fresh food and solitude, but not today. The prospect of spending a fifth day on land tipped the scales in favour of the sea, but I am no fool.

It's one thing to be pushed down a bay under the influence of a down draft and another to be broadsided by it as you cross. Even in the sheltered tickle, I could hear the winds howling above and the inland clouds were flying out to sea, in warp drive. It was a risky business. The bay in front was almost 13 kilometres across, open, and made for high winds. With this in mind, I beached, climbed a hill and planned my crossing of Lewis Sound.

Choppy it was, dangerous it wasn't. A cool head I have, and today's conditions would test it, but not to the limit. I decided on tacking into the wind first, to Saint Anthony's Island, then turning and surfing the remainder to the point of Cape Saint Lewis. Easier said than done, but after taking stock of the situation and of weighing up my option of another day on dry land, I was down the hill and into my kayak before any second thoughts could gain momentum.

I got soaked within seconds of leaving the sheltered tickle, and by the time I had reached the island, I was shivering with cold. Half way across, I got my second wind. Maybe it was the sight of Fox Harbour's dominating radio tower mounted on the cape's bald point ahead that raised my spirits. Whatever the reason, I was warming to the task, and no sooner had I crossed, gained a finger hold on its cape and rounded the point into the sheltered waters at its feet, than once again I relaxed into the scenery, and what a scene it was. The soaring cliffs may not have had the shock value of Cape Saint Charles, but with a backdrop of menacing black clouds, they looked just as impressive.

That day, the conditions required a steady nerve and total concentration, but I found it impossible. Overwhelmed at times, as much by its extremes of beauty and tranquility as by the danger, that it wasn't until it was all over, and I'd made camp and lit a fire, that I was able to reflect fully on the details of the day's highs and lows.

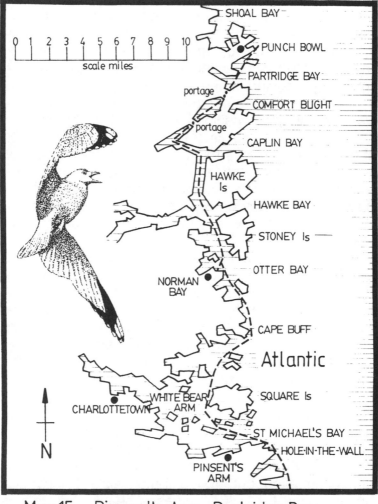

SHOAL BAY

PUNCH BOWL

PARTRIDGE BAY

portage

COMFORT BLIGHT

portage

CAPLIN BAY

HAWKE
Is

HAWKE BAY

STONEY Is

OTTER BAY

NORMAN
BAY

CAPE BUFF

Atlantic

WHITE BEAR
ARM

SQUARE Is

CHARLOTTETOWN

ST MICHAEL'S BAY

HOLE-IN-THE-WALL

PINSENT'S
ARM

N

0 1 2 3 4 5 6 7 8 9 10
scale miles

Map 15   Pinsent's Arm – Partridge Bay

That night, I camped in the sheltered waters at the head of Gilbert River behind Ship Harbour Head. I was miles off course. The moon was already down and it was dark. A light mist had rolled in from the sea and my camp fire was starting to halo in the gloom. Above, the night sky looked disjointed and out of focus. In fact my whole day could be summed up in the same way. Twelve hours before, I had left Lodge Bay and plotted a point to point course from Cape Saint Lewis to Cape Saint Francis, but at the end of the day I had found myself 8 kilometres off course, inland from the open sea. Instead of allowing myself some distance from the shoreline and going point to point as I had planned, I'd hugged it. The strong offshore winds and the funnelling effect caused by the shallow fiords had forced me to follow the contours of land like a tracer. I now knew every nook and cranny, every nest and safe harbour from Lewis Sound to Alex River. I had planned a 50 kilometre day, but probably put in over sixty, making only thirty as the crow flies, but what a day it had been. The towering statues of rock at Northern Head had entranced me, yet the waters its high walls stood guard over had beaten the snot-out of me. I had been seduced into taking a break in the sheltered waters of Spear Harbour, then almost lost it to huge clapping waves as I rounded its point. I had come within a hair's breath of accepting an invitation at sea from a family returning home by speedboat to Williams Harbour, but my pride had stopped me. I had sought shelter down tickles and inlets whenever possible, then I got lost paddling behind Granby Island to escape some surf; not completely, but enough to take the wind out of my sails. It was time to call it quits.

The next day was a carbon copy of the previous day, with one exception; a 'sea was on'. I could hear the surf pounding away like the dull rhythmic claps of distant thunder from inside my tent. The whole coastline had turned from one calmed by an offshore wind into one underlined by a thick brushwork of white surf. Today, more than any other, I was glad that my 'baptism by fire' into the mysteries of the 'clapping wave' had come in the relative calm waters of Quebec's Lower North Shore, because today's clapping waves were both enormous and extremely powerful. The seas around Ship Harbour, aided and abetted by a huge sea swell, now made their Quebec counterpart look tame in comparison. It was this dangerous cocktail of shoal and sea swell, and the frequency I swallowed its spray that eventually wore me down to the point of submission.

It had all started innocently enough, I had made it through the locally named Chimney - a narrow tidal channel set between a coastal ridge of rock - to the open sea. I had skirted as best I could the sea of clapping waves around Ship Harbour Head. I passed the unusual rock formation called Hole in the Wall, and was edging my way around the False Cape into Saint Michael Bay. That day, I wanted desperately to put in some good distance. To get home before the weather changed and the easterlies became an every day feature of my trip, I would have to take some calculated risks, and my traverse across Saint Michael Bay was one of them. I was closing in on the Sisters - two islands at the far end of the bay, and had completed what I thought was the worst part of the crossing, when suddenly something caught my eye and my nerves cracked.

Until that moment, I had never once taken my eyes off the shoreline ahead, holding it in my vision with a vice-like grip. I had been paddling with my blinkers on, telescoping all my thoughts and concentration down a narrow passage of water. My paddle had got caught in some half-submerged kelp, and stopped. I was just shaking it free from my blade when I saw the huge cresting wave out to sea. No longer could I ignore the dangerous shoal waters that studded the bay's entrance. I watched as yet another wave built, crested, then rushed towards me. Momentarily, I froze. The action was taking place more than three hundred yards away to my right, but the sight of a wall of water rising out of nowhere, eclipsing against another onrush of surf, and the clap and roar of its wave smashing on rock finally broke the spell. Within seconds my tail had dropped. I turned and gingerly headed down wind, to seek shelter behind a curtain of islands at the bottom of White Bear Arm.

Curse those easterlies! If I didn't know any better, I would have sworn they were laughing at me. Today, I was sorely tempted to stay in my sleeping bag. The seas looked no worse than yesterday, but once the waves rocked me as I rounded Cape Bluff, my confidence dropped.

As a result, my paddle finished before it had even started. I had hoped to be camped somewhere down Fisherman's Run before nightfall. I had planned to kayak 50 kilometres, but hadn't even paddled twenty. My plans to visit the old abandoned whale station on Hawke Island, and visit Calvin's brother Earl in Styles Harbour had gone up in smoke with the weather. Taking the easy way out, I'd scooted down Lady's Arm to the settlement of Norman Bay at the first hint of rain.

I was now beginning to question my sanity. The constant wind and waves were wearing me down, physically and mentally. I knew that another day stormbound would only compound my present state, but the thought of continuing looked no better. It wasn't that I needed a break from kayaking, but one from the sea. I needed a change of scenery. I needed something to take my mind off the weather; to inject my trip with renewed vigour. That evening, when I sat down in Philip Snow's kitchen, he must have read my mind.

"Remember when you passed through here some winters back on snowshoes? That time you got lost up Peter's Hill en route to Cartwright? Well, in summer it's a piece of cake to follow. You can make it all the way to Patridge Bay without getting your feet wet."

I can't stress enough my reliance on local knowledge. Had I not heard that this inland route could be portaged from the horse's mouth, so to speak, I wouldn't even have entertained the thought.

That evening Philip, and I poured over my sea charts. Tomorrow, no matter what the weather, I would leave. I would be exchanging the open sea for a network of salt water channels up Squasho Run, and a couple of fresh water ponds behind the hills around Comfort Blight. I would have to make three portages, but they all looked short and Philip assured me they were all cut (they are used as winter snowmobile trails) and easy to spot. This inland route seemed just what the doctor ordered. I gave into the idea immediately and that evening fell soundly asleep on his living room sofa without a care in the world.

It was here, six years ago, trapped in a storm with Philip as my aide du corp, that I truly understood why the people of Labrador are a breed unto themselves. It was here that I first heard the term resettlement and truly understood the pros and cons of isolation. Before I turn the page on a new day, I would like to take this opportunity to quote my first impressions of its community as written in my book Journey through Labrador. What I wrote about them is just as relevant today as it was then.

Until Mary's Harbour, Norman's Bay had been a mystery. My map called it Lady's Arm. It wasn't even a dot. I originally took it for a summer fishing community, deserted in winter, now I was about to be swallowed by its sleepy generosity. After days of scentless travel, communities were always announced by the sweet smell of burning wood and, once I was spotted, by a chorus of barking dogs. The first thing that struck me on the coast were the homes. They were all wood. Most were box-like, four convenient corners and a roof, but here and there the odd one still retained that add-on look and a few more had the picture postcard window and door moldings painted in vivid red and green. Central heating and microwaves were the norm, no different from a city family with its one point two children. That was on the surface, but you only had to see past their Nintendo games to find the East Coast's flip side. Norman's Bay community of eleven families was a prime example.

To cross their threshold was like entering a time machine. The first door opened into a storage area of wood and hardware called the porch. You were now one step away from the inner cloister, because the next door opened into the kitchen.   Here I found wood burning cast iron stoves still in use for heating and cooking, black and white televisions constantly crackled and clothes hung as they fell on the floor.   Every room had that lived-in look, where you could just as easily see a ski-doo engine stripped for repair on the kitchen floor as baking on its table. Life in these communities continue to go forward but with one eye on the rear view mirror.   Isolation helps this view and blood lines cement it.

Blood ties on the Labrador coast run deep.   In Lodge Bay, nearly all the surnames were Pye. In Mary's Harbour every other one was a Rumbolt and in Port Hope Simpson, the Pennys ran everything from the post office-cum-store to the Alexis Hotel.   In Charlottetown the Campbells and Turnbulls were evenly matched and here in Norman's Bay all except two were Wards.

I was now definitely in tea country; invitations were sealed with it.   Tea wasn't just a tradition, it was a religion, and God forbid you ask for the herbal variety. Water was always on the boil and it wouldn't be long before the kitchen table was full of oven-fresh bread and homemade jams. The next ritual would take me into the living room. Here I would receive a lesson in genealogy as family histories were recorded in picture frames,from B & W to colour, and it didn't take a family planning expert to work out that the old-fashioned bed had more uses than for sleep.

Norman's Bay is one of those isolated outposts that cable TV forgot about and that Bell Canada is just getting to.   They still have no wharf, no indoor plumbing and the brook is the only reliable source of water.   That's one side of the equation. The other has no fences, an abundant wilderness and a quality of life that can only be judged if you can swim in many cultures.

I ate an early breakfast of toast and jam, in a good mood. Outside the sky was pale, but yesterday's strong easterlies had dropped back a peg a two. Even the thought of another easterly front, forecast to arrive by mid afternoon, couldn't spoil my mood. If anything, I was hoping for a hurricane. Today, I would be paddling in sheltered waters. The sea's influence would be zero and the only thing that morning that played on my mind was mosquitoes.

I made it across the sheltered waters of Otter Bay and Hawke's Bay, behind Stoney Island, before the sun was half up, then paddled down the tree-topped narrow gorge of Squasho Run before noon. The portages over the first two fresh water ponds posed no difficulty and it was mid after-noon before I took my first break. So far, so good, just as I was indulging myself in a little back slapping, I hit a snag.

I had been following Philip's instructions to the letter, but as I approached my third and final portage to Partridge Bay, I got confused. I'd just surprised a flock of ducks. I had my eyes trained on a low point of land in front, and had seen the makings of a brook in a shallow pass between two hills. I'd been committing its course through the willows to mem-ory, but I lost it. I now couldn't tell east from west, or which of the three points of low land led to Partridge Bay. If only I had not thrown away my compass!!!

I headed towards the first break I saw in willows and tied up my kayak on a branch, but after wading half a dozen steps, I was halted by a wall of its knotted roots and branch-es. Now I was too close to the bank to see where the brook entered the pond, or if this narrow break in the willows was, in fact, the one I'd seen earlier.

One thing was for certain, snowmobiles had cut a path over its tops. I was now totally confused. Snowmobiles require only a dusting of snow over frost-hardened ground to travel on, but by the looks of the broken branches, above a snowmobile would have had to be either flying or tracking over a five foot snow drift to make those marks. Although snowmobiles had passed this way, surely this couldn't be the cut snowmobile trail Philip had talked about. I was begin-ning to think it had returned to nature. I didn't like the idea of being cut to ribbons, portaging my kayak through the wil-lows, but if it had to be done, it had to be done. I marked a branch with some red surveyor's tape, then paddled back into the pond.

I'd been right the first time. The red tape I'd left should have been, for all intents and purposes, where the brook emptied into the pond and where the snowmobile trail should have been. By now, the sense of well-being I'd built up during the day had crumbled. The thought of having to fight my way through the willows with my kayak was too much to contemplate. I'd taken the inside passage to escape the stormy seas only to find it blocked by a tidal wave of willows. It was 5:00 pm, and I hadn't eaten all day. My chocolate bars were stored away out of reach, lost to the morning's laziness, and my flask was empty of Philip's wife's coffee. I didn't fancy leaving the portage until morning. I didn't want a night of tossing and turning, replaying the day's events out in my head, but just as I was giving way to weariness, I spotted a small man-made cut.

Yes me'boy. Cut three metres wide and twelve metres deep. I found the snowmobile trail some distance from the willows, above the bank. I didn't even have to unpack my kayak. It glided over the neatly laid out trunks and branches that filled in all the rougher sections, and when it opened onto acres of ankle-deep blueberry bushes and wind dried moss, I knew I was home and dry.

By seven o'clock, I made camp on a ridge overlooking the sea channel between two islands called Fisherman's Run. My good humour had returned, and with it, a renewed vigour to explore. I climbed an adjacent ridge, ascended another hill, and a blast of wind announced the summit. There, stretched out for as far as the eye could see - to Spotted Island, some 50 kilometres away - lay the maze of islands and channels I would be paddling through tomorrow.

I don't know what it is about me and land, but I never seem to escape a portage without encountering a bear - and not any kind of bear, but angry ones. Maybe they sense that I am unarmed and that my testosterone levels have shot through the roof, or maybe its just that I am an unlucky man, but I have yet to meet a bear that's more frightened of me than I am of him. This bugger looked larger than life and twice as angry. I had startled him on the forage, and he didn't look at all pleased.

They say ownership at sea is nine-tenths of the law.

I shared the dilemma of a captain who abandons his ship only to find it occupied on his return. The bear was standing over my kayak, and it was obvious from its demeanour it was after something. His snout had been buried in my cockpit, and it was now pointing in my direction.

My first instinct had been to put as much distance between me and it as possible, but the bear was standing guard over my getaway vehicle, and then there was my tent. To the casual bystander, our standoff must have looked ludicrous. We had both stopped what we were doing, and were now just staring at each other. Like two bar antagonists locked in an arm wrestle of wills, neither of us was willing to admit defeat, but I wasn't going to back down. I was the one cornered. I had the most to lose. In fact, running away hadn't even crossed my mind. It's not that I wasn't scared, but at that instant it would have been a luxury. My brain was working overtime; noise; exaggerated movements. I even thought of throwing my remaining Mars bar at him. Each notion was analysed and dumped. He was just too close to my kayak. If he stood on it, I would be left with a gaping hole, and if I left him to forage inside my cockpit, God knows what damage he could do.

I was now slowly edging towards him. He had turned from my kayak and had latched onto some equipment I'd left on the beach. He seemed to take one step forward, then two steps back. Maybe for the first time, he'd caught my scent, but for whatever reason I was grateful, as no sooner had his snout turned up when he turned away from the beach. The standoff was broken, but I didn't relax until he had disappeared down a ravine, then over a hill, out of sight.

I must admit, I didn't sleep well that night. Now, I saw fresh bear droppings everywhere. I could only assume from his blue-dyed shit that the blue berries had attracted him to the clearing, and not the sight or the scent of my camp, but I wasn't taking any chances. I lit a huge fire, after collecting enough driftwood to keep it going for a week. I woke twice to rekindle it and once into a nightmare of blood and guts, but come the morning, all was O.K. All except the weather.

The day spent in sheltered waters hadn't shaken the easterlies. The weather that morning was dreadful. Cold, windy and wet. The labyrinth of channels, tickles and islands that looked so distinct last night in the clear crisp atmosphere of early evening had now fused into a milky grey drizzle. I was in a half mind to stay, but no sooner had I decided to leave and break camp when it started to rain, and I mean rain. It came down in buckets-full, and kept right on coming. Even with my dry suit I felt cold. The rain was taking away my body heat faster than I could generate it by paddling and if that wasn't enough, its thick haze was obliterating sight of the land. Within an hour, I had no clue where I was other than I was on the leeward side of some islands. Even the sea lane buoys that marked the safe deep water passage to the mothballed fish plant at Punch Bowl offered up little in the way of my position. Seldom have I felt such an overpowering sense of helplessness. It was aided by the fact that I was feeling increasingly unwell, and also because I had convinced myself that I had missed Punch Bowl. Suddenly, I heard a speedboat, then the deep drone of a generator, and through the gloom appeared a huge white satellite dish.

Thirty minutes, later I was sitting down with Punch Bowl's skeleton staff, catching up on the latest weather forecast and feeling as sick as a dog. I must have drunk some infected water because for the next hour I was up and down like a yo-yo, alternately glued to the toilet seat or shivering besides a stove. I didn't even have the energy to accept their food, and when offered a bunk to lay down on, died on it.

That night, I must have lost a gallon of fluids, because the following morning, I ate and drank like there was no tomorrow. I know I should have taken the day off - miracles only happen in the bible - but the weather had cleared and the window of opportunity was too good to pass. True, I had this incredible appetite for all things sweet, but other than that, I felt my old self.

Sometimes I can be as stubborn as a mule. I had not even finished the day's first page when a call-of-nature had me scuttling ashore. Half the morning's breakfast exited in a stream of piping hot fluids, but it was when I got caught out down in Porcupine Bay, failed to beat the flood gates and shit my britches, that I called it quits. It was not yet noon. I beached at the first sandy cove, and erected my tent. I was depressed. If it wasn't one thing, then it was another. August was not half over, yet it felt like the September easterlies had already arrived. The dry chill of last week had turned into a penetrating cold damp air. I was beginning to will myself onto the end. I was rushing things, and I knew it. Like today, when I should have stayed instead of leaving, I was beginning to spend more time looking at tomorrow and to escape the worries of the day, but then something happened.

'IS THERE ANYBODY OUT THERE?'

I'm not a religious man, by a long shot, but there are times, and tonight was one of them, when life skips without warning onto another plane. It was one of those glorious nights. There was a touch of frost in the air and the mosquitoes, for once, were quiet. I could sit outside in peace and watch the sky go technicolor. Blood reds changed into deep purple, then into the ink black cloak of night. It was a childhood fantasy come true. My own observatory. The night was crystal clear. I traced the Big Dipper, found the North Star and lined in the likes of Scorpio, Aries and Taurus the Bull. I must have tracked half a dozen satellites, named three planets and gazed in wonder at the Milky Way before the main event started. It began with a distant glow, like the far off haze of city lights. It slipped over some low hills, grew in brightness, then exploded into life. Lines, tails, curls, it was everywhere. A curtain one minute, an old man's whiskers the next. It went from white to fluorescent green to dull amber. For sixty minutes, the Northern Lights massaged my tired limbs and fed my spirit. Once again, the unseen doctor of good luck had come knocking at my door and once again not a day too soon.

There is a saying on the Labrador coast that the Island of Ponds manufactures storms for export to the mainland and that morning its saying rang true. It was blowing a gale. Any other island and I could have expected some kind of shelter on its leeward side, but not this one. There's not a single bush, twig, blade of grass, or cliff outcrop to be found anywhere. Nothing to soak up the 30 to 40 knot easterly winds that were sweeping over its smooth bald hills and tearing up the seas down Porcupine Bay. It had been my intention to call in on the island community of Black Tickle. I had fallen in love while under the influence during a visit there four years before, and wanted to pick up where I had left off, but today the Gods were against me.

Once again a steady head wind wore me down. It froze my fingers, chapped my cheeks and geared my progress down to a crawl. It took me almost six hours to cover the 16 kilometres from Porcupine Bay to Rocky Bay, around the backside of the Island of Ponds. It was both frustrating and boring, with little to excite my interest on either land or sea, and I was almost ready to pack it in. Turning away from the wind, I was angling over to the magnificent silhouette of rock called Indian Island when a splash of colour and some waving hands caught my attention.

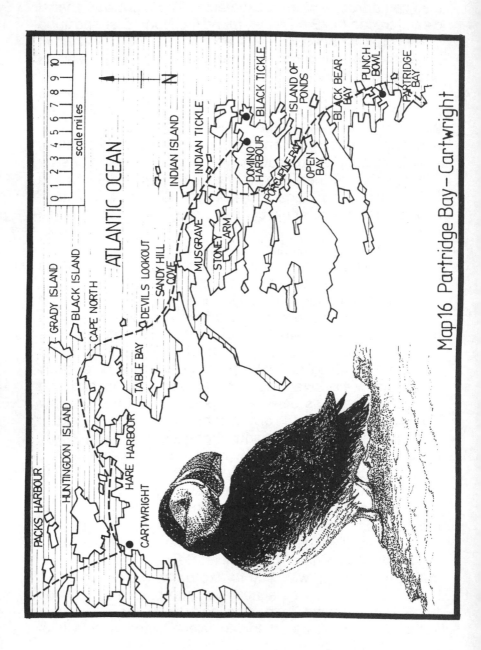

Map16 Partridge Bay–Cartwright

Immediately my day picked up. I had been spotted by a family out bake apple picking. They were an answer to a maiden's prayer, for no sooner had my name a.k.a. 'The Walking Man' past my lips, when I was being sped across open water to the quiet little settlement of Domino Run.

That night, I didn't so much fall asleep under the influence of food and drink as be lulled by its music. Bless 'em. I had spotted their squeeze boxes the moment my feet crossed the threshold of their kitchen, but seeing and hearing are worlds apart. There are three things a Labradorian cannot live without: food, drink and his music. If you thought Cape Breton had cornered the market on the fiddle and the squeeze box, then you haven't heard the transplanted Newfies of Labrador's Southern Coast play. I am no stranger to centre stage. I am the kind of person who can fall flat on his face and turn it into an artistic pirouette. In short, I am not frightened of making a fool of myself, but that's me, and I tend to forget that others are less fortunate. I must have tried everything from praise to guilt, in my efforts to persuade them to play me a tune, but once they had started to rock and roll, there was no stopping them.

I would like to think it was my name that filled their kitchen with bodies that night, but I know better. By ten o'clock the room was bursting at the seams. Feet were tapping, spoons rapping and off-key singing was the order of the night. This time, I kept my mouth shut, filled it with food, and the only steps I took that evening were to bed, where not until the early hours of the morning did I eventually close my ears, drop my lids and fall asleep.

It was impossible to sleep in. Reveille, I had been told, would be at 5:30 am. And reveille I got. I was too tired to get up, but too restless to sleep in. I was caught in a no-man's land of fatigue. It's not that the sounds emanating down the hall were loud. It was the constant background hum of chatter, and the revolving door of toilet ablutions taking place next door to my bedroom. There weren't many of them, but they made up for their weakness in number by an incredible variety of sounds that resembled a band tuning.

The party had fallen asleep where they had sat the night before, and were now gathering themselves for an early start to catch the Northern Ranger ferry over to St Anthony's in Newfoundland. There was an urgency in the air. The ferry had left Cartwright that morning, and as I downed my first cup of coffee. I could hear its engines approaching out at sea, near Wolf Island. Last night, I had been told that one of the ladies in the settlement had been flown out to St Anthony's and was now a patient in its Grenfell Mission Hospital. She had a history of complicated births and because there are no doctors on the Labrador coast, she had been flown out just to be on the safe side. Now all her brothers and sisters, lock, stock and barrel, were heading over on the ferry, to pay her a visit. Last night's party had been an excuse for a little steam blowing but now the mood was somber. I offered my good wishes and said my goodbyes on the doorstep, and as they left up Domino Run to Black Tickle in a flotilla of speed boats, I too was transported by speedboat to where I had left my kayak, above the beach at Salmon Point.

The bottom half of the day was brilliant, but I never managed to make inroads past noon. The short narrow passage of Indian Tickle cut between its island namesake and the mainland under clear blue skies, with only a ripple in its sheltered waters. The tickle was full of rocky shoal, mini gardens of sand, stunted trees and huge faces of rock. One scene eclipsed the next in a never-ending panorama of gold, green and blue. No sooner had my eyes latched onto one frame of its interesting detail when another popped into focus.

The word 'TICKLE' originates in the description of a body of water between islands or the mainland where the passage is so narrow that it tickles the side of one's boat, and today's ripple-filled waters - stroked by a strong current fluting through its narrows - did just that. The calm lulled me into a false sense of security, as once I had paddled out of its shadows, the scene and its conditions changed rapidly. I

had just turned the corner at White Point, giving the pounding waves a wide birth and was resting in some quiet sea
swells, lapping up the amazing sight of the Devil's Lookout
(a huge island of rock in Table Bay), when the back of my
neck felt the first flutter of a sea squall. Within minutes
waves were being squeezed-up and cresting in the shallows. The tide was out, and I was being pushed dangerous-
ly close to some shoal. Rocks were exposing themselves
everywhere. I was now being broadsided and slapped by
waves identical to those I had experienced leaving Sept-
Îles, but this time I was ready. I was angling, ever so slowly,
towards the shore. Sometimes bypassing rocks and sometimes foolhardily allowing myself to be carried over their
ragged tops on the crest of waves. If anything, I was enjoying myself. I had already made up my mind I would beach,
put up my tent and wait out the squall. I even caught a rough
wave to surf in on. Having made it ashore with downtime on
my hands, I spent the next hour practicing my take-offs and
landings through its increasing surf.

By noon, I had called it a day. I was tucked in North
Shore Bay under a high hill burn on the Musgrave
Peninsula. I had accepted my day was finished. The squall
had turned into a full-blown easterly. Waves were building
and queuing up, ready to crest on the beach, and the two
points of land at either end of the bay were awash in surf. I
was now content to explore my whale bone-filled sandy
beach and after collecting enough specimens to fill the
Smithsonian Museum, I turned my attention to collecting
driftwood.

When the mood strikes me, and I have the time to
indulge its appetite, I love building 'bonfires'. The bonfire is
an old British tradition stemming from the day almost four
hundred years ago when 'Guy Fawkes' attempted to burn
down the Houses of Parliament in London. British people
are a peculiar race. We love runners up and people who
swim against the current, but most of all we love our anti-
heroes. In fact, we downright worship them. Guy Fawkes is
to the rebel what Robin Hood Is to the compassionate.

Being a rebel at heart, I always looked forward to 'Bonfire Night' and although today wasn't November 5th (the day set aside in Great Britain to celebrate Guy Fawkes infamous deed), I wasn't going to let that small detail spoil my fun.

From a distance, my bonfire of driftwood must have looked like an Egyptian pyramid set in a desert of sand. I had found the spring high tide mark above the beach's lip to be a depository of twisted roots, tree trunks, floats and lobster traps, and I even found the skeleton remains of a fishing boat. By sunset I was ready, and so was the sky. I watched, entranced, as the light drained rapidly from the sea. I had already cooked and eaten my supper, and was toasting my bum on a small fire I had built to do my cooking. It was now time to ignite its big brother and within minutes - fed by a stiff offshore breeze - it was soon crackling and exploding under the force of its heat-expanded sand-filled skin, sending up snakes of sparkling embers one minute and illuminating the evening sky the next, like that of some rocket propelled firework.

I set off the next day bright and early. I had already broken camp and was paddling when the sun pushed its way to the surface. The flock of male eider ducks which had lulled me to sleep with their chatter but had also, intermittently woken me through the night, rose in a huge formation of black and white feathers on seeing me approach, but they were only the tip of the iceberg. Maybe two hours had passed. I was closing in on Cape Green. The view ahead of Table Bay was awesome. The sea was still becalmed and my eyes had been resting on a humpback whale smacking the surface of the sea with its large dorsal fin, but something else caught my eye. It had started as a smudge in the sky, then as it closed in, turned into a wavering line of motion. It was coming at speed and skimming the waters in a broken V. If only I knew my ducks. You name them, and that morning, I saw them. They came in low-flying squadrons of whistling noise. Terns, puffins, and God knows what others. Some formations came so close that I saw their heads turn, their eyes popping out of their heads, staring in my direction with a child's curiosity. I had heard the rich waters around Table Bay was home to colonies of ducks and that the Devil's Lookout Island's shear rock faces were their favourite nesting grounds, but if I hadn't seen it with my own eyes, I wouldn't have believed it.

Once again I dawdled. I had paddled two kilometres out into their flight lane. I had drifted, tried my hand at picture taking, and even put pencil to paper trying to describe the events unfolding around me. But, as I said a few pages back; 'Labrador waits for no man, especially the weather.' I was probably half way across Sandy Hill Cove, five kilometres off land and angling my way over to the Devil's Lookout when a stiff breeze came out of nowhere.

That night found me camped out on the tip of Sandy Hill Cove, with an unrestricted view of Table Bay. The wind that morning had been strong; strong enough to force me ashore, but hadn't lasted long. I had beached, put up my tent and catnapped to wait out the wind, but instead of waking when the wind died, I had slept through the whole afternoon. They say that 'idle hands are mischievous hands', but in my case, foolish ones. I should have stayed in my sleeping bag and filled in the time with letters, but my body had energy to burn and a play ground of rock and sea to expend it on. I decided to go for a swim. I chose an outcrop of rock boarded by deep water, but no sooner had I dived in than I was out. The sea was so cold, it was like stepping on fire. I was now numb to the bone, and to make matters worse, a dark bulbous cloud passing overhead started to spit rain, then it poured down.

I ran all the way back to my tent like a lunatic, with as many dry twigs clasped to my chest as I could carry. Why I decided on building a fire in the rain is anyone's guess. Maybe it was a knee-jerk reaction from past experience. My life seemed so flexible back then, that the only constant I had was my evening fire. Now it seemed that no amount of rain was going to spoil it. Three times, I made scavenging forays in the rain, and each time I carefully stored away the twigs in hope that the downpour would pass. It was worth it. By the time the sun had set, I had kindled a roaring fire, and by the time the drizzle had stopped, it once again become the hook to hang my thoughts on.

I was now three quarters of my way home. I had rounded the Straight of Belle Isle without mishap. My old confidence had finally returned and Sept-Îles had become a distant memory. I was sure if I remained cautious, I could cope with any condition a strong east wind could blow my way, and for the first time in my trip I allowed myself thoughts of finishing; of kayaking down Lake Melville to Mud Lake; of seeing my 'tent city home' down the back channel, and of Chuck, Dean and the boys. What stories I would be able to tell. I would stretch them to the limit, get drunk and enjoy every minute of it, and now having thought it, I knew for certain it would happen.

I woke into another beautiful day, but it wouldn't last. I broke camp before sunrise and was in the water and within striking distance of Devil's Lookout Island. The sun had just started to force its way through the early morning's blanket of light mist. Overhead I could still see the thin silvery moon, but as the mist evaporated, so did its outline. By 10:00 am, I had crossed the bay and a mid afternoon heat replaced the early morning chill. For once, the sun's rays warmed my back, and for the first time since leaving the Saint Lawrence, I allowed myself the pleasure of catching its rays. I took an extended break while tanning myself in the kayak. I drifted for maybe an hour, then the clouds that I had seen earlier, floating over the horizon, rolled in from the sea, and the sun was lost for the rest of the day.I had not listened to the weather forecast since Punch Bowl and had forgotten, in all the excitement in Domino, to ask, so when I popped my head round Grady Island and was greeted by the biggest sea swells I had ever paddled in, I was both surprised and elated.

Imagine tobogganing down a hill in slow motion, skimming across its valley at speed, then being carried by your own momentum to the top of its twin. It's like your whole world tilts, flattens, then you kiss the sky. I could only guess as to the wave's height, but in their troughs - even though I was less than half a mile from shore - the land was lost to the sea. At Cape North, I cut right into the cliffs. The noise of the huge waves pounding and echoing from its face sounded like the rapport of canon fire, but it was when I got within a stone's throw of its powerful reflective waves that its awesome power finally struck home.

When soapy water is married to air, you get bubbles. But when Atlantic surf is married to rock, then divorces itself and is carried by the wind, you get flying blobs of foam. I was now paddling in a blizzard of thick spongy bubbles, cutting a course through its wide channel of froth. Once again I lingered. It's not everyday the elements push huge sea swells through becalmed waters. I knew Cape North would be my last opportunity to witness such a dramatic scene, and I wanted to commit it to memory before continuing. I must have replayed my approach three times. I knew from my sea charts that once I had rounded the cape, I would be back in protected waters with only the exposed sandy beaches of the Strand to worry about, so who could blame me?.........THE WIND

I was now past the thought of 'beginning to think'. I now knew 'for certain' the wind was conspiring to make my last chapter a memorable one, for no sooner had I rounded the cape than the wind turned ninety degrees, dropped ten in fahrenheit, geared up six notches and took off big time. I was now surfing with a freezing cold tail wind at my back, and I do mean surfing. Again I was caught in two minds. I had spotted a cluster of smoke-topped cabins in the cape's cove behind its shear face of rock. I was neither tired, thirsty or hungry, but when one of its anchored speedboats unlashed its moorings and sped my way with an invite, I gave into its messenger and joined him for a plate of fried cod.

By late afternoon it had started to rain. My hands were numb, and the pinched nerve that the week before had caused me so much pain had returned. Even my toes, encased in rubber protective stockings, had lost all feelings to numbness. Any moment I expected it to snow, and when I got soaked by a shoal-breaking wave from behind, while crossing Backguard Bay, I gave up all thoughts of reaching Cartwright before nightfall. Once again I lowered my horizons, changed course and sprinted for Hare Harbour.

There are times, when survival outweighs any feelings of guilt about breaking the law. I have lived in Labrador long enough to understand why some cabins in remote areas are left opened under the honour system of pinned notes for unknown users - to 'wash up', 'replace fire wood', and 'shut the door before leaving', while others, closer to home, are boarded and locked against everyone. Cabins left open close to settlements are quickly becoming open invitations for abuse, so I wasn't surprised to find that the dozen or so cabins scattered around the Hare Harbour were all locked.

Cartwright was less than 16 kilometres away, and in the wind, probably less than two hours by paddle, but I was running on empty. My stomach had lost all its reserves to constant shivering and I was frozen to the bone. My hands were so cold that my paddle strokes had taken on a life of their own, and my feet - unable to fine tune my rudder's movement to less than a full turn - felt like blocks of lead.

Before I commited the dastardly deed and broke into the cabin, I did try to light a fire, but to no avail. For all my efforts, I only found a few emaciated twigs, everything else had been saturated with rain - which was by now almost certainly entertaining thoughts of freezing into ice pellets. Twice, I tried to light one, but both times it took off like a limp squid, only to douse itself in its own air-throttling fumes of smoke. I even tried to set light to an old spruce tree, whose branches had obviously seen better days. Its underbelly at once took off, but once its old pine needles had singed themselves out down to their branches, it too was extinguished by the rain. By this time I was past the point of caring. I had already lost one full box of matches to my arthritic fingers and another box to rain. Even my flame throwing - never say die, survival lighter had packed in on me.

The only quality the cabin I chose to break into had over the rest was its proximity to my kayak. Thank Christ, its door offered up little resistance. The lock's bolted hinges required only a minimum force to prize their nails out of the wood ,and once inside, I soon had the stove fired and the room roasting. I still wasn't in a fit state to cook. My finger tips and toes hurt like hell, and when blood eventually started to circulate in my cheeks, they too flushed and burned with pain. Full recovery took longer than I thought it should have, but when my body normalized, and I had dropped back into my old skin, the late afternoon grey had turned into a dark misty gloom.

That evening, I decorated every hook and twine in the cabin, with everything from my sea-soaked wet suit to my dew dampened tent. I cooked in the gloom, ate under candlelight and indulged myself with hours of radio news before hitting the sack. That night, I dreamed in technicolor, but when the first rays of dawn woke me the scene outside was black on white.

The morning was a carbon copy of yesterday afternoon's wind and rain, and had I have not been so close to Cartwright, with an invitation to stay in its nursing station, I would have rolled back into my dream and stayed put.

Before leaving the cabin, I wrote a quick letter of explanation to its owner. I apologized for busting its lock's hinges, tried to explain about the weather, my health and the reason for using up most of its dry wood. I left him two dinners of freeze-dried food as payment for my stay, then secured the door shut as best I could.

I made it to Cartwright bright and early, but once my feet touched dry land, they became sodden. The threatened easterly storm - the first of the year, that every one on the coast had been praying would blow itself out to sea, and that had caused yesterday's mountainous ocean swells - had finally arrived as promised.

For the first three days, I actually liked being storm-bound. I had cosy quarters at the nursing station, receptive ears in their nurses, and numerous friends and friends of friends to call on and fill in my days.

By now the reader must think I know everybody on the Labrador coast, if not intimately, at least by sight. It's not the case, but I did forewarn the reader that almost every-body is related one way or another and you could say that Cartwright is its melting pot.

Situated in the headwaters of Sandwich Bay with mountains as its backdrop and a barrier of islands at its mouth. Cartwright is closed in from the outside world as tight as a drum. For me it was neither its harbour or its size - although its population of 600 plus put it second only to Nain as the coast's most populated settlement - that set it apart from the other settlements I had visited. It wasn't its services either - even though it was a home away from home to a who's who of government facilities including an RCMP detachment, Fish and Wildlife offices, volunteer coast guards, a nursing station, the second largest high school, largest hotel on the southern shore, largest airport and a deep water harbour second to none. Impressive as these statistics read, it was its potpourri of resettled families that stood out the most, and it's this strange genealogical jour-ney that has always captivated me.

If you believe all you read in the newspapers, Toronto and Vancouver have cornered the market on multicultural-ism. Islam, Sikh turbans and Somali refugees are a fact of life these days. It is easy to overlook the fact that you don't have to come from another country, be black, disabled or homosexual to have a social problem. Imposed resettlement in Cartwright stretched its facilities to the breaking point and pushed Labrador's brotherly love to the limit. Before reset-tlement in the '60s, Cartwright was mostly home to the Birds, Martins and Pardys. This was before the Williams family was uprooted from North West River, the Winters from Muddy Bay, the Browns from Separation Point, the

Meshers from Paradise River, the Lethbridges and Learnings from Eagle River, the Reeves from Hare Harbour, the Elsons from Spotted Island, the Dysons and Webbers from Batteau and the Howells from Porcupine Bay. It all added up to a strange mixture and the single most important reason why I couldn't turn a corner within its boundaries without encountering someone's relative. Ironically this very fact, this daily rub of goodwill, of not being able to turn a corner without someone wanting a part of my story was what did me in.

By my fifth day, I was starting to listen to the weather forecast on an hourly basis. It hung on my lips, occupied my mind and was slowly becoming the only topic of conversation I had ears for. I had become a worn-out record in only four days. Even the people who had opened their doors to me only yesterday were starting to dread my appearance at their doorstep. That is all except for one, and for the sake of anonymity, I will call him Henry.

Every small town and village has one. He's the kind of person who walks around as if attached to a rubber band, giving the strong impression that if he strayed too far he'd snapped right back, and if he eventually left, everybody in turn would leave as well. Henry knew everybody and everybody knew him.

That particular morning, I wasn't exactly in a good mood. I had just heard the weather forecast and it was full of strong winds, low pressure this and that and rain, more bloody rain. I was beginning to think that that was it. That autumn had finally arrived, and I would be stuck in Cartwright, if not for the winter, then at least for the next two weeks. By now, I had got into the habit of packing everything away in my kayak more out of a morning routine than in hope that the weather would change during the day, and has it hadn't stopped raining since my arrival, I had also taken to wearing my wet suit during daylight hours, only changing for the evening's meal in someone's house.

I had just switched off my radio. I had not even taken a dozen steps outside when Henry appeared out of nowhere. I give Henry his due. The guy was a veritable reference library of useful information, with volumes of experience at his fingertips, but it came with a price. He just hadn't learned to shut up. He had the appearance of a dried out raisin. It was as if life had been vacuumed out of his body. Maybe he was living on borrowed time, but by the look in his eyes and his square shoulders, he wasn't leaving without a fight, and I was beginning to believe he'd chosen me as his last hurrah. He spoke in short crisp sentences, pausing more to let his words sink in, than to gauge my response. This man was not a pleaser. I doubt if this man had ever responded to a joke or told one in his life, but it wasn't his lack of humour that drove me crazy or that he had turned, if only for the duration of my stay, into his pet subject. No, it was none of the above. It was his complete indifference to the pleasures of shelter that finally killed it for me. He would always catch me in the most exposed areas of town when the wind and rain was at its strongest. On these occasions, and they had become more numerous of late, the last thing I wanted to indulge in was polite conversation and today was the straw that broke the camel's back.

"Don't it feel good ta'be alive me boy?"

"What!!!!!" Once again, he'd appeared from nowhere, just as the rain was being carried horizontally. Even the dogs were quiet that morning and that's saying something.

"Lord gentle Jesus I've never seen it better."

He sounded like a blue bottle fly buzzing around my head. I was in no mood to feel good. In fact, I liked my present state of depression. I felt I deserved at least another day in that state.

"If only I was a young'n again, I'd be out there paddling with ya' right now."

Yeh, right, I thought. There were white caps everywhere, and any moment I expected to hear thunder. I hated him, his enthusiasm, his bravado. Were we looking at the same ocean? Were we even on the same planet? Once again he had bit my ankle bottoms with the tenacity of a fox terrier. For ten minutes I couldn't shake him. 'Don't you have something better to do?' I thought about saying, but under the circumstances, kept it to myself. He kept up this steady dialogue, only pausing to catch breath before racing through another subject. His enthusiasm was killing me. I could have murdered him right there and then except he was probably already spoken for. I wanted to swat him like a fly, or even better reverse the torture. I could remember myself thinking it's him or me, then!..

"Yes me'boy. If only I was a young'n again."

That did it. I could have gone straight for his jugular. Surely any court this side of hell would have acquitted me. It was so ludicrous. His words, my thoughts and the weather, that I broke out laughing.I had been making a mountain out of a mole hill. Maybe he had chewed my ankles to the bone and steam blasted my ears red raw, but this man, like everyone, deserves their moment in the sun.

"So you'd like to go for a paddle would you?"

My words had not even fallen out of my lips when he bit.

"I'd like nothing better me'boy."

Thirty minutes later, beaming from ear to ear, encouraged on by a gathering crowd of his cronies, I watched as this old man - years having fallen off his shoulders and his muscles of Popeye fed not by spinach but by the shouts of encouragement from the gathering crowd, paddled out into the bay for his one last shot at the big time.

It was apparent from the very outset that he'd never been in a kayak, but he wasn't going to allow this small detail to spoil his fun. It was ludicrous. He could have capsized at any second. He was living for the moment, swept along by the enthusiasm of his audience, and I am certain had he flipped, he wouldn't have cared less. In fact for all his efforts, he never made it past the first few waves. He could neither find the strength to puncture them, or the head wind that was wagging his tail. I do believe that had Henry capsized and drowned in two feet of water he would have died a happy man. And no sooner was he ashore, boasting of his exploits and breathing life into the gathering flames of enthusiasm that were sweeping through his friends when they too wanted a turn in my kayak. I let them all have a go and one eventually did capsize. I had to wade out thigh deep to retrieve him, but that morning nothing could have spoiled their fun.

I left on the sixth day. The winds were still gale force, but I had been offered a cabin across the bay down North River at Sandy Point. I had accepted the invitation more out to escape prying eyes than out of frustration at being storm-bound, and I wasn't surprised when Henry materialized out of the wind and rain to see me off.

I spent two pleasant days stormbound at Sandy Point. I had the whole place to myself. I read and wrote and indulged myself in hours of radio, but still it was hard to escape thoughts of the weather. On the first night the wind blew so hard it threatened to rip off the cabin's roof, and the rain was not only continuous, but on occasions deafening. However I had a fire, my chocolate bars and my smokes.

There was also time to reflect, and I didn't exactly fill this time with good thoughts. I had already spent more than two months on the water. I had turned the corner at Red Bay, but hadn't beaten the weather. It was only mid August, but already the easterly winds had arrived. Henry had told me the winds were two weeks ahead of schedule. Damp biting winds were becoming a daily occurrence. Rain was more on than off; the sun more hidden than exposed, and although my time in Labrador had told me that storms at this time of year were uncommon, I knew for certain that from here to Goose Bay, I would be in for a rough ride. Since Cape Charles, I had experienced only two clear nights. The late afternoons were now oppressively cold, and if it wasn't the wind and rain that was wearing me down, it was the inevitability that some errant wave would slap me with such force that my wet suit and cockpit skirt seals would let me down, and all my stored up warmth would immediately be washed away. I just wasn't looking forward to the day's pad-dle anymore. I felt it worse first thing in the morning. I didn't have the drive, that 'get out of bed and attack the rising sun'

Hamilton Inlet

FLAT WATER COVE

FLATWATER POND

portage

BACKWAY

BIG HILL

NEW HARBOUR

Atlantic Ocean

FISH COVE

WEST BAY

WOODY POINT

CAPE PORCUPINE

TRUNMORE BAY

Mealey Mountains

0 1 2 3 4 5 6 7 8 9 10
scale miles

NORTH RIVER

SANDY POINT

EARL Is

CARTWRIGHT

Sandwich Bay

N

EAGLE RIVER

PARADISE SETTLEMENT

Map 17
Cartwright–Backway

PARADISE RIVER

anymore. Uptil Cartwright, I had always had something during the day to look forward to, a roaring fire; a dry sleeping bag, and more often than not a cabin or someone's house, but from Cartwright to Goose Bay it would be anyone's guess. I had already decided to miss out Hamilton Inlet, its numerous coves, cabins and the settlement of Rigolet at the headwaters of Lake Melville and to take the old winter snowmobile trail down Flat Water Pond from its mouth just above West Bay to the Back Way (a tidal lake that joins into Lake Melville). If the weather cleared up, it could turn into the highlight of my trip, but if the weather stayed the same, it would be a complete waste of time.

The storm finally broke on the third day. For all intents and purposes I had lost a week to it, but I knew it would return. That morning the Marine Weather Forecast was all gloom and doom; yet another low pressure system was on the way, another dreaded north easterly.

That morning, I got my first view of the Mealie Mountains. Wrapped in a haze at their base and topped by a dusting of fresh snow, the sight only added to the feeling of urgency that was growing like a cancer in my head. I now had to take full advantage of whatever gaps of calm the bad weather offered, and paddled without a break over the Foul Ground shallow shoals behind Horse Chop Island. I was under the gun. The wind was rising with the sun, and before I crossed the horseshoe bay of Trunmore, it had picked up from the morning's light winds to a strong north westerly breeze.

Noontime found me toasting my buns over a fire in the heavily wooded armpit of Porcupine Bay. The sky was checkered with black and white clouds and anytime soon, I expected it to rain. Not for the first time on this trip, I was undecided. Every now and then the clouds would open, the sun flash, and the sea sparkle, but no sooner would the thought of leaving enter my head than the clouds would close rank, the seas darken and once again the waves would look menacing.

By mid afternoon, I'd had enough. The Tavener's (Labrador's second ferry) engines had seduced me from my sheltered perch onto the water and although Cape Porcupine's point was awash in surf, I rounded it.

The view ahead up the Strand was dismal. I felt betrayed, not because of the surf that was pounding the shore for as far as the eye could see, or the eerie, fine mist that its racing breakers caused, which was obscuring the sands. No, it was what I had left behind. The spot on Cape Porcupine facing south, sheltered from the wind and sur-rounded by lush green ferns with a spectacular view of the Mealie Mountains. It had not only been picture perfect; its brook and ample driftwood offered all the facilities I could hope for. Now not only was I facing the inevitability of hav-ing to paddle at least 14 kilometres into the teeth of a bitingly cold north west breeze, but also that the Strand's flat shore-line, dotted only with the occasional stunted pine and low lying bush, promised little in the way of shelter.

The Strand is 32 kilometres long, completely open to Atlantic storm swells and noted for its breakers. If it was any-where other than Labrador with its short summers and frigid waters, the golden beaches would be a surfer's paradise, but today it looked desolate. My sea chart only showed two small outcrops of land on which, in today's conditions I could safely beach, but once I had resigned myself to the inevitable 13-k paddle to Paradise Point and erased the pic-ture of the campsite I had left behind, I felt better.

Soon, I was skirting the shoreline with great enthusi-asm. The forming waves rising up to greet the shore rocked me as if in a cradle, and their racing breakers provided a hypnotic target for my eyes to follow. I was now a seasoned veteran in the art of surfing and beaching and today it was child's play. From a distance, the only feature that set Paradise Point apart from the beach was a cabin, but as soon as I approached, the rest fell into shape.

I judged the landing at the point would be in two parts. A huge rock guarded its nipple and its mini lagoon of still waters were protected by a high wall of sand. First, I rode in on a gathering wave, then nipped in behind the rock, just as the wave started to crest. Phase two was a waiting game. I watched and counted for the rough waves. It was all a matter of timing. I darted out between waves, paddled like crazy down a trough and just as a crested onrush of surf caught me, I squirted out of its grip behind the sheltered arm of sand into the calm waters of the lagoon.

I may have made a brilliant landing under the circumstances, but my choice of campsite was pathetic. The stunted bushes that surrounded my tent, their twisted shape resembling melted candles more than wind bent trees, were even worse in reality than seen from the sea.

I woke to find the rain - that had picked up during the night - puddling inside my tent. It was sponging time, but my heart wasn't up to the task. If anything the wind felt fresher than yesterday's and although the black clouds above looked pregnant with rain, I broke camp and left.

Sometimes there is method to my madness and it can't be judged until the day is finished. I chose to brave the elements that morning in hope that the next outcrop of land at Shag Rocks would hold better protection. I judged the point only 8 kilometres away. A one hour sprint under normal conditions, but these weren't normal conditions. It took what felt like hours to get there. The strong north west winds were sling shooting around the Mealies. There was hardly an undergrowth of bush, hillock, or mound to arrest its progress across the plains of land between them and the sea. It chopped up the waters and slapped its airborne spray in my face. Soon, my knuckles were red raw from the wind and my eyes sore from its salt water spit, but once I had beached, found a neat little cluster of heavy pines to camp under and lit a roaring fire, I was soon applauding my decision. Seeing two sea otters inspecting my kayak, down on the beach, was just icing on the cake.

There is nothing more disheartening than waking up warm and refreshed from a good night's sleep, only to be slapped by the prospect of putting on a skintight wet suit whose temperature is no different than the morning dew. That morning, I put on every stitch of clothing I had. I was determined to get out of the Strand. I was determined to make Flat Water Bay, rest up in 'Uncle Tom's Cabin', and dry everything out.

It was hard to keep the thought of a warm sleeping bag out of my head. The sky was clear, but the wind, if anything, felt stronger than yesterday. The breakers were still unrelenting and their surf scarred everything in sight. If it wasn't for the fact that I had lost over one week to bad weather, and that yesterday I had only paddled 8 kilometres, I would have followed the dull ache in my head back to its pillow.

I broke camp at a snail's pace. My hands were already cold from the morning dew, and by the time I'd stuck everything back into my kayak, I had about as much grip in them as a boxer has wearing his gloves. I set off in a sorry state. I shut down the obvious, trained my eyes on Ship Harbour some 16 kilometres to the north and dug in for the long haul to its point.

It was a hard slog. My knuckles still raw from yesterday's pounding now gripped the paddle with little force, and my protective poggies were nothing more than receptors for the never-ending waves that swept over them. What the frigid waters couldn't touch that morning, the bitter cold headwind made up for in spades. Twice, I skirted too close to shore and twice breakers broke over me. The scene was one of unrelenting surf close to shore, and counter waves pushed up by the wind and clapping against each other offshore. When I looked up at the Mealie Mountains I cursed their cold, and the Strand's beautiful sandy beaches, half hidden in fine mist, its unprotected shoreline. Even the rhythmic thunderclap of its breakers held no solace. It was as if nothing short of glass calm would satisfy me, and it wasn't until I had rounded Fish Cove Point, nipped into West Bay and found an anchorage of stilled waters, that I could relax.

Slowly the realization dawned that the worst of my trip was over, and to celebrate the occasion, I cracked open a small bottle of vodka. The Strand had been my last major hurdle. My last stretch of open sea. Tomorrow, I would be starting my inland portage, then it would be the sheltered tidal waters of The Back Way, then Lake Melville and home.

I was now entering Hamilton Inlet (the huge expanse of water where Lake Melville flows into the sea), and as I turned into its mouth the wind died away completely. I now covered the distance to Flat Water Cove as if in a dream. For only the second time in two weeks, the late afternoon sun carried heat. Once again, I hugged the coast, skirted point to point and even flirted with the coastal shoal waters of exposed rocks, but it wasn't until the impressive rock face of Saddle Island came into view that I finally gave into my emotions and started to cry.

By now the sea was glass calm and full of interesting diversions, and as this would be my last opportunity to experience an Atlantic horizon, I decided to stop and savour it. I paddled out to a small island close to shore, beached, lit a fire and waited for the sunset.

I knew all the islands in the inlet by name and also their stories. Cut Throat Island spoke for itself and everybody in these parts knew of the safe anchorage at Brig Harbour. The old fish plant at Smokey was hidden from view, but its radio tower was beaconed in light. I could just make out the small cluster of islands called White Bear, some 30 kilometres away on the far shore, and the pale blue vertical slabs of rock, called George Island, which dominated its mouth like two darkened twin towers. That evening, enhanced by the setting sun's prism of colours and mellowed by the smell and sounds of my fire, turned into a sunset to remember. It wasn't until the sun eventually dipped below the Mealies that I reluctantly left the scene and paddled down Flat Water Cove to Uncle Tom's cabin.

I first heard of Uncle Tom's cabin during my snow shoe trip up the Labrador coast. I had missed it because of a blizzard, but today I was going to pay it a visit. I knew the chances of meeting Tom were slim. His year round home was in Rigolet and the salmon fishing season had closed, but I knew for certain his cabin would be open. Tom, like many people on the coast, is a cast back to the days when hospitality was not only a word, but a way of life. That's why I was one hundred percent certain that even if Tom couldn't warm my heart with his presence, his cabin's open door of hospitality would. I had been told that due to its location, just off the coastal snowmobile trail from Goose Bay to Cartwright, it had become over the years quite literally the all-season drop-in centre for tired and weary travellers, and lost souls like myself, and that evening's only disappointment came in a note from Tom............he'd just that day left for Rigolet.

That morning, I was about to start my portage from Flat Water Cove to The Back Way. Three years before, I had walked its frozen trail on snowshoe. I wasn't taking this route to save time or to cut out dangerous waters, on the contrary. Hamilton Inlet is not only spectacular, but also home to hundreds of feeding whales. No, I wanted to mix-up my trip. I had already portaged two locks on the Saint Lawrence Seaway, but had been aided by pick-up trucks. The portage behind Mutton Bay was man-made, and the sheltered shortcut down Squasho Run from Caplin Bay to Partridge Bay had been too short to give me any sense of challenge.

I judged today's portage would take two days. First, I would have to follow Flat Water Brook to its headwaters at Flat Water Pond, then follow a natural dip of land over a treeless wasteland before joining a narrow man-made cut through a tree-filled valley before reaching The Back Way. I didn't have to take this route. I had both the time, food and equipment to take alternate routes. My main objective in taking this portage was to see if I could spot some mountain caribou that I knew roamed this area during summer. (Unlike their neighbours, the Georges River Herd that migrate in their hundreds of thousands through central Labrador to northern Quebec, this small herd don't migrate north during fall. They stay year round in the mountains and are bigger, more timid and fewer in number), and I was excited at the prospect of seeing them.

I planned my departure to perfection, paddled the reversing rapids at the mouth of Flat Water Brook during high tide, and managed to gain whatever favours it offered me until the next step up, some twenty minutes into my paddle. The day was glorious. The morning chill had killed off the flies, and the light breeze coming off the cool waters of Lake Melville were just enough to make paddling in the confined waters on the brook comfortable. The whole area was teeming with wild life - loons, canvas backs and a lone crane coughing like a deep-throated baritone suffering the flu. I even saw a pair of osprey circling above, hunting for trout. They would circle one spot for four to five minutes then move to another. Deep brown in colour, tinged in white freckles, and with heads turning this way and that, they made a captivating sight. For thirty minutes I watched them spiralling above, then suddenly one stopped; fluttered, then with wings folded, dropped like a dart into the water. It was amazing, and when moments later it surfaced empty handed, I was disappointed. I continued to watch but now felt like an intruder. Once I started paddling, they took off for greener pastures and dropped out of sight.

One hour into my paddle, the open brook narrowed into two channels around a small island. The willows at this point completely disappeared, and I had an unrestricted view of a huge open area blanketed in deep green moss. I was just trying to make up my mind which channel to take when my eye caught a movement ahead. It was a moose. Framed in the backdrop of the Mealie Mountains, it looked magnificent. It was a full grown male with a huge set of antlers. I watched his disjointed steps for some minutes. He seemed to be going nowhere in particular and oblivious to my presence, then I spotted another, then it spotted me. What happened next was both amusing and disappointing. Both moose took off as if someone had let off a fire cracker between their legs. Then a beaver slapped its tail on the water, and within seconds its crack had set off a chain reaction of noise that threatened to burst the brook's banks. First a cloud of ducks, more heard than seen, took off behind the island. Next, two bushes wavered, fluttered, then burst into life, disgorging scores of birds from its branches, who on seeing me peeled away from my kayak, in brilliant white streamers of motion. Then a crow appeared. I was cooked. I now knew that every living creature within ear shot of the commotion, would know I was in the neighbourhood.

The brook was now opening and closing like the pages of a book, and when it finally shut tight at the third set of rapids, I decided to leave it for good. For all this time, I had been keeping an eye on a cone-shaped hill to my right. It was one of those easy points of reference you could latch onto and not fail to recognize, from whatever direction you viewed it. I have always searched out these unique points of land. I use them no differently than a person uses stepping stones to cross water. Now that I had left the brook and started to pull my kayak over the slippery moss away from water, I was confident I wouldn't get lost.

I was now thoroughly enjoying the day - its solitude - that edge of uncertainty that only solo voyageurs get, and the knowledge that I owned the place. I had all the life ingredients that a man travelling in the bush craves. Once I had spotted my campsite, pulled my kayak up to it and put up my tent, I stripped naked, and, with all the intoxicating feelings of the first man on the moon, I went for a walk.

By early evening I had a blazing fire. I had chosen a place between two stunted black spruce, with a clear view of Flat Water Pond ahead. I had chosen well. The area offered up an abundance of dead wood for my evening fire, the pond for my water supply, and my elevated position had just enough exposure to gain full measure out of the cool breeze from the Mealie Mountains. The black flies were non-existent and the early evening breeze carried enough chill to keep the mosquitoes away, but still I felt a little uneasy. The bear dropping I had seen earlier in the day looked fresh, and behind my campsite, blanketing a small bog, were row upon of their favorite berry; the bake apple.

The sun had already set behind the Mealies but there was still plenty of light. I'd eaten well. The fire I'd built on a platform of collected rocks was still going strong. I now judged it safe enough to go on the forage. I'd not gone far. I'd just swept clean a small clearing of its bake apples. Facing the mountains, I was checking visually a heavy thicket of willows when I heard a noise. It was a muffled grunting sound, then I heard it again. I stood perfectly still. I could feel the excitement inside me starting to build, then I heard a crack, then another grunting sound. Could it be a caribou?

Immediately, common sense flew out of the window. Within seconds, I was knee-deep in undergrowth, and within minutes struggling to climb over the knotted branches of willows that lay ahead. I must have sounded like a bull in a china shop. I knew it was stupid, but my excitement had got the upper hand. Slowly I picked my way into the thicket, but I was starting to have this disagreeable feeling of being watched. Branches were closing in. I was now not certain what direction I was going in, but I was quite certain that the source of the noise did, then I tripped and fell. A branch slapped my eyes. I knew I wasn't blinded, but it hurt like hell, then I heard the noise again.

All reason now flew out of the window. I wanted out. I wanted to get back to my fire, but where was it? I sat and blinked like crazy. The pain was excruciating, but there was nothing else I could do. My mind was racing. What was the noise? An old bad tempered bear with a toothache? A young bull moose on the rut? I tried to push these thoughts away, but they came right back. I had now definitely made up my mind it was a lone wolf and he was playing with me, then I saw the source....a crow? Once I saw it, everything else fell into place. My eyes cleared and my route out of the thicket opened up like a six-lane freeway. I walked out and back to my tent as if nothing had ever happened, but the writing was on the wall.

My instincts were failing me. I was starting to hear

things that weren't there. Nature has a way of weeding out the weak and weary, and this animal was dog-tired. But it was more than physical fatigue. I just wanted it all to end. Three months on the water is long enough for anyone. I wanted to go home.

That night I made up my mind to end the trip as quickly as possible. No more side trips; no more foolish wanderings or contemplative stops. You can't win every battle, but it's important to win the last one. Lake Melville was just around the corner and Mud Lake's finishing line at its throat was probably less than a week's paddle away.

Another day, another chapter. Goodbye sun, hello wind and rain. The sun had risen like a frosted bell and had been almost immediately extinguished by clouds. A cool wind rose and the dark billowing clouds only made the corridor of wind that much sharper.

That morning, I had decided to portage my kayak to the pond first. I left my tent up, wanting to take advantage of the wind to dry off the morning dew, but almost immediately cursed my decision. Reaching my kayak at the pond's edge, I turned, to see my tent take off like an inflatable balloon.

Things went from bad to worse. The wind chopped up the pond like a bathtub of playful children and then it started to drizzle. The whole scene turned grey, but thank God I knew where I was going.

Once across the pond, I knew the winter snowmobile trail would be easy to follow to the Back Way, but the same couldn't be said for its surface. Years of snowmobile travel had left its mark. The bog's delicate surface of moss had been torn to shreds, and instead of gliding over its surface, my kayak sunk. After thirty minutes, I had a change of plan. I decided to empty my kayak and split my work into three loads, which immediately tripled the distance of my portage.

After five hours, fatigue was starting to nibble away at the corners of my endurance. I had just left the bog behind, and was starting the climb to the Back Way's lip. The trail had narrowed into a cut and was rising steeply. I

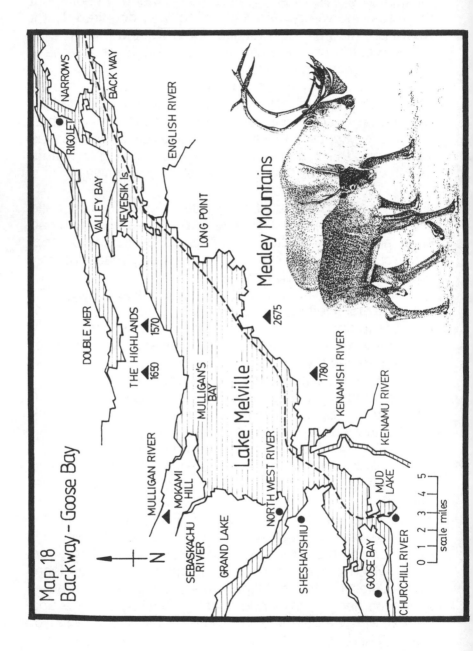

Map 18
Backway – Goose Bay

was passing through a rough section in the snowmobile trail. Some trees lay as they must have fallen when cut, whilst others, once neatly laid out to even the bumps and hollows, had long since found other resting places. In fact, the whole section looked like the aftermath of a pulp mill forestry truck accident, and it looked infinitely easier to break a new trail than follow the one ahead. I was beginning to feel very low, and I knew what it was.

The sea had become so much a part of my life that even this temporary separation was beginning to play on my nerves. This abandonment now felt contrary to the spirit of my trip, or was it fatigue? I took a rest, then five minutes later the question answered itself. I got this incredible urge to crest the hill above, so I left my kayak and broke a new trail. As soon as I saw the huge expanse of water down the Back Way, I was renewed with a sudden burst of energy.... then I saw my caribou............

I covered the remainder of the portage with no difficulty and put up my tent on a soft blanket of red berry bushes with a magnificent view down the Back Way from my bedroom window. The view through the early evening haze was eerie. Bordered to the east by the Mealie Mountains and to the west by the huge Gnat Mountain, this inland arm of sea seemed to stretch into infinity. Not for the first time on this trip, I stood alone in it, but not for long.

That evening the clouds disappeared and the stars came out, but just as I was starting to relax into my full stomach, a crow dropped by for a visit. I was probably 65 kilometres from Cartwright; 48 kilometres from Rigolet and 130 kilometres as the crow flies from Goose Bay, so why here?

If the playful grey jay is the outdoor man's friend, then certainly the raven is his biggest nuisance. These pesky creatures don't take no for an answer. You can't leave anything laying about. If it's not tied or nailed down, it is theirs for the picking. Before I turned in for the night, his constant crowing had attracted three more of his friends. By nightfall the whole place seemed to be festooned with them. I was beginning to feel as if I had strayed on some ancient

Inuit burial site - that the large oval rock adjacent to my camp was some medieval headstone, and that maybe there was some unearthed remains close by that only the ravens knew about. Pherhaps I was camped on tomorrow's breakfast. There seemed seem to be no rhyme nor reason for their behaviour or for their numbers.

During the night, I had a terrible dream in which the crows got into my tent and were pecking out my eyes. In terror to get out, I almost ripped my tent in two. The noise woke the crows and the whole scene replayed itself.

I made little progress the following day. The wind grew in force as the morning crept by, and by noon I was forced ashore. I had put up my tent to wait out the wind, but instead of catnapping, I died to the world, and it wasn't until the sun's shadow stretched from shore to shore that I stirred. It was late afternoon. The wind had blown itself out and the lake now mirrored the shoreline. Its surface was picture perfect and too good to spoil with a paddle. I yielded to its portrait and even though the magnetic pull to put in more mileage was strong, I watched entranced as it bronzed and framed under the setting sun.

The next day, I fared no better. I woke into a torrential downpour, that came in dark swirling curtains across the lake. It was a full-blown storm, but I didn't care. That morning I was prepared. I wore almost every stitch of clothes I had - thermal underwear, wet suit, pullover, mittens, poggies, socks, boots and my dry suit top. I cocooned myself in layers of insulation, and with no sea swells or breakers to contend with, I felt great. For starters, I hadn't see anyone for over a week, and I wanted to keep it that way. I didn't want my surprise homecoming spoiled by an errant visitor. I wanted to finish unannounced and I didn't want my stories diluted by a third party.

All day, I replayed the highs and lows of my trip, and I couldn't have chosen a better day to rehearse them. The rain's mist cut down my views to all but the shoreline, and the darker my reality became, the more fertile my imagination flourished.

If the day belonged to reflective thought, then the night belonged to the here and now. I had paddled from sunrise to almost sunset, to get out of the Back Way. I had climbed the mountain, so to speak, and now I could lay back and enjoy the view. That night found me camped at the T junction of two great bodies of tidal water: The Back Way and Lake Melville. Tomorrow, I would turn west. My final leg was just around the corner and I could smell the finish line in Mud Lake. I had never felt fitter or so much at peace as I did that night. It made the huge expanse of water look that much sweeter and when the Northern Ranger came into view up the Narrows, en route west to Goose Bay, 130 kilometres down at the bottom of Lake Melville, it was icing on the cake.

Thank God, I was paddling in my own backyard. It's not that I knew the lake's shoreline like the back of my hand, but I had been up and down it enough to know both its character and its temperament. As it turned out, it was a good thing I did, for the only constant over the next two days was the weather: rain, rain, rain. It rained continuously, and what the rain didn't obscure, the heavy mist that accompanied it did. Lake Melville closed its curtains. I only caught a glimpse of the Mealies and the magnificent falls at the bottom of Etagaulet Bay were completely hidden. It was late into the second day before it offered up its endless horizon of inland sea.

The weather actually broke not a moment too soon. I had just paddled past the mouth of English River. The monstrous cliffs at Long Point, where the Mealie Mountains rise vertically out of the lake, were just starting to materialize out of the gloom. The tide was falling and shoal rock was starting to pepper the water ahead. The sun had long since dropped below the mountains and the southern shore was blanketed in shade. I was now in a race between the tide and the setting sun. I had to find a campsite, and quickly.

The further west I paddled, the further north I was steering to skirt the rocks. I was already three hundred yards from shore, and angling out further with every stroke. It was already difficult enough to spot a campsite. If forced any further into the lake, I wouldn't stand a chance. Twice, I'd turned ashore in hopes of finding some open ground, but was thwarted. Once, I'd mistaken a grassy knoll for tidal marsh reeds, and on the other occasion, a bleached white line of driftwood exposed by the falling tide for sand. It was frustrating. I was wasting precious daylight, and it was only when the early evening's dark blue skies tinged red that I finally turned ashore for the last time. It seemed to take me forever to break through the blockade of exposed rocks that lined the shore, but no sooner had I reached the open water, when I bottomed out.

By the time I'd dragged my kayak ashore, the night sky was racing down the lake. I would have to make do with whatever I found. Beggars can't be choosers when the day is almost up, but then my luck turned. Had I have been in my kayak, I doubt I would have seen it. It was a lagoon. It had been hidden from the lake by a border of willows, and its sandy beach by a bank of driftwood at its mouth. The lagoon was horseshoe in shape, with enough room at its throat above the hide tide mark to pitch my tent on its sands. It was a sight for sore eyes, but I couldn't linger. Light was draining fast from the sky. It was damp and cold and my feet smelt like rotting eggs from the bog-like mud, but I was as high as a kite. I was just too close to home to keep anything back. I had been immunized too many times to care about my mood swings. I had turned a losing cause into a glorious victory in a matter of minutes. I had been forced ashore by the setting sun, had to portage my equipment through mud to my present campsite, but what a campsite.

That night the whole lagoon danced in the light of my driftwood fire. The night sky flickered like snow flakes in sun, and a female moose who didn't seem to care less about my presence, grazed in the boggy shore. For the first time in eight nights I caught the evening news. It was full of storm warnings, but even that couldn't earth me from my present high.

The next morning, I was mindful of what lay ahead, but nothing outside a hurricane was going to keep me ashore and although the signs were against me, I chose to reject their signals and left.

Fools rush in where angels fear to tread. That's Bernie for you. The weather seemed hell bent on prolonging my trip. I hadn't been paddling thirty minutes when the checkered quilt of black and white clouds blended into a gloomy grey, then descended, opened and dumped on me. The wind, as predicted, came directly out of the east. I had fallen asleep with my fingers crossed. I had second-guessed the weather and lost.

At this time of year the southern shore of Lake Melville is open to easterly winds. Its shores offer little protection, as they are mined with jagged shoal rocks and unlike its northern shore, its banks of thick undergrowth are not exactly camper-friendly. My decision to paddle down its southern shore had been based on the simple fact that I had paddled its northern shore before. I had wanted a new challenge and today's conditions were, to say the least, challenging.

At that very moment, my brain was telling me to cross the 16 kilometres of open water to Charle's Point on Lake Melville's northern shore. The thought of its sheltered shoreline was seductive, but I knew my shoulders weren't up to the task. I knew I hadn't the upper body strength or endurance to crash through the wall of easterly wind. I knew it would be suicidal, as the view ahead looked only marginally better.

It's impossible to win every battle at sea, but it's all-important to win the last one, and that's crossing the finishing line. Like a marathon runner who enters the stadium hours after everyone has left, it's a personal battle. Long-distance travel is not a sport of winners and losers. There are no accolades for being the fastest, there's no one look ing over your shoulder to record your daily triumphs or failures. What might be easy one day may look unsurmountable the next, and like today, it's no good beating yourself up with those 'if onlys'........ If only I had crossed yesterday when the conditions were ideal. If only I had bigger shoulders. I am no god. I have been doing this travel lark, for that's what it is for over twenty years and these 'if onlys' have always plagued my ego, and although it pains me to own up to it, I still felt like a wimp for not at least trying to cross the lake. Now that would have been a test worth writing about.

By mid morning the wind had torn up the lake, pushed up its surface into steep short waves and was beating me to pulp. The conditions were dreadful, and even worse when I caught sight of the surf-washed shore. The wind was squally, sometimes very strong, but always relentless. Wave after wave broadsided my kayak. They weren't big, but they were big enough. I was getting drenched from head to foot. I was cold wet, and dejected. My arms were going through the motions, but my hands, even with wool mittens and protected against the wind in my poggie paddle covers, had lost nearly all sense of touch. The sting of windchill crept from finger tip to knuckle and now enveloped my hand like a vice. The pain, acute in the morning, had dulled to a throbbing ache by noon. It wore away at my senses, and when it turned to pins and needles rounding Long Point, I knew it was time to stop, but where?

Long Point may be one of Lake Melville's little known visual treasures, but it certainly doesn't offer up much in the form of campsites. It seemed to go on for ever, but once I had rounded its rocky cliffs, I had my spirits raised by a plume of smoke, and I broke into a sprint. That day, I learned my lesson the hard way, and that evening, paid for my supper with the day's story.

I was now just over 65 kilometres from home and that was the only fact that pried me from my pillow the next day, but I shouldn't have bothered. I had not even paddled 8 kilometres when I threw in the towel and beached next to a cluster of deserted cabins adjacent to Big Brook. It wasn't official, but as far as I was concerned, summer was over. My trip was now in the lap of the gods. The easterlies had set in. I could be stormbound for a day or a week, but one thing was certain, I couldn't afford it to stretch into two. I only had food for the next four days, and to make matters worse, my tobacco was running low.

For three long days it blew. Then my patience snapped. I spotted a freighter. I watched it come and I watched it go. It appeared through the shield of rain only to be lost behind a point of land. Its sight had raised my spirits, but its departure had left me limp. The last thing I wanted was to finish this trip with my tail between my legs. Then I noticed the waves.

'Wake up Bernie and smell the roses. The winds has changed, me'boy'

I had completely forgotten that my camp was facing down the lake not across it. If it hadn't been for the freighter, I would never have noticed it in a month of Sundays. I only had to round the next point of land and I could surf home in no time

'What are you waiting for Bernie?'

It was the thought of kayaking over 65 kilometres in one day, aided by a stiff tail wind, that did it.

'After three months at sea you should have nerves off steel,' I told myself.

What a ride I had! I couldn't have planned my last day any better. I flew past the settlement of North West River in over-drive, skipped over the rough waves at the mouth of the Kenamu River and literally hydroplaned the water of Hamilton Basin to the Churchill River. I covered almost 50 kilometres in less than six hours, not even breaking a sweat, and it wasn't until I had paddled down the back channel to Mud Lake, within sight of my home, that I gave into my nerves and stopped paddling.

I neither felt sad nor excited at finishing, just glad to be home. I know most people suffer withdrawal symptoms at the end of a trip, but I don't. It was a wonderful lark and that's all it was.

I could have happily stayed where I was drifting, in the lake, but my stomach started to complain.

"Eh, Clara, any food on the go?"